To Your Good Health®

Bob Moore

AN EMPLOYEE-OWNED COMPANY

Everyday
Gluten-Free
Cookbook

FOR KATE & NICK
TO YOUR
WHOLE GRAIN
GOOD HEALTH!
Bob Moore
LONDON
8 JULY 2016

Everyday
Gluten-Free
Cookbook

281 delicious
whole-grain recipes

Camilla V. Saulsbury

Robert
ROSE

For complete cataloguing information, see page 336.

Disclaimer
The recipes in this book have been carefully tested by our kitchen and our tasters. To the best of our knowledge, they are safe and nutritious for ordinary use and users. For those people with food or other allergies, or who have special food requirements or health issues, please read the suggested contents of each recipe carefully and determine whether or not they may create a problem for you. All recipes are used at the risk of the consumer.

We cannot be responsible for any hazards, loss or damage that may occur as a result of any recipe use.

For those with special needs, allergies, requirements or health problems, in the event of any doubt, please contact your medical adviser prior to the use of any recipe.

Design and production: Daniella Zanchetta/PageWave Graphics Inc.
Editor: Sue Sumeraj
Recipe editor: Jennifer MacKenzie
Proofreader: Kelly Jones
Indexer: Gillian Watts
Photographer: Colin Erricson
Associate photographer: Matt Johannsson
Food stylist: Michael Elliott
Prop stylist: Charlene Erricson

Cover image: Multigrain Blueberry Muffins (page 273)

The publisher gratefully acknowledges the financial support of our publishing program by the Government of Canada through the Canada Book Fund.

Published by Robert Rose Inc.
120 Eglinton Avenue East, Suite 800, Toronto, Ontario, Canada M4P 1E2
Tel: (416) 322-6552 Fax: (416) 322-6936
www.robertrose.ca

Printed and bound in Canada

4 5 6 7 8 9 MI 23 22 21 20 19 18 17 16

Contents

Go with the Grain

When most people remember the comfort foods of their youth, they think of macaroni and cheese, rich soups and stews, and decadent sweets. It's another story for me and my siblings. We get nostalgic over whole-grain molasses spice cookies, thick-cut oatmeal with plump raisins, coarse, dark bread slathered with homemade plum jam, and my mother's extraordinary bulgur salad with oranges, herbs and cashews. The credit goes to my parents. Both are enthusiastic home cooks and avid gardeners who made modest yet scrumptious meals built on a foundation of fresh fruits and vegetables, a minimal amount of meat and a variety of whole grains. That's how I continue to cook today for myself and my family.

So when the chance came to write this book, showcasing the breadth, depth and versatility of Bob's Red Mill's gluten-free grains, I was thrilled. (Full disclosure: I may have screamed.) I grew up eating Bob's Red Mill grains and, should you open my pantry, refrigerator and freezer on any given day, you will undoubtedly see Bob Moore's iconic image staring back at you from the copious bags of their products, which I always have on hand.

Although I have been eating a diet rich in whole grains my entire life, it is the opportunity to highlight naturally gluten-free grains and grain flours in this book that excites me most. More people than ever before are seeking ways to cut back on gluten or completely eliminate it from their diet, whether because of celiac disease, an array of allergies or a variety of other health reasons. And one of the simplest and most delicious ways to make the transition to a gluten-free diet is not to eliminate all grains, but rather to embrace the wealth of ancient grains that are naturally gluten-free.

The bounty of these nutrient-dense ancient grains is astounding, from amaranth to quinoa, millet, teff and so much more, and Bob's Red Mill is dedicated to making these once unfamiliar grains readily available. The introductory sections of this book teach you everything you need to know about the gluten-free grains and flours used in the recipes, as well as a diverse array of other natural ingredients that can help turn those grains into an extraordinary variety of entrées, side dishes and treats. So read up, and then dive in and start cooking your way to delicious, naturally gluten-free, easy-to-make everyday meals!

Gluten-Free Grains Primer

A **wide variety** of naturally gluten-free, nutrient-dense grains are now readily available for enjoying in countless dishes designed for every day of the week. The majority of the grains featured in this collection have been consumed, and heralded, in different cultures around the world for thousands of years. Now their status as some of the most nutritious foods on the planet is supported by extensive scientific research linking them to multiple health benefits, from reducing the risks of cardiovascular disease, certain cancers and diabetes to supporting digestive health, a strong immune system and a healthy body weight.

Amaranth

Petite in size and tan in color, amaranth was a staple food of the pre-Columbian Aztecs in Mexico and Peru. The Aztecs — who called the seeds *huaudi* — believed that, in addition to providing general sustenance, amaranth consumption increased both energy and strength. It was also an integral part of their religious practice: they made figurines from the puffed seeds, mixing them with honey or blood, as offerings to the gods.

The crops were almost completely eradicated by Spanish conquistadors in the 16th century, but the few remaining plants made a slow and steady comeback in Mexico. Amaranth is now cultivated in the United States, South America, Europe and China.

The Aztecs' prescience is remarkable: scientific research suggests that amaranth may indeed increase energy, strength and overall health in multiple ways. Amaranth is loaded with calcium, magnesium, iron, phosphorus, potassium and B vitamins. It is also high in protein. Further, unlike many other grains, amaranth is a rich source of essential fatty acids, including the heart-healthy oleic acid normally associated with olive oil. Amaranth is particularly beneficial for those following a vegetarian or vegan diet, thanks to its high levels of iron.

The nutrient-rich properties of amaranth only go further. For starters, a growing body of research indicates that amaranth can help fend off a variety of cancers. Lunasin, a bioactive peptide in amaranth, has been shown to inhibit the development of cancer cells. Soy also contains lunasin, but researchers are discovering that the lunasin in amaranth penetrates the nucleus of cancer cells more rapidly. Adding good news to good news, scientists have further discovered that squalene, an antioxidant compound present in amaranth, may halt the blood supply to tumors.

Like buckwheat, amaranth is excellent for supporting myriad aspects of heart health. Studies of both animals and humans indicates that consuming amaranth may significantly lower blood pressure, triglycerides and low-density lipoprotein (LDL) cholesterol, as well as aid in heart rhythm normalization. Not surprisingly, researchers reached the conclusion that amaranth should be considered a functional food in the prevention and treatment of cardiovascular disease.

What's good for the heart is also good for the brain, at least in the case of amaranth. Rutin and nicotiflorin, two polyphenols found in amaranth, have established anti-inflammatory and antioxidant properties; new scientific research indicates that they also have a neuro-protective effect. A recent study found that they not only decreased inflammatory cytokines, but also aided in the repair of damaged brain cells.

When it comes to bone health, amaranth offers a mother lode of support. In addition to being rich in calcium, magnesium, phosphorus and manganese, amaranth also has high levels of the amino acid lysine, which helps the body absorb calcium and decreases the amount of calcium lost in waste fluids. Lysine also plays a role in the formation of collagen, a substance crucial for sturdy bones. Furthermore, studies indicate that lysine and L-arginine, another amino acid in amaranth, work together to make bone-building cells more active.

Amaranth Cooking Methods

Cooked amaranth strongly resembles tiny pearls of caviar. The tiny seeds can also be popped. Popping amaranth seeds takes a few minutes, as you can only pop one spoonful at a time, but the result looks like the world's teeniest, tiniest popcorn. It's a wonderful addition to all sorts of baked goods and treats. It's delicious eaten out of hand, too, but more than a little challenging to get the tiny popped kernels into your mouth without half of them falling on the floor (just keep a vacuum close).

The Simmer Method

To prepare 2 cups (500 mL) cooked amaranth, bring 3 cups (750 mL) water to a boil in a medium saucepan. Stir in 1 cup (250 mL) amaranth, reduce heat to low, cover and simmer for 17 to 20 minutes or until liquid is just absorbed. Remove from heat and let stand, covered, for 5 minutes. Fluff with a fork.

Freezing Cooked Whole Grains

One of my favorite tricks, if you can call it that, to make eating whole grains extra easy and convenient for everyday cooking is to make double or triple what I need for a given recipe and freeze the rest. A great number of recipes in this collection call for cooked grains. With the grains precooked and frozen, recipe assembly is super-swift.

After cooking the grains of your choice, let them cool completely. I prefer to spread the grains out in a thin layer on a baking sheet (lined with plastic wrap, for easy transfer and cleanup). Not only does this help the grains cool more quickly than if left in the pan, it also prevents them from becoming mushy. Once the grains are cooled, store them in a tightly sealed zip-top plastic bag (press out as much air as possible before sealing the bag) or airtight container in the freezer for up to 3 months. Clearly label the bag or container with the grain, quantity and date the grains were prepared.

Thawing Grains

Frozen grains can be thawed overnight in the refrigerator or, if you want to use them right away, defrosted in the microwave. Transfer the frozen grains to a microwave-safe bowl and thaw on Medium (50%) in 1-minute intervals until completely defrosted. It will take between 3 and 8 minutes, depending on the size of the grains.

Reheating Grains

To reheat grains, whether for a recipe calling for hot cooked grains or simply to enjoy as a side dish or for breakfast, heat the thawed grains in the microwave on High for 30 seconds. Stir the grains and repeat as needed, stopping to stir after each interval, until the grains are heated through. Alternatively, place the thawed grains in a nonstick skillet and add 1 tbsp (15 mL) water for every 2 cups (500 mL) cooked grains. Cook over medium heat, stirring, for 2 to 5 minutes or until heated through.

Popped Amaranth

To prepare 2¼ cups (550 mL) popped amaranth, you will need ⅔ cup (150 mL) amaranth. Heat a large dry skillet over medium-high heat. Add 1 tbsp (15 mL) amaranth and vigorously shake the pan for 12 to 18 seconds or until the seeds have popped (they should begin to pop within 1 to 2 seconds after being added to the pan); watch closely, as the amaranth will burn quickly once it has finished popping. Immediately transfer the popped seeds to a medium bowl to cool. Continue popping the remaining amaranth, 1 tbsp (15 mL) at a time, making sure the pan remains very hot in between batches.

Store any extra popped amaranth in a tightly sealed zip-top plastic bag or airtight container at room temperature for up to 1 week.

Buckwheat

Buckwheat grains, known as groats, are the hulled seeds of the buckwheat plant. First cultivated in Southeast Asia thousands of years ago, soft white buckwheat groats have a naturally mild flavor. However, once they are toasted or roasted, groats darken dramatically and their flavor becomes intense and robust. In Eastern Europe, where buckwheat was later transported, toasted buckwheat (typically called by its Russian name, kasha) is an ubiquitous ingredient in soups, side dishes, porridge and, when ground into flour, copious baked goods.

Despite its name, buckwheat has no relation to wheat whatsoever. Rather, this naturally gluten-free grain is the seed of a plant related to rhubarb. It is packed with protein, fiber and flavonoids — disease-fighting antioxidants found in green tea and dark chocolate.

Buckwheat is naturally low on the glycemic index, but research reveals that it helps to manage the body's blood sugar in additional ways. First, recent findings suggest that buckwheat actually has a glucose-lowering effect. This is credited to a compound in buckwheat called d-chiro-inositol, which is documented in other foods as an effective agent in glucose metabolism and cell signaling. Second, like other whole grains, buckwheat is high in fiber (more than 4 grams per cup/250 mL), which benefits blood sugar and body weight maintenance because it is absorbed slowly from the gut into the bloodstream.

The benefits of buckwheat also extend to its mineral and antioxidant composition. Buckwheat is high in both magnesium and rutin. The former contributes to overall heart health by relaxing blood vessels, improving blood flow and reducing blood pressure; the latter protects against disease by strengthening capillaries and preventing blood clotting. In addition, a study in the *American Journal of Clinical Nutrition* showed that eating 100 grams of buckwheat (about ½ cup/125 mL raw groats or about 1¼ cups/300 mL cooked buckwheat) per day improved heart health by lowering total cholesterol and low-density lipoprotein (LDL) cholesterol and increasing the ratio of high-density lipoprotein (HDL) cholesterol to total cholesterol.

Buckwheat Cooking Methods

Use the simmer method to make cooked buckwheat for salads, side dish, pilafs or anywhere else you need cooked buckwheat groats. Removing the pan from the heat and letting the buckwheat steam during the final minutes of cooking helps to keep the groats from becoming mushy.

If you wish to ensure that the cooked groats remain separate, use the egg method instead.

The Simmer Method

To prepare 2½ cups (625 mL) cooked buckwheat, combine 1 cup (250 mL) buckwheat groats and 2 cups (500 mL) water in a medium saucepan. Bring to a boil over medium-high heat. Reduce heat to low, cover and simmer for 10 to 12 minutes or until liquid is just barely absorbed. Remove from heat and let stand, covered, for 5 minutes. Fluff with a fork.

If a creamier, porridge-type consistency is desired, prepare the groats as directed above, but simmer for 14 to 18 minutes, stirring occasionally, or until almost all of the liquid is absorbed.

Quickly Cooling Cooked Grains

If a recipe calls for cooked grains that have been cooled, you can cool them quickly by rinsing them under cold water and draining them thoroughly before adding them to the recipe. This will not affect the nutrients of the grain. The nutrients in whole grains are found in the oils in the outer, protein-rich layer of the endosperm (the aleuronic layer) and within the endosperm, both of which are dense enough that the nutrients cannot seep out to the outer layer of the grain. Hence, nutrient loss from rinsing grains is negligible.

The Egg Method

To prepare 3½ cups (875 mL) cooked buckwheat, lightly beat 1 large egg in a medium bowl. Add 1 cup (250 mL) buckwheat groats, tossing to coat. Heat a large nonstick skillet over medium heat. Add egg-coated groats and cook, stirring, for 1 to 2 minutes or until groats appear completely dry. Add 2 cups (500 mL) water, increase heat to medium-high and bring to a boil. Reduce heat to low, cover and simmer for 10 to 12 minutes or until liquid is just barely absorbed. Remove from heat and let stand, covered, for 5 minutes. Fluff with a fork.

Chia Seeds

Chia seeds were once a power food of the ancient Aztec civilization. Early Spanish manuscripts note that the Aztecs routinely ate chia seeds to improve their endurance, calling chia their "running food" because messengers reportedly could run all day on a mere handful. The seeds were also prized for medicinal purposes and were used as a form of currency in lieu of gold. The decline of the Aztec civilization forced chia seeds into relative obscurity for hundreds of years (with the exception of corny pottery animals). Now scientists and consumers alike are excited about what the Aztecs knew for hundreds of years.

A wide body of scientific research, beginning in the 1990s, reveals that chia seeds are incredibly nutritious. Superior in protein quality to wheat, corn, rice, oats, barley, amaranth and soy, chia also offers a disease-fighting arsenal of antioxidants, including chlorogenic acid, caffeic acid, myricetin, quercetin and flavonols. A 2-tbsp (30 mL) serving of chia seeds provides 10 grams of fiber, 5 grams of protein and 18% of the daily value for calcium. Initial clinical research also indicates that chia seeds may be beneficial for appetite control and weight loss, as well as reduced blood glucose and triglyceride levels.

Of particularly keen interest at present, however, is the abundance of alpha-linoleic omega-3 fatty acids in chia seeds: 4,500 milligrams per ounce (30 g), far exceeding the amount in flax seeds. These fatty acids may promote a wide range of cardiovascular and mental health benefits.

Chia seeds are like flax seeds in that they have a mild flavor, but unlike flax seeds, chia seeds do not need to be ground to maximize the availability of their nutrients. The whole seeds can be used as a thickener in a broad range of drinks, from traditional Mexican *agua fresca* to newfangled smoothies, or to make almost-instant jams, puddings and porridges.

When combined with liquid, chia seeds swell and form a gel that can be used as an egg substitute in baked goods. Ground chia seeds can also be used to thicken sauces, soups and stews.

Millet

Millet is a tiny, pale yellow and almost perfectly spherical grain — technically a seed — that is most familiar to North Americans as birdseed. Yet millet's history as a cultivated crop dates back to 6000 BC in China, where it was once considered one of the five sacred crops and was, for thousands of years, the primary grain of northern China. Marco Polo recorded his observance of millet consumption in China, noting that millet was plentiful and was often prepared as a gruel cooked in milk.

Millet was later cultivated all over northern Europe, Egypt and India. It is estimated that millet presently sustains roughly one-third of the world's population, and it is widely used in Asian, African and Eastern European cuisine. In particular, millet plays a prominent role in the diet of the Hunza people, a Himalayan tribe whose members are known for leading very long, healthy lives.

Millet is gaining popularity in North America in large part thanks to its mild, subtly grassy flavor and incredible versatility. For example, it can be creamy (think porridge or polenta), light and fluffy (almost identical to couscous) or, when toasted, a crunchy alternative to nuts in baked goods and granolas. Although there are several types of commonly eaten millet, pearl millet, which is what is usually eaten in North American and European countries, accounts for 50% of the world's millet crop.

But millet's nutritional properties are what make it a slam dunk for many modern consumers. Millet isn't just gluten-free, it is also easy to digest in general. High in fiber and protein, it helps to keep the digestive tract operating smoothly and lowers the risk of diabetes and heart disease. Plus, it is one of the only grains that is alkalizing to the body. Millet is a great source of B vitamins (especially niacin, thiamin and vitamin B_6), and is rich in manganese (an enzyme activator that improves bone structure), magnesium (which lowers cholesterol and the risk of heart attack and type 2 diabetes), phosphorous (which helps the body efficiently process carbohydrates, fats and proteins) and copper (which supports a strong metabolism).

Millet Cooking Methods

Use the simmer method to yield millet grains that remain separate and fluffy, for use in recipes such as salads, side dishes and stuffing. Use the creamy millet recipe for breakfast porridge — simply add the spices and toppings of your choice — or as a basic "polenta" that is wonderful as a side dish or accompaniment to stews or ragùs.

The Simmer Method

To prepare 2½ cups (625 mL) cooked millet, bring 2 cups (500 mL) water to a boil in a medium saucepan. Stir in 1 cup (250 mL) millet, reduce heat to low, cover and simmer for 17 to 20 minutes or until liquid is just absorbed. Remove from heat and let stand, covered, for 5 minutes. Fluff with a fork.

Creamy Millet

To prepare 3 cups (750 mL) creamy millet, bring 3 cups (750 mL) water to a boil in a medium saucepan. Stir in 1 cup (250 mL) millet, reduce heat to low and simmer, stirring, for 25 to 30 minutes or until thick and creamy. Remove from heat and, if desired, stir in 1 tbsp (15 mL) unsalted butter or olive oil.

Oats

The Celts have had it right for centuries: oats are one of the most nutritious, powerful foods you can eat. Oats are annual grasses that probably originated from the Asian wild red oat, which grew as a weed in other grain crops, such as barley. The oldest known oat grains were found in Egypt, dating from 2000 BC; however, it is likely they were weeds and were not actually cultivated by the Egyptians. The oldest known cultivated oats were found in caves in Switzerland that are believed to belong to the Bronze Age. But up until a few centuries ago, oats were used mostly to feed livestock, not for human consumption.

Although they eventually became a staple food in parts of Northern Europe, especially Scotland and Ireland, oats still received little praise. In Samuel Johnson's 18th-century dictionary, for example, oats were said to be "eaten by people in Scotland, but fit only for horses in England." The Scotsman's retort to this is: "That's why England has such good horses, and Scotland has such fine men!"

Oats were first brought to, and planted in, the New World in 1602, off the southern coast of Massachusetts, but it took another 250 years for them to acquire acclaim. Ferdinand Schumacher, a German immigrant and miller from Akron, Ohio, is largely responsible for the sea change. In 1854, Schumacher made it his mission to introduce the world to the wonders of oatmeal. He began by selling oats in his small general store, but then took to traveling the United States to promote the virtues of oatmeal as a flavorful, frugal and healthful food. The notion stuck (much as a good bowl of oatmeal does to your ribs), and oat porridge and other oat cereals became, and continue to be, some of the most popular breakfast foods in North America.

Oats are worthy of all of Schumacher's praise, and now the hype is backed by significant scientific research. Rich in complex carbohydrates and high in protein, oats contain all of the B vitamins, including traces of B_{12}, are rich in vitamin E and contain trace amounts of vitamin K. They are also the only cereal containing saponin, a hormone-like substance that helps the pancreas regulate insulin production. If that was not enough, oats are also loaded with minerals, silica and other trace elements the body needs to build strong bones and muscles and to maintain joint elasticity.

What really sets oats apart is how they benefit digestion. Oats contain more soluble fiber than any other grain. Soluble fiber dissolves, which slows down digestion. Not only does this make you feel fuller (and more satisfied) for longer, it allows for greater absorption of nutrients and may contribute to lower blood pressure.

Fiber is also the key to oats' cholesterol-lowering abilities. Oats are packed with a particular type of soluble fiber called beta-glucan, which prevents cholesterol-rich bile acids from being reabsorbed into the body. Beta-glucan has antimicrobial and antioxidant capabilities, too, which may boost immunity, accelerate wound healing and improve the functionality of antibiotics.

Rolled Oats

Large-flake (old-fashioned) rolled oats are oat groats (hulled and cleaned whole oats) that have been steamed and flattened with huge rollers. Quick-cooking rolled oats are groats that have been cut into several pieces before being steamed and rolled into thinner flakes. For the best results, it is important to use the type of rolled oats specified in the recipe.

If you're following a gluten-free diet, it is imperative to buy oats that are certified gluten-free, as oats can easily be contaminated with wheat during harvest, storage or other stages of processing. Certified gluten-free oats are available in large-flake (old-fashioned) and quick-cooking.

A Note about Oat Tolerance

A small number of people with celiac disease may not tolerate oats. If you are unsure about your oat tolerance, consult your doctor.

Rolled Oats Cooking Methods

In case you need another reason to love rolled oats, add quick and easy preparation to the list. Both quick-cooking and large-flake (old-fashioned) rolled oats cook in a matter of minutes. In addition, they can be made on the stovetop, in the microwave or in a slow cooker. All three methods yield creamy results.

Simmering oats on the stovetop is likely the most familiar method, and is ideal for cooking one to four servings. The microwave method is best for making one or two servings at most. It is imperative to use a larger-than-usual bowl (as directed) because the oats bubble up and can make a grand mess if they overflow. A slow cooker is ideal for cooking larger quantities; the fact that it is hands-off cooking is a great bonus.

The Stovetop Method

- *Quick-cooking rolled oats:* To prepare $2\frac{1}{2}$ cups (625 mL) cooked oats porridge, bring 2 cups (500 mL) water and a pinch of fine sea salt to a boil over medium-high heat. Stir in 1 cup (250 mL) quick-cooking rolled oats and reduce heat to medium-low. Cook, stirring occasionally, for 3 to 5 minutes or until porridge is creamy. Remove from heat, cover and let stand for 2 minutes.

- *Large-flake (old-fashioned) rolled oats:* To prepare $2\frac{1}{2}$ cups (625 mL) cooked oats porridge, bring 2 cups (500 mL) water and a pinch of fine sea salt to a boil over medium-high heat. Stir in 1 cup (250 mL) large-flake (old-fashioned) rolled oats and reduce heat to medium-low. Cook, stirring occasionally, for 10 to 20 minutes or until porridge reaches desired amount of creaminess. Remove from heat, cover and let stand for 2 minutes.

The Microwave Method

- *Quick-cooking rolled oats:* To prepare $1\frac{1}{4}$ cups (300 mL) cooked oats porridge, combine $\frac{1}{2}$ cup (125 mL) quick-cooking rolled oats, a pinch of fine sea salt and 1 cup (250 mL) water in a 4-cup (1 L) microwave-safe bowl. Microwave on High for 2 to 3 minutes or until water is boiling and mixture is thickened and somewhat creamy. Let stand for 2 minutes (mixture will continue to thicken as it stands), then stir well before serving.

- *Large-flake (old-fashioned) rolled oats:* To prepare $1\frac{1}{4}$ cups (300 mL) cooked oats porridge, combine $\frac{1}{2}$ cup (125 mL) large-flake (old-fashioned) rolled oats, a pinch of fine sea salt and 1 cup (250 mL) water in a 4-cup (1 L) microwave-safe bowl. Microwave on High for 3 to 5 minutes or until water is boiling and mixture is thickened and somewhat creamy. Let stand for 2 minutes (mixture will continue to thicken as it stands), then stir well before serving.

The Slow Cooker Method

- *Quick-cooking rolled oats:* To prepare 2½ cups (625 mL) cooked oats porridge, combine 1 cup (250 mL) quick-cooking rolled oats, a pinch of fine sea salt and 2 cups (500 mL) water in a slow cooker. Cook on Low for 2 to 2½ hours or until mixture is thickened and creamy. Stir well before serving.

- *Large-flake (old-fashioned) rolled oats:* To prepare 2½ cups (625 mL) cooked oats porridge, combine 1 cup (250 mL) large-flake (old-fashioned) rolled oats, a pinch of fine sea salt and 2 cups (500 mL) water in a slow cooker. Cook on Low for 3 to 3½ hours or until mixture is thickened and creamy. Stir well before serving.

Quinoa

Although cooked and eaten like a grain, quinoa (pronounced *KEEN-wah*) is technically a seed, classified as a "pseudocereal." Quinoa seeds are harvested from a broadleaf plant that belongs to the goosefoot (*Chenopodium*) family, which is closely related to spinach, beets and chard. Quinoa plants can grow upwards of 7 feet (2.1 m) and have brilliantly colored, flowering seed heads in shades ranging from orange, yellow and pink to red, purple and black. Once the seed head is dried, the small quinoa seeds are simply shaken out. The edible seeds are typically white or pale golden, but can be pink, red, orange, purple or black. They are coated in saponin, a bitter, resin-like substance that protects the plant from insects and birds.

Quinoa is classified a superfood by nutritionists and a "super-crop" by the United Nations for multiple reasons. First, it boasts a near-perfect balance of protein, carbohydrates and dietary fiber. Second, it is rich in vitamins and minerals, namely thiamine, riboflavin, vitamin B_6, folate, magnesium and vitamin E, and is a good source of iron, calcium, phosphorus and zinc. And third, of all whole grains, quinoa is also highest in potassium, a mineral that is essential for optimal brain function, blood sugar regulation, muscle function and sound mental health.

Quinoa's protein content has garnered considerable attention because it includes all of the essential amino acids humans need. The National Academy of Sciences calls quinoa "one of the best sources of protein in the vegetable kingdom" and the World Health Organization rates the protein in quinoa as comparable to milk protein (casein), a position supported by extensive nutritional research. Quinoa is an especially good source of the amino acid lysine (linoleic acid), a member of the omega-6 group of essential fatty acids. Rarely found in plants, lysine assists in the building of muscle protein and is important in the production of antibodies, hormones and enzymes, collagen formation and tissue repair.

Quinoa can be particularly valuable for those with celiac disease, who are often deficient in calcium and magnesium. Quinoa is a good source of calcium, and its lysine content assists in the absorption and storage of calcium. Quinoa also offers a good source of magnesium: 1 cup (250 mL) of cooked quinoa provides about 30% of the daily requirement.

Quinoa Cooking Methods

To cook quinoa for a side dish or breakfast porridge, or for use in a recipe that calls for cooked quinoa, you can use the simmer method or the pasta method. Both yield equally good results.

The Simmer Method

To prepare 3 cups (750 mL) cooked quinoa, combine 1 cup (250 mL) quinoa and $1\frac{2}{3}$ cups (400 mL) water in a medium saucepan. Bring to a boil over medium-high heat. Reduce heat to low, cover and simmer for 10 to 12 minutes or until liquid is just barely absorbed. Remove from heat and let stand, covered — 4 to 5 minutes for an al dente texture, ideal for salads; 6 to 7 minutes for a light, fluffy texture, ideal for side dishes; or 8 to 9 minutes for a softer texture best suited to desserts, breakfasts and incorporation into baked goods. Fluff with a fork.

Darker quinoa seeds — particularly red and black seeds — use the same quinoa-to-water ratio as the more common white quinoa. However, they do not always absorb all of the water in the designated cooking time. If excess liquid remains at the end of the cooking time, simply drain it off.

The Pasta Method

The easiest way to cook quinoa is to boil it like pasta. This method is particularly good for individuals who detect residual bitterness from the quinoa saponin. It is not necessary to rinse the quinoa before using this method.

Fill a large pot with water, add salt if desired and bring to a boil. Add the desired amount of quinoa and cook for 10 to 13 minutes or until tender. Drain the quinoa through a fine-mesh sieve. Return the quinoa to the still-warm pot (off the heat), cover and let stand for 2 to 3 minutes. The moisture in the cooked quinoa will steam it slightly, producing a light and fluffy texture.

If using this method to prepare quinoa for a salad, do not return the drained quinoa to the pot. Instead, rinse it under cold water until cooled. Shake the sieve to remove as much water as possible, then transfer the quinoa to a bowl and fluff with a fork.

Are Nutrients Lost with the Pasta Method?

The moisture-bound nutrients in quinoa and other whole grains are found in the oils in the outer, protein-rich layer of the endosperm (the aleuronic layer) and within the endosperm, both of which are dense enough that the nutrients cannot seep out to the outer layer of the grain. Hence, nutrient loss from boiling and draining quinoa (the pasta method) is negligible.

Rice

Rice is one of the most ancient cultivated foods. Pottery shards believed to be more than 4,000 years old have been discovered in Thailand bearing the imprint of both grains and husks of cultivated rice, and rice plant remains found near the border between Thailand and Myanmar are believed to date to 10,000 BC. In China, extensive archeological evidence, including rice grains, rice husks and rice farming implements, point to the existence of cultivated rice for more than 8,000 years. At present, rice sustains billions of people worldwide and is cultivated on every continent except Antarctica.

Prior to the 19th century, only a small fraction of people consumed white rice; the only rice they knew was what we now call "brown rice." Brown rice is the "unrefined" version of white rice. Brown rice is a whole grain because, unlike refined white rice, it still has the side hull and bran. It is the side hulls and brans that are naturally rich in protein, thiamine, calcium, magnesium, fiber and potassium. By contrast, white rice has very little nutritive value beyond calories. Even though some white rice is "fortified" to make it moderately more nutritious, the vitamins and minerals are typically synthetic additions, and one serving still falls far below minimum nutritional requirements set forth by entities such as the U.S. Food and Drug Administration (FDA).

The reason for the preference for white rice over brown rice is largely due to importing. When Westerners brought rice mills to Asian countries in the 19th century, they demanded that white, polished rice be the norm for export. The reasons were about business more than taste: white rice weighs less and can be stored longer without spoiling. With time, white rice became the norm — considered the refined and modern option — not only in Western countries, but in Asian countries as well. But the tables are slowly turning toward a preference for brown rice as consumers discover the many nutritional benefits it offers, as well as the naturally delicious, nutty flavor it imparts to recipes.

Beyond being naturally gluten-free, brown rice is rich in antioxidants and minerals such as selenium and manganese. An extensive body of scientific research indicates that selenium may reduce the risk of developing common illnesses such as cancer, heart disease and arthritis, while manganese benefits the nervous system and reproductive system, and helps the body synthesize fats.

Like many other whole grains, brown rice is high in fiber, which assists in weight loss and maintenance, digestive health and stabilization of the body's blood sugar levels. New research indicates that the natural digestibility of brown rice, combined with its high fiber content, can help the digestive tract recover from an overgrowth of candida organisms.

Brown Rice Cooking Methods

Brown rice requires a longer cooking time than white rice, but it is well worth the wait. The following methods can be used for any variety of brown rice (long-grain, basmati, medium-grain or short-grain), with the exception of quick-cooking or instant rice (which are not used in this collection). Both methods yield equally good results.

The Simmer Method

To prepare 3 cups (750 mL) cooked brown rice, combine 1 cup (250 mL) brown rice and 2 1/2 cups (625 mL) water in a medium saucepan with a tight-fitting lid. Bring to a boil over high heat. Stir once or twice, then reduce heat to low, cover and simmer for 45 to 55 minutes or until liquid is just absorbed and rice is tender (do not uncover while cooking). Remove from heat and let stand, covered, for 5 minutes. Fluff with a fork.

The Pasta Method

Fill a large pot with water, add salt if desired and bring to a boil. Add the desired amount of brown rice and cook for 45 to 55 minutes or until tender. Drain thoroughly.

Sorghum

Sorghum, an ancient cereal grain that's a staple crop in India and throughout Africa, has long been considered a safe grain alternative for people who cannot tolerate gluten. New molecular evidence confirms that sorghum is completely gluten-free, and a growing body of research reveals its multiple health benefits.

Sorghum most likely made its way to North America in the 18th century via slave ships to the United States. At the time, it was known as "Guinea corn." Sorghum soon became a significant crop in the Southern states, but for its cane, not its grain. Farmers would remove the leaves and seeds (grains) from the plant, then boil the cane to make a thick syrup known as either sorghum syrup or sorghum molasses.

These days, sorghum grain is once again the star. The plump, tender cooked grains and the faintly sweet flour are an excellent source of complex carbohydrates, and are rich in thiamin, riboflavin, niacin and trace minerals such as iron, phosphorus and potassium. Sorghum promotes a healthy metabolism, thanks to its high magnesium and copper levels. Magnesium also contributes to healthy bone tissue and regulates the body's calcium levels, while copper boosts the immune system and promotes red blood development.

In addition to being free of gluten, sorghum contains tannins that interact with carbohydrates and cause the formation of resistant starch. Resistant starch is digested far more slowly than other starches, especially refined starches. It is slowly fermented in the intestinal tract, which improves the environment for healthful bacteria, allowing them to thrive. These bacteria have multiple benefits, including the production of vitamins, detoxification of potential carcinogens and the activation of health-promoting compounds. Further research also indicates that sorghum extracts inhibit amylase, the enzyme produced with saliva and pancreatic juice that breaks down starch; this allows for a slower conversion of starch into sugars, which is beneficial for the maintenance of healthy blood sugar levels.

Sorghum Cooking Methods

Sorghum takes longer to cook than grains such as quinoa and millet, but it is worth the wait. The plump, chewy grains are reminiscent of Israeli couscous pearls and are delicious hot and cold. Both the simmer method and the pasta method produce equally excellent results.

Like amaranth, sorghum can also be popped, but I cannot recommend it. Popped amaranth is almost ethereal in texture and pops with ease. Sorghum is more of a challenge to pop — it takes longer than amaranth and is prone to burning — and the results taste like the hulls of popcorn, absent most of the puff.

The Simmer Method

To prepare $2\frac{1}{2}$ cups (625 mL) cooked sorghum, combine 1 cup (250 mL) sorghum and 3 cups (750 mL) water in a medium saucepan. Bring to a boil over medium-high heat. Reduce heat to low, cover and simmer for 50 to 60 minutes or until tender. Drain off any excess liquid.

The Pasta Method

Fill a large pot with water, add salt if desired and bring to a boil. Add the desired amount of sorghum and cook for 45 to 55 minutes or until tender. Drain thoroughly.

Teff

Teff, native to Ethiopia and smaller than any other grain, has origins that can be traced back between 4000 and 1000 BC. Its name comes from the Amharic (Ethiopian) word *teffa*, meaning "lost": the saying goes that if you drop a grain of teff, you'll never find it again. But the tiny, naturally gluten-free grain is a nutritional leviathan, high in protein, fiber, vitamins and minerals.

Teff is a northeast African mainstay. It is prepared in multiple ways, but is very often ground into a flour and fermented to make injera, a spongy sourdough flatbread that is soft, porous and thin like a pancake. It is estimated that Ethiopians and Eritreans get about two-thirds of their dietary protein from teff, and long-distance runners from Ethiopia and Eritrea credit their energy, health and athletic prowess to the grain. But teff only became known in other parts of the world in the late 20th century when farmers began to cultivate it in Australia and the United States. Teff varies in color, from light to dark, but the dark red variety — which has an earthy flavor with hints of malt and hazelnuts — is the most commonly available outside of Ethiopia.

The nutrient-packed bran and germ make up the majority of the teff grain, which explains why its nutrient content is so high compared with other grains. One serving of dry teff (1/4 cup/60 mL) offers 7 grams of protein, 4 grams of dietary fiber, 25% of the daily recommended magnesium, 20% of your daily iron and 10% of your daily calcium, vitamin B_6 and zinc. Unlike other grains, teff is also an excellent source of vitamin C. Plus, teff is high in resistant starch, a type of dietary fiber that benefits blood sugar management, weight control and colon health.

Teff Cooking Methods

Because of its tiny size, teff does not cook into light, fluffy, separate grains. It makes up for that with what it *can* do. It can be cooked into a creamy porridge that works equally well as a sweet breakfast, pudding or savory polenta; a few spoonfuls can be added to soups and stews to achieve a thicker texture; or it can be "dry-cooked," producing crunchy grains suitable for topping salads, breads, hot cereal, muffins and more.

Porridge/Soft Polenta-Style Teff

To prepare 3 cups (750 mL) cooked porridge- or polenta-style teff, combine 1 cup (250 mL) teff and 3 cups (750 mL) water in a medium saucepan. Bring to a boil over medium-high heat. Reduce heat to low, cover and simmer, stirring occasionally, for 15 to 20 minutes or until liquid is absorbed and mixture appears creamy. Remove from heat and let stand, covered, for 5 minutes before serving.

Dry-Cooked Teff

To make 1 cup (250 mL) dry-cooked teff, place 1/2 cup (125 mL) teff in a medium skillet. Cook, stirring, over medium-low heat until the grains begin to make a popping sound. Stir in 3/4 cup (175 mL) water and a pinch of fine sea salt; reduce heat to low, cover and cook for 5 to 8 minutes or until all of the water is absorbed. Remove from heat and let stand, covered, for 5 minutes. Spread teff out on a small rimmed baking sheet and let cool completely. Use immediately in a recipe or store in an airtight container in the refrigerator for up to 1 week.

Gluten-Free Flours, Starches and Psyllium Husk

The whole-grain flours used in this collection open up new worlds in baking, and not only for those looking for recipes free of gluten. Each of the following flours has subtle and distinct nuances, leading to enchanting new flavors, as well as enticing textures, in the resulting baked goods.

Amaranth Flour

Amaranth has a grassy, almost herbal flavor, which makes it particularly well suited to baked goods with other herbal qualities, such as honey, fresh herbs and sweet spices. Store amaranth flour in a tightly sealed zip-top plastic bag or airtight container in the refrigerator for up to 3 months or in the freezer for up to 6 months.

Brown Rice Flour

Brown rice flour is milled from unpolished brown rice and has a higher nutrient value than white rice flour. Since it contains bran, it has a short shelf life and should be refrigerated. It is extremely important to choose a brown rice flour with a fine, powdery texture. Rub the flour between your fingers: it should feel powdery, not gritty. If you use a grittier brown rice flour, the resulting baked goods will have a gritty texture. Store brown rice flour in a tightly sealed zip-top plastic bag or airtight container in the refrigerator for up to 3 months or in the freezer for up to 12 months.

Buckwheat Flour

The small seeds of the buckwheat plant are ground to make a strongly nutty-flavored flour that is unmistakably delicious and distinctive in pancakes, quick breads, cookies and cakes. Store buckwheat flour in a tightly sealed zip-top plastic bag or airtight container in the refrigerator for up to 6 months or in the freezer for up to 12 months.

Millet Flour

Millet flour is light and versatile, with a flavor reminiscent of corn or hominy. It makes a great alternative to cornmeal for those with sensitivities to corn, but is neutral enough that it can be used in a broad range of sweet and savory recipes. Store millet flour in a tightly sealed zip-top plastic bag or airtight container in the refrigerator for up to 3 months or in the freezer for up to 12 months.

Oat Flour

Oat flour has a mild, gently sweet, almost creamy flavor that is scrumptious in everything from cookies to muffins to tortillas. You can easily make oat flour at home from rolled oats (see box, below), but you can also buy it ready-made. Be sure to check that the flour is made from certified gluten-free oats. Store oat flour in a tightly sealed zip-top plastic bag or airtight container in the refrigerator for up to 6 months or in the freezer for up to 12 months.

> **Making Your Own Oat Flour**
>
> To make about 1 cup (250 mL) oat flour, place 1⅓ cups (325 mL) certified GF rolled oats (large-flake or quick-cooking) in a food processor or blender and process to the consistency of flour.

Quinoa Flour

Quinoa flour has a distinctive, earthy-sesame flavor that is stronger than cooked whole quinoa. It pairs well with hearty and assertive flavors in both sweet and savory baked goods. Quinoa flour rivals wheat flour for versatility, making it possible to create myriad gluten-free baked goods that bake up quickly and easily, with excellent flavor and texture. Store quinoa flour in a tightly sealed zip-top plastic bag or airtight container in the refrigerator for up to 3 months or in the freezer for up to 6 months.

Sorghum Flour

When ground into flour, sorghum adds a superb, slightly sweet flavor to baked goods and is highly nutritious. Store sorghum flour in a tightly sealed zip-top plastic bag or airtight container in the refrigerator for up to 2 months or in the freezer for up to 4 months.

Teff Flour

Teff flour gives baked goods a light, springy texture. It has a subtle sweetness, with hints of malt and cocoa, that is exceptional in combination with flavors such as chocolate, molasses, strong sweet spices (such as cloves and allspice) and dark beer. Store teff flour in a tightly sealed zip-top plastic bag or airtight container in the refrigerator for up to 3 months or in the freezer for up to 6 months.

Potato Starch

Potato starch is used in combination with other flours, rarely by itself. Be careful not to buy potato flour (it can be a bit confusing, since potato starch is occasionally labeled "potato starch flour"). Potato flour has a strong potato taste and a heavy texture; it is rarely used in gluten-free baking. Store potato starch in a tightly sealed zip-top plastic bag or airtight container in the refrigerator for up to 6 months or in the freezer for up to 1 year.

Tapioca Starch

Tapioca starch (also called tapioca flour) is a light, velvety flour milled from the cassava root. It lightens gluten-free baked goods and gives them a texture more like that of baked goods made with wheat flour. Store tapioca starch in a tightly sealed zip-top plastic bag or airtight container in the refrigerator for up to 6 months or in the freezer for up to 1 year.

Psyllium Husk

You may not have heard of psyllium as a binder for gluten-free baked goods, but it will soon become one of your favorite products. It is an all-natural, easy-to-use alternative to gums such as xanthan gum and guar gum.

Psyllium (*Plantago ovata*) is an annual herb that is grown in India and some European countries. Its seeds contain large quantities of a type of soluble fiber known as mucilage, which absorbs liquid to produce a thick gel. It is this thick gel that provides structure and volume in the absence of gluten.

Psyllium husk can be purchased at health food stores, pharmacies and online health food purveyors. Be sure to select whole psyllium husk (preferably organic), not psyllium husk powder. Store psyllium husk in a tightly sealed zip-top plastic bag or airtight container at room temperature for up to 6 months or in the freezer for up to 1 year.

Making a Psyllium "Egg"

Psyllium husk can also be used as an egg substitute for those with egg sensitivities. To make a psyllium "egg," mix 1 tbsp (15 mL) psyllium husk with 3 tbsp (45 mL) water or other liquid, then let stand for 5 minutes to thicken.

The Everyday Gluten-Free Pantry

Although all of the recipes in this collection feature one or more of the ancient grains highlighted in the previous section, the delicious, healthful dishes are not made from grains alone. Use this guide to help you choose the other ingredients you need to stock your pantry, fridge and freezer with wholesome ingredients that will make gluten-free food preparation a breeze.

When following a gluten-free diet, make sure to use gluten-free versions of the following ingredients:

- Almond extract
- Baking powder
- Broth
- Chocolate
- Miso paste
- Soy sauce
- Tamari
- Vanilla extract

Hidden Gluten

Gluten is found in many obvious places (breads and bread products), but it is also hidden in thousands of products you would never think to suspect, from meats to flavorings to Popsicles. Reading labels is critically important, as is becoming familiar with the names of potential gluten ingredients. Celiac organizations such as the National Foundation for Celiac Awareness, Celiac.com, The Center for Celiac Research and Celiac Disease Center offer information about hidden gluten ingredients on their websites.

To help you remember, when I call for any of these ingredients in the recipes, I specify "GF" — for "gluten-free" — in the ingredient list, reminding you to check for hidden gluten when restocking your supply of these items.

Fruits and Vegetables

Whole grains and fresh produce go hand in hand. Here are some go-to options that will help you prepare a wealth of healthy whole-grain meals.

Fresh Fruits and Vegetables

Fresh fruits and vegetables are packed with essential vitamins and nutrients, so it's a good idea to always have some on hand. Place a bowl of fresh fruit on the counter, and keep washed and cut vegetables in the refrigerator for ready-to-eat snacks. Store hardy vegetables, such as onions, potatoes, carrots and celery, in the pantry and crisper — they're a great foundation for countless recipes.

For the freshest fruits and vegetables at the best prices, buy what is in season. In most cases, you can buy fruits a few days before their peak ripeness and let them ripen at home before use. If you choose to buy them at or past peak, use them right away — within a day or two.

Fresh Dates

Fresh dates — the fruit of the date palm tree — are among the sweetest fruits in the world, with a flavor similar to brown sugar. They can be used in desserts, snacks, sauces and even soups, stews and chilis to add sweetness. The most commonly available soft dates in the United States and Canada are Medjool dates, which are plump and tender, and Deglet Noor dates, which are semi-soft, slender and a bit chewy; both varieties have often been left on the tree for a while after they are ripe to dry a bit (and thus last longer after harvest). When choosing fresh dates, select those that are plump-looking; it is okay if they are slightly wrinkled, but they shouldn't feel hard.

Delicate fruits and vegetables, such as berries, cherries, plums, asparagus, bell peppers, corn, cucumbers, mushrooms, yellow summer squash and zucchini, should be used close to the day of purchase. By contrast, apples, bananas, cabbage, carrots, celery, citrus fruits (such as oranges, lemons, limes and grapefruits), garlic, onions, potatoes (yellow and russet) and sweet potatoes keep well.

Ask your grocery store's produce manager what the delivery days are, so you can purchase your favorite fruits and vegetables before their quality declines. Alternatively, buy your produce at a local farmers' market. Many communities sponsor weekly farmers' markets to provide a central, in-town site for small farms to sell their produce directly to consumers.

The Dirty Dozen and the Clean Fifteen

The Environmental Working Group (EWG), a nonprofit organization, created the *Shoppers Guide to Pesticides in Produce*. The 2014 edition of the guide is based on the results of 28,000 tests for pesticides on produce by the U.S. Department of Agriculture and the federal Food and Drug Administration. It's important to note that the EWG states that almost all of the tests were performed on produce that had been rinsed or peeled. For more information, visit www.ewg.org.

The Dirty Dozen (Plus Two)

Here are the top 12 most pesticide-contaminated fruits and vegetables in America, along with two additional suspects, summer squash and kale. When shopping for these items, buy organic whenever possible.

1. Apples
2. Strawberries
3. Grapes
4. Celery
5. Peaches
6. Spinach
7. Bell peppers
8. Nectarines (imported)
9. Cucumbers
10. Potatoes
11. Cherry tomatoes
12. Hot peppers
13. Summer squash
14. Kale

The Clean Fifteen

These fruits and vegetables are the least contaminated by pesticides, so it's not as crucial to buy organic.

1. Sweet corn
2. Onions
3. Pineapples
4. Avocados
5. Cabbage
6. Sweet peas (frozen)
7. Papayas
8. Mangos
9. Asparagus
10. Eggplants
11. Kiwifruit
12. Grapefruit
13. Cantaloupe
14. Sweet potatoes
15. Mushrooms

Frozen Fruits and Vegetables

Keeping a selection of frozen fruits and vegetables in the freezer is a great way to make quick and simple grain dishes in an instant, whether for quick soups or for morning smoothies.

In addition to its convenience, frozen produce can sometimes be more nutritious than fresh. When fresh fruits and vegetables are shipped long distances, they rapidly lose vitamins and minerals thanks to exposure to heat and light; by contrast, frozen fruits and vegetables are frozen immediately after being picked, ensuring that all of the vitamins and minerals are preserved.

Whenever possible, choose organic frozen fruits and vegetables. Some varieties to keep on hand include:

- Winter squash purée (typically a blend of acorn and butternut squash)
- Petite peas
- Chopped greens (e.g., spinach, Swiss chard, mustard greens)
- Chopped onions
- Vegetable stir-fry blends
- Broccoli florets
- Shelled edamame
- Corn
- Lima beans
- Berries (blueberries, blackberries, raspberries, strawberries)

- Diced mangos
- Diced pineapples
- Sliced peaches

Shelf-Stable Tomato Products

Choose organic tomato products whenever possible, as they tend to be lower in sodium and residual chemicals.

Diced Tomatoes

Canned diced tomatoes can replace diced fresh tomatoes in most recipes, especially soups and stews. Stock up on diced fire-roasted tomatoes, too, as they add a subtle smoky flavor to dishes.

Interpreting Organic Labels

Understanding the various organic labels can be a challenge. Here's what the four most common labels and claims mean:

"100% Organic" USDA ORGANIC	For a food product to be 100% organic and be able to bear the USDA organic seal, it must be made with 100% organic ingredients. The food product also must have an ingredient list and list the name of the certifying agency.
"Organic" USDA ORGANIC	For a food product to be labeled as "organic" and be able to bear the USDA organic seal, it must be made with 95% organic ingredients. The food product also must list the name of the certifying agency and have an ingredient statement on the label where organic ingredients are identified as organic.
"Made with Organic Ingredients"	To make this claim, a food product must be made with at least 70% organic ingredients. The food product also must list the name of the certifying agency and have an ingredient statement on the label where organic ingredients are identified as organic.
"Some Organic Ingredients"	Food products with less than 70% organic ingredients cannot bear the USDA seal nor have information about a certifying agency, or any reference to organic content.

Crushed Tomatoes

Canned crushed tomatoes (sometimes called ground tomatoes) are a convenient way to add fresh tomato flavor to soups, stews and pastas without the separate step of puréeing.

Tomato Sauce

Tomato sauce can be used to make delicious sauces, stews and soups when you want to give them a distinct tomato flavor. For true tomato flavor with minimal processing, be sure to select a variety of tomato sauce that is low in sodium and has no added seasonings.

Tomato Paste

Tomato paste is made from tomatoes that have been cooked for several hours, then strained and reduced to a deep red, richly flavored concentrate. It is available in both cans and convenient squeeze tubes. Just a tablespoon or two (15 or 30 mL) can greatly enrich a wide variety of dishes, adding acidity, depth and a hint of sweetness. Select a brand that is low in sodium, has no added seasonings and is clearly labeled gluten-free (a small number of brands use wheat-based additives as thickening agents).

Sun-Dried Tomatoes

Sun-dried tomatoes are a flavorful and nutritious way to add an extra bit of zest to grain recipes. Look for organic sun-dried tomatoes, which are often processed at a lower temperature than most commercial varieties, preserving some of the nutrients.

Marinara Sauce

Jarred marinara sauce — a highly seasoned Italian tomato sauce made with onions, garlic, basil and oregano — is typically used on pasta and meat, but it is also a great pantry staple for creating a range of whole-grain meals in minutes. For the best tomato flavor and the most versatility, choose a variety with minimal ingredients and low sodium. The majority of marinara sauces on the market are gluten-free, but check the label to be certain.

Chunky Tomato Salsa

Like marinara sauce, ready-made chunky salsa — rich with tomatoes, peppers, onions and spices but low in calories — packs tremendous flavor into grain recipes in an instant. For the best flavor and nutrition, select a brand that is low in sodium and has a short list of easily identifiable ingredients.

Dried Fruit

A variety of dried fruit is essential for adding depth of flavor and sweetness to grain recipes. Whenever possible, opt for organic dried fruit. The following are top picks:

- Raisins (both dark and golden)
- Dried currants (sometimes labeled Zante currants)
- Dried cranberries (preferably sweetened with fruit juice)
- Dried cherries
- Dried apricots
- Dried apples
- Dried figs
- Prunes (dried plums)

Legumes

Legumes are nutritional powerhouses, very low in cost and easy to prepare for use in a wide variety of grain recipes. In this collection, legumes are used in many forms, from canned beans to dried split peas to tofu.

Canned Beans

With their high protein content, wide availability, low cost and convenience, canned beans are ideal in combination with grains for quick, healthy meals. For the best flavor and versatility, select varieties that are low in sodium and have no added seasonings. The following varieties are great choices to keep on hand for everything from dips to entrées:

- Black beans
- White beans (e.g., cannellini and white navy beans)
- Pinto beans
- Red kidney beans
- Chickpeas

Dried Split Peas (Green and Yellow)

A variety of yellow and green peas are grown specifically for drying. These peas are dried and split along a natural seam (hence, "split peas"). Split peas are very inexpensive and are loaded with good nutrition, including a significant amount of protein. They are available packaged in supermarkets and in bulk in health food stores. Unlike dried beans, they do not require presoaking.

Dried Lentils

Lentils are inexpensive, require no presoaking, cook in about 30 to 45 minutes and are very high in nutrients (soybeans are the only legume with more protein). Lentils come in a variety of sizes and colors: common brown lentils and French green lentils can be found in supermarkets, and increasingly, so can red and black lentils.

Tofu

Tofu, or bean curd, is made from soy beans that have been cooked, made into milk and then coagulated. The soy milk curdles when heated, and the curds are skimmed off and pressed into blocks.

The recipes in this collection were tested with refrigerated tofu. While shelf-stable tofu is convenient, the flavor and texture are markedly inferior. Tofu can be found in extra-firm, firm and soft varieties in the refrigerated section of the supermarket. For optimal results, be sure to use the variety specified in the recipe.

Nuts, Seeds and Nut/Seed Butters

Nuts and seeds — including natural nut and seed butters — are very nutritious and are a perfect complement to a wide range of grains. In addition to being excellent sources of protein, nuts and seeds contain vitamins, minerals, fiber and essential fatty acids (such as omega-3 and omega-6).

Nuts

A wide variety of nuts are used in this collection, including walnuts, cashews, pecans, almonds, hazelnuts and pistachios. Many of the recipes call for the nuts to be toasted before they are used. Toasting nuts deepens their flavor and makes them crisp.

Toasting Whole Nuts

To toast whole nuts, spread the amount needed for the recipe on a rimmed baking sheet. Bake in a preheated 350°F (180°C) oven for 8 to 10 minutes or until golden and fragrant. Alternatively, toast the nuts in a dry skillet over low heat, stirring constantly for 2 to 4 minutes or until golden and fragrant. Transfer the toasted nuts to a plate and let them cool before chopping.

Ground Flax Seeds (Flaxseed Meal)

Flax seeds are highly nutritious, tiny seeds from the flax plant. They have gained tremendous popularity in recent years thanks to their high levels of omega-3 fatty acids. But to reap the most benefits from the seeds, they must be ground into meal. Look for packages of ready-ground flax seeds, which may be labeled "flaxseed meal," or use a clean spice or coffee grinder to grind whole flax seeds to a very fine meal. The meal adds a warm, nutty flavor to a wide range of recipes. Store ground flax seeds in an airtight container in the refrigerator for up to 5 months or in the freezer for up to 8 months.

Green Pumpkin Seeds (Pepitas)

Pepitas are pumpkin seeds with the white hull removed, leaving the flat, dark green inner seed. They are subtly sweet and nutty, with a slightly chewy texture when raw and a crisp, crunchy texture when toasted or roasted. They can be used much as nuts are used — sprinkled atop salads, soups and entrées for a pleasant, contrasting crunch, or added to muffins, cookies or breads. All of the recipes in this collection use raw green pumpkin seeds unless otherwise specified.

Shelled Sunflower Seeds

Sunflower seeds are highly nutritious and have a mild, nutty flavor. The recipes in this collection call for seeds that have been removed from their shells, and are raw, rather than roasted, unless otherwise specified. They can be used in place of nuts in both sweet and savory dishes.

Sesame Seeds

The flavor of tiny, delicate sesame seeds increases exponentially when they are toasted. Used as a flavoring in many Asian preparations, sesame seeds are also delicious in sweet and savory baked goods.

Toasting Seeds

Seeds toast more quickly than most nuts, so toasting them in a skillet on the stovetop is the best option. Spread the amount needed for a recipe in a dry skillet and cook over low heat, stirring constantly, for 1 to 4 minutes or until golden and fragrant. (Sesame seeds and green pumpkin seeds will also make a popping sound when they are fully toasted.) Immediately transfer the toasted seeds to a plate and let them cool completely before adding them to the recipe.

Nut and Seed Butters

Delicious, nutritious, ultra-convenient nut and seed butters are a boon for any meal of the day, as well as for snacks, desserts and quick breads. They can also impart instant richness to a wide range of sauces and dressings. A wide variety of all-natural, unsweetened, unsalted nut and seed butters is increasingly available at well-stocked supermarkets, co-ops and natural food stores. Seed butters, such as tahini and sunflower seed butter, are an excellent substitution for nut butters for those with tree nut allergies or sensitivities. Store opened jars in the refrigerator.

Eggs, Dairy and Non-Dairy Milks

Eggs, dairy products and non-dairy milks are essential ingredients in any healthy pantry, helping you prepare everything from short-order breakfasts and dinners to countless baked goods.

Eggs

All of the recipes in this book were tested with large eggs. Select clean, fresh eggs that have been handled properly and refrigerated.

Do not use dirty, cracked or leaking eggs, or eggs that have a bad odor or unnatural color when cracked open; they may have become contaminated with harmful bacteria, such as salmonella.

Dairy Products

Dairy products are used in a wide range of recipes in this book. All of the recipes were tested with both whole and lower-fat milk and other dairy products; you may use either. I do not recommend using nonfat dairy products, as the lack of fat can significantly alter the texture and flavor of the finished product. In addition, nonfat dairy products such as

Decoding Egg Labels

These days, egg cartons are covered in labels ranging from "organic" to "cage-free" to "animal welfare approved." It's confusing, to say the least. Here's a quick guide to the terms you need to know, according to USDA guidelines:

- *Organic:* Chickens must be cage-free with some outdoor access (amount not defined), cannot be given antibiotics, and must be fed organic, vegetarian food. The USDA Organic seal is the only official egg label claim that's backed by federal regulations.
- *Free Range:* Chickens are out of cages, and can roam freely around a farmyard for at least part of the day, but there is no regulation in the U.S. about the amount or quality of outdoor access. There are no restrictions on what the birds can be fed.
- *Cage Free:* Chickens have continuous access to food and water and are out of cages, but do not necessarily have access to the outdoors. They may be tightly packed into a shed, with no access to a farmyard.
- *Certified Humane:* Chickens are out of cages inside barns or warehouses, but may not have access to the outdoors. There are regulations to ensure that the chickens can perform natural behaviors and to limit the density of birds. More information is available at www.certifiedhumane.com.
- *Animal Welfare Approved:* This term is given to independent family farmers with flocks of up to 500 chickens, who are free to spend unlimited time outside on pesticide-free pasture and cannot have their beaks cut (beak cutting is allowed in all the previous definitions and is very common). Eggs from these farms are most commonly found at specialty or health food stores and at farmers' markets.

The following terms are unregulated and therefore mean nothing:

- Natural
- Naturally Raised
- No Hormones
- No Antibiotics

cheeses often contain starches and gums that are less than healthy or tasty.

Buttermilk

Commercially prepared buttermilk has a delicious and distinctive tang. It is made by culturing 1% milk with bacteria. When added to baked goods, it yields a tender, moist result and a slightly buttery flavor.

Making a Buttermilk Substitute

If you don't have buttermilk, it's easy to make a substitute. Mix 1 tbsp (15 mL) lemon juice or white vinegar into 1 cup (250 mL) milk or plain non-dairy milk. Let stand for at least 15 minutes before using, to allow the milk to curdle. Any extra can be stored in the refrigerator for the same amount of time as the milk from which it was made.

Yogurt

Yogurt, like buttermilk, is acidic and adds a distinctive tang to recipes. It tenderizes meats and baked goods, and makes an excellent substitution for sour cream in a wide range of recipes. Greek yogurt is a thick, creamy yogurt similar in texture to sour cream. It is made by straining the whey from yogurt and is very high in protein, not to mention incredibly delicious.

Non-dairy yogurt can be used in place of dairy yogurt for any of the recipes in this collection. Try rice, coconut or soy yogurt.

Non-Dairy Milks

Non-dairy milks are essential for vegans, as well as those who are lactose intolerant or are allergic to dairy. But they are also a delicious option for all of us, whether to use in cooking or baking, or to drink straight up. The variety and availability of non-dairy milks is greater than ever, and you cannot beat their shelf-stable convenience. Although non-dairy milks are available in a variety of flavors, opt for plain when substituting them for milk in any of the recipes in this collection.

Almond Milk

Almond milk is made from almonds, water, sea salt and typically a small amount of sweetener. It works particularly well as a substitute for dairy milk in recipes for baked goods.

Rice Milk

Rice milk is made from brown rice, water, sea salt and typically a small amount of oil. It is a very light, sweet beverage that can replace cow's milk in most recipes.

Hemp Milk

Hemp milk is a thick, rich milk made from hemp seeds, water and a touch of brown rice syrup. It is rich in healthy omega-3 fatty acids, protein and essential vitamins and minerals. Because of its neutral taste, it can be used in a broad range of sweet and savory dishes.

Coconut Milk

All of the recipes calling for coconut milk in this collection specify full-fat (typically 17% fat or slightly higher). Its rich, full-flavor, snow-white liquid is produced by grating and pressing fresh coconut meat. Be careful not to use "light" coconut milk or coconut milk beverage in place of full-fat coconut milk; both have a much lower fat content, and using them will lead to markedly different results, especially in baked goods.

If you choose to use coconut milk where non-dairy milk is specified, use half full-fat coconut milk and half water. For example, for 1 cup (250 mL) non-dairy milk, use 1/2 cup (125 mL) full-fat coconut milk mixed with 1/2 cup (125 mL) water.

Coconut milk is available in cans and, occasionally, in Tetra Paks. It remains mostly liquid at room temperature. Some of the liquid and fat separate, even at room temperature, so it is important to stir or gently whisk the milk upon opening until it is blended smooth. Transfer any unused coconut milk to an airtight container and refrigerate for up to 5 days or freeze for up to 6 months.

Flax Milk

In comparison to other non-dairy milks, flax milk has a flavor and texture most similar to cow's milk. It is made by mixing cold-pressed flaxseed oil with water. Flax milk is high in omega-3 fatty acids and calcium. It is also a good source of vitamin A, vitamin B_{12} and vitamin D.

> ### Making Your Own Flax Milk
>
> In a blender, combine 1/3 cup (75 mL) flax seeds with 6 cups (1.5 L) filtered water and blend on high for 1 minute. Strain through cheesecloth into an airtight container and refrigerate for 3 to 5 days.

> ### Making Your Own Sunflower Seed Milk
>
> Soak 1 cup (250 mL) raw sunflower seeds in filtered water overnight. Drain and add the seeds to a blender with 3 cups (750 mL) water, then blend until smooth. Strain through cheesecloth into an airtight container and refrigerate for 3 to 5 days. Shake well before using. The same method may also be used to make milk with sesame seeds or green pumpkin seeds (pepitas).

Sunflower Seed Milk

Sunflower seed milk has a rich texture and a faint sunflower seed taste. It is a good source of calcium and also has small amounts of vitamin A and iron.

Fats and Oils

Fats and oils can be healthy or unhealthy; it all depends on the type you use and how much you consume. Some oils, such as those that contain essential fatty acids (omega-3s and omega-6s, for example), are an absolutely necessary part of your diet. And when it comes to eating healthier over the long term, you'll feel happy and satisfied when you cook your food with a healthy amount of good fats.

Butter

Fresh butter has a delicate cream flavor and a pale yellow color, and adds tremendous flavor to a wide range of recipes. I recommend buying and using only unsalted butter for the recipes in this collection. The obvious reason is the added salt. Different manufacturers use different amounts of salt in their butter, so it's not possible to reliably determine how much salt is in any given stick or cube. The less obvious reason is that salt is a preservative: salted butter has a longer shelf life in the refrigerator (as much as 2 or 3 months). As such, the salted butter at the supermarket may be far less fresh than the unsalted option, and has sometimes been made from cream that is less fresh too. If you are concerned about keeping unsalted butter fresh once you've purchased it, you can store it in the freezer for up to 6 months.

Butter quickly picks up off-flavors during storage and when exposed to oxygen, so once the carton or wrap is opened, place it in a sealable plastic food bag or other airtight container. Store it away from foods with strong odors, especially items such as onions or garlic.

Olive Oil

Olive oil is monounsaturated oil that is prized for its use in a wide range of dishes. Extra virgin olive oil is the cold-pressed result of the first pressing of the olives and is considered the finest and fruitiest of the olive oils. The subtle nuances of extra virgin olive oil shine best when it is uncooked, whether in salad dressings or drizzled on top of soup. Consider using olive oil simply labeled "olive oil" — produced from additional pressings of the olives and far less expensive than extra virgin — for general cooking purposes.

Virgin Coconut Oil

Virgin coconut oil is harvested from fresh, young coconuts with a minimal amount of processing. A bonus of this minimal processing is that the oil retains a delicate coconut scent and aroma. Unlike other plant oils, many of which are prone to rancidity and must be refrigerated, coconut oil can be stored at room temperature. In cool regions, during winter months, or in the refrigerator, the oil is solid, but in warm climates, such as the tropical regions in which coconuts grow, it remains a clear liquid year-round. When kept at room temperature, the oil will fluctuate from liquid to solid; this is completely normal and, unlike other oils, it does not affect the oil's quality.

It is simple to scrape out a teaspoon or tablespoon (5 or 15 mL) of coconut oil when it is solid, but when a larger amount is needed for a recipe, it is easier to melt the oil before measuring. As noted above, it does not harm coconut oil to be warmed to a liquid state, so you can quickly liquefy the entire jar of oil. To do this, simply hold the sealed jar under warm running water, or place it in a bowl of warm water, until there is enough liquid oil to measure out. Coconut oil can also be warmed in the microwave. Scrape out the approximate amount needed for the recipe into a microwave-safe bowl. Microwave in 3- to 4-second intervals until warm enough to measure easily.

Toasted Sesame Oil

Toasted sesame oil has a dark brown color and a rich, nutty flavor. It is used sparingly, mostly in Asian-inspired recipes, to add a tremendous amount of flavor.

Vegetable Oil

"Vegetable oil" is a generic term used to describe any neutral, plant-based oil that is liquid at room temperature. You can choose from a variety of vegetable oils (such as safflower, sunflower or canola), but opt for those that are:

- Expeller-pressed or cold-pressed. Expeller-pressed oils are pressed simply by crushing the seeds, while cold-pressed oils are expeller-pressed oils that are produced in a heat-controlled environment.
- High in healthful unsaturated fats (no more than 7% saturated fat).

Nonstick Cooking Spray

A number of recipes in this collection call for the use of nonstick cooking spray, which helps keep foods from sticking while simultaneously cutting back on fat and calories in a dish. While any variety of cooking spray may be used, I recommend using an organic cooking spray for two reasons: first, these sprays are typically made with higher-quality oils (in many cases expeller-pressed or cold-pressed oils) than most commercial brands; second, they are more likely to use compressed gas to expel the propellant, so no hydrocarbons are released into the environment. Read the label and choose wisely.

Minimally Processed Sweeteners

Minimally processed sweeteners are closer to their whole form than highly refined sweeteners, which have most or all of their natural vitamins and minerals removed during the refining process. Minimally processed sweeteners contain a broader spectrum of flavors than refined sugar; hence, they add more than sweetness alone to sweet and savory dishes.

Fine Crystal Cane Sugar

Fine crystal cane sugar, also called natural cane sugar, evaporated cane sugar, whole cane sugar or dried cane juice, is made by extracting, clarifying, evaporating and crystalizing sugar cane juice. Many of the minerals from the plant are still present, which helps the human body digest the sugars.

Cane sugars come in a wide variety of colors, from pale blond to dark brown, and textures, from coarse and dry to fine and somewhat moist. At present, there is no standardization for the processing and labeling of cane sugars, so the best option is to choose the type that suits your needs and tastes. The recipes in this collection were tested using fine crystal cane sugar, which is fine-grained, pale in color and similar in texture to granulated sugar.

Brown Sugar

Brown sugar is granulated sugar with some molasses added to it. The molasses gives the brown sugar a soft texture. Light brown sugar (also known as golden yellow sugar) has less molasses and a more delicate flavor than dark brown sugar. Once opened, store brown sugar in an airtight container or a tightly sealed zip-top plastic bag to prevent clumping.

Coconut Sugar

Coconut sugar is an all-natural, unrefined sugar made from coconut nectar. Once the coconut nectar is collected, it is air-dried to form a crystalline sugar that looks and tastes much like brown sugar, with a very faint coconut flavor. It dissolves and melts the same as other sugars and can be used measure for measure in place of granulated or brown sugar. Since coconut sugar is not refined, it retains a number of key vitamins, minerals and phytonutrients, including potassium, zinc, iron and vitamins B_1, B_2, B_3 and B_6. It also has a low glycemic index.

If you have shopped in Southeast Asian, Indian or Central American markets, you may have seen coconut sugar labeled as jaggery, palm sugar or Java sugar and shaped into cones or cakes. Where coconut sugar is called for in this collection, use bagged granules of coconut sugar that can be scooped and measured.

Turbinado Sugar

Turbinado sugar is raw sugar that has been steam-cleaned. The coarse crystals are blond in color and have a delicate molasses flavor. They are typically used for decoration and texture atop baked goods.

Pure Cane Confectioners' (Icing) Sugar

Confectioners' (icing) sugar (also called powdered sugar) is granulated sugar that has been ground to a fine powder. Cornstarch is added to prevent the sugar from clumping together. Pure cane confectioners' (icing) sugar, sometimes labeled "powdered sugar," is made using the same process as regular confectioners' sugar, but is made with less processed cane sugar. Several brands also use tapioca starch or potato starch in place of cornstarch. Regular confectioners' sugar may be used in its place. It is used very minimally in a couple of recipes in this collection.

Brown Rice Syrup

Brown rice syrup is made from brown rice that has been soaked, sprouted and cooked with an enzyme that breaks the starches into maltose. Brown rice syrup has a light, mild flavor and a similar appearance to honey, though it is less sweet. Rice syrup can be substituted one for one for honey or maple syrup.

Honey

Honey is plant nectar that has been gathered and concentrated by honey bees. Any variety of honey may be used in the recipes in this collection. Unopened containers of honey may be stored at room temperature. After opening, store honey in the refrigerator to protect against mold. Honey will keep indefinitely when stored properly.

Maple Syrup

Maple syrup is a thick liquid sweetener made by boiling the sap from maple trees. It has a strong, pure maple flavor. Maple-flavored pancake syrup is just corn syrup with coloring and artificial maple flavoring added, and it is not recommended as a substitute for pure maple syrup. Unopened containers of maple syrup may be stored at room temperature. After opening, store maple syrup in the refrigerator to protect against mold. Maple syrup will keep indefinitely when stored properly.

Molasses

Molasses is made from the juice of sugar cane or sugar beets, which is boiled until a syrupy mixture remains. The recipes in this collection were tested using dark (cooking) molasses, but you can substitute light (fancy) molasses if you prefer. Blackstrap molasses is thick and very dark, and it has a bitter flavor; it is not recommended for the recipes in this collection. Unopened containers of molasses may be stored at room temperature. After opening, store molasses in the refrigerator to protect against mold. Molasses will keep indefinitely when stored properly.

Agave Nectar

Agave nectar (or agave syrup) is a plant-based sweetener derived from the agave cactus, native to Mexico. Used for centuries to make tequila, agave juice produces a light golden syrup.

Chemical Leaveners

Chemical leaveners lighten dough, causing it to rise. In the baking recipes in this collection, baking powder and baking soda are used as the leaveners.

Baking Powder

Baking powder is a chemical leavening agent made from a blend of alkali (sodium bicarbonate, known commonly as baking soda) and acid (most commonly calcium acid phosphate, sodium aluminum sulfate or cream of tartar), plus some form of starch to absorb any moisture so a reaction does not take place until a liquid is added. When baking powder is combined with a liquid, a chemical reaction produces carbon dioxide, which is trapped in tiny air pockets in the dough or batter. Heat releases additional carbon dioxide and expands the trapped gas and air to create steam. The pressure expands the air pockets, thus expanding the food.

The alkali and acid components of baking powder are naturally gluten-free, but in some cases, the starch that is added contains gluten. Most of the brands found in supermarkets are gluten-free, but if you are following a gluten-free diet, check with the manufacturer to be certain.

If you find yourself without baking powder as you prepare to bake, use this simple substitution: for every 1 tsp (5 mL) commercial baking powder, use a combination of $\frac{1}{4}$ tsp (1 mL) baking soda, $\frac{1}{2}$ tsp (2 mL) cream of tartar and $\frac{1}{4}$ tsp (1 mL) cornstarch.

Testing the Potency of Baking Powder

Baking powder loses its potency over time. To test your supply before using it in a recipe, pour $\frac{1}{3}$ cup (75 mL) hot water over $\frac{1}{2}$ tsp (2 mL) baking powder in a cup. The mixture should bubble vigorously. If it does not, toss the baking powder out and purchase a new container.

Baking Soda

Baking soda is a chemical leavener consisting of bicarbonate of soda. It is alkaline in nature and, when combined with an acidic ingredient such as buttermilk, yogurt, citrus juice, honey or molasses, it creates carbon dioxide bubbles, giving baked goods a dramatic rise. Baking soda is naturally gluten-free.

There is no accurate way to test the potency of baking soda. As a general rule, though, replace the box every 6 months for optimal freshness. Write the date the box was opened on the front, for an easy reminder.

Fresh Herbs

Fresh herbs add an aromatic backbone to cooked food. When added during the cooking process, they willingly surrender their flavors and aromas in minutes. Alternatively, you can add them as a final flourish for a bright note of fresh flavor and color.

Flat-leaf (Italian) parsley, cilantro and chives are readily available and inexpensive, and they store well in the produce bin of the refrigerator, so keep them on hand year-round. Basil, mint and thyme are best in the spring and summer, when they are in season in your own garden or at the farmers' market.

Flavorings

Elevating healthy, everyday dishes to exceptional levels of deliciousness can be as easy as creating a harmonious balance of simple flavorings — even if you're just adding salt and pepper. Here are my top recommendations for ingredients that will make the ordinary extraordinary.

Fine Sea Salt

Unless otherwise specified, the recipes in this collection were tested using fine-grain sea salt. Conventional salt production uses chemicals, additives and heat processing to achieve the end product commonly called table salt. By contrast, unrefined sea salt contains an abundance of naturally occurring trace minerals.

Black Pepper

Black pepper is made by grinding black peppercorns, which have been picked when the berry is not quite ripe, then dried until it shrivels and the skin turns dark brown to black. Black pepper has a strong, slightly hot flavor, with a hint of sweetness.

Spices and Dried Herbs

Spices and dried herbs can turn the simplest of meals into masterpieces. They should be stored in light- and air-proof containers, away from direct sunlight and heat, to preserve their flavors. Co-ops, health food stores and mail order sources that sell herbs and spices in bulk are all excellent options for purchasing very fresh, organic spices and dried herbs, often at a low cost.

With ground spices and dried herbs, freshness is everything. To determine whether a ground spice or dried herb is fresh, open the container and sniff. A strong fragrance means it is still acceptable for use.

Note that ground spices, not whole, are used throughout this collection. Here are my favorite ground spices and dried herbs:

Ground Spices
- Black pepper (cracked and ground)
- Cardamom
- Cayenne pepper (also labeled "ground red pepper")
- Chili powder
- Chinese five-spice powder
- Chipotle chile powder
- Cinnamon
- Coriander
- Cumin
- Garam masala
- Ginger
- Hot pepper flakes
- Mild curry powder
- Nutmeg
- Paprika
- Smoked paprika (both hot and sweet)
- Turmeric

Dried Herbs
- Bay leaves
- Oregano
- Rosemary
- Rubbed sage
- Thyme

Citrus Zest

Zest is the name for the colored outer layer of citrus peel. The oils in zest are intense in flavor. Use a zester, a rasp grater (such as a Microplane) or the small holes of a box grater to grate zest. Avoid grating the white layer (pith) just below the zest; it is very bitter.

Cocoa Powder

Select natural cocoa powder rather than Dutch process for the recipes in this collection. Natural cocoa powder has a deep, true chocolate flavor. The packaging should state whether it is Dutch process or not, but you can also tell the difference by sight: if it is dark to almost black, it is Dutch process; natural cocoa powder is much lighter and is typically brownish red in color.

Chocolate

It is becoming easier to find gluten-free chocolate, in both bar and chip form. Nevertheless, the best way to make sure your chocolate is gluten-free is to double-check the label and contact the manufacturer if necessary. Bars of gluten-free chocolate are sometimes easier to find than gluten-free chocolate chips. If necessary, use 3 oz (90 g) chocolate, chopped, for every 1/2 cup (125 mL) chocolate chips.

Vanilla Extract

Vanilla extract adds a sweet, fragrant flavor to dishes, especially baked goods. It is produced by combining an extraction from dried vanilla beans with an alcohol and water mixture. It is then aged for several months. The three most common types of vanilla beans used to make vanilla extract are Bourbon-Madagascar, Mexican and Tahitian. Select a brand that is clearly labeled as gluten-free.

Almond Extract

Almond extract is a flavoring manufactured by combining bitter almond oil with ethyl alcohol. It is used in much the same way as vanilla extract. Almond extract has a highly concentrated, intense flavor, so measure with care. Select a brand that is clearly labeled as gluten-free.

Tamari and Soy Sauce

Both tamari and soy sauce are natural products made from soybeans, water and sea salt; the two are very similar, but tamari has a deeper color and flavor. Wheat is sometimes added to the mix of ingredients in the fermenting process, so select a brand that is clearly labeled as gluten-free.

Miso Paste

Miso is a sweet, fermented soybean paste. It comes unpasteurized and in several varieties, from golden yellow to deep red to sweet white. It can be made into a soup or a sauce or used as a salt substitute. Select a variety that is clearly labeled as gluten-free.

Dijon Mustard

Dijon mustard adds depth of flavor to a wide range of dishes. It is particularly useful in salad dressings because it facilitates the emulsification of oil and vinegar.

Vinegars

Vinegars are multipurpose flavor powerhouses. Delicious in vinaigrettes and dressings, they are also stealth ingredients for use at the end of cooking time to enhance and balance the natural flavors of dishes. Store vinegars in a dark place, away from heat or light.

Cider Vinegar

Cider vinegar is made from the juice of crushed apples. After the juice is collected, it is allowed to age in wooden barrels.

Unseasoned Rice Vinegar

Rice vinegar is made from an alcohol fermentation of mashed rice. It then undergoes another fermentation to produce vinegar. In general, rice vinegar tends to be more acidic than other vinegars. Be sure to check the label to make sure it is unseasoned; seasoned rice vinegar has added salt and sugar.

Red Wine Vinegar

Red wine vinegar is produced by fermenting red wine in wooden barrels. This produces acetic acid, which gives red wine vinegar its distinctive taste. Red wine vinegar has a characteristic dark red color and red wine flavor.

White Wine Vinegar

White wine vinegar is a moderately tangy vinegar made from a blend of white wines. The wine is fermented, aged and filtered to produce a vinegar with a slightly lower acidity level than red wine vinegar.

Sherry Vinegar

Sherry vinegar has a deep, complex flavor and a dark reddish color. It is made from three different white grape varieties grown in the Jerez region of Spain. Most of the sherry vinegar produced comes from this region, making it a popular ingredient in Spanish cooking.

Balsamic Vinegar

Balsamic vinegar is a thick, aromatic vinegar made from concentrated grape must. Grape must is the freshly pressed juice of the grape, and also contains pulp, skins, stems and seeds. The must is boiled down to a sap and aged in wooden barrels for 6 months to 12 years. Some very expensive balsamic vinegars are aged for up to 25 years.

Ready-to-Use Broths

Ready-made chicken, beef and vegetable broths are essential for many of the recipes in this collection. Opt for certified organic broths that are clearly labeled as gluten-free, reduced-sodium and MSG-free. For chicken and beef broths, look for brands that are made from chicken or cattle raised without hormones or antibiotics.

For convenience, look for broths in Tetra Paks, which typically come in 32-oz (900 mL) and occasionally 48-oz (1.5 L) or 16-oz (500 mL) sizes. Once opened, these can be stored in the refrigerator for up to 1 week.

Buying Gluten-Free Groceries

The more you know about food, the easier it is to determine hidden sources of gluten. This is not as much of an issue when you're cooking with raw ingredients, but when it comes to processed foods with long ingredient lists, reading labels is a must. However, labels can be difficult to interpret. The Food Allergen and Labeling Consumer Protection Act requires that the top eight food allergens be clearly identified as ingredients, but not so for gluten. An August 2013 update to the law (effective as of August 2014) provides a definition for "gluten-free," as well as rules for the use of "gluten-free" on product packaging, but has no mandate for calling out the presence of gluten.

If a label does not state that the product is gluten-free but the ingredient list contains no gluten, wheat, barley, rye or wheat relatives such as spelt, triticale or Kamut, contact the manufacturer to assess the risks. Look for well-sealed plastic or metal packaging, as products in unlined paper can become contaminated if they're stored near wheat.

Measuring Ingredients

Accurate measurements are important for cooking — and essential for baking — to achieve consistent results time and again. So take both time and care as you measure.

Measuring Dry Ingredients

When measuring a dry ingredient, such as flour, cocoa powder, sugar, spices or salt, spoon it into the appropriate-size dry measuring cup or measuring spoon, heaping it up over the top. Slide a straight-edged utensil, such as a knife, across the top to level off the extra. Be careful not to shake or tap the cup or spoon to settle the ingredient, or you will have more than you need.

Measuring Moist Ingredients

Moist ingredients, such as brown sugar, coconut and dried fruit, must be firmly packed in a measuring cup or spoon to be measured accurately. Use a dry measuring cup for these ingredients. Fill the measuring cup to slightly overflowing, then pack down the ingredient firmly with the back of a spoon. Add more of the ingredient and pack down again until the cup is full and even with the top of the measure.

Measuring Liquid Ingredients

Use a clear plastic or glass measuring cup or container with lines up the sides to measure liquid ingredients. Set the container on the counter and pour the liquid to the appropriate mark. Lower your head to read the measurement at eye level.

Breakfasts

Ancient Grains Granola

With this crispy and
crunchy granola, the
possibilities for variation
are endless, so have fun
with spices, sweeteners,
nuts, seeds, flaked
coconut and dried fruit.

Tips

An equal amount of melted
virgin coconut oil, or unsalted
butter, melted, can be used in
place of the olive oil.

For the chopped dried fruit,
try apricots, cherries or raisins.

- Preheat oven to 325°F (160°C)
- Large rimmed baking sheet, lined with parchment paper

2 cups	certified GF large-flake (old-fashioned) rolled oats	500 mL
1 cup	amaranth or quinoa, rinsed	250 mL
½ cup	teff or millet	125 mL
½ cup	chia seeds	125 mL
⅓ cup	packed light brown sugar	75 mL
2 tsp	ground cinnamon	10 mL
1 tsp	fine sea salt	5 mL
½ cup	olive oil	125 mL
½ cup	pure maple syrup, liquid honey or brown rice syrup	125 mL
1 cup	chopped dried fruit	250 mL

1. In a large bowl, combine oats, amaranth, teff and chia seeds.

2. In a medium bowl, whisk together brown sugar, cinnamon, salt, oil and maple syrup until well blended.

3. Add the brown sugar mixture to the oat mixture and stir until well coated. Spread mixture evenly on prepared baking sheet.

4. Bake in preheated oven for 22 to 27 minutes or until oats are golden brown. Let cool completely on pan.

5. Transfer granola to an airtight container and stir in dried fruit. Store at room temperature for up to 2 weeks.

Chocolate Buckwheat Granola

If you love granola that forms clusters, then you will love this granola, because it does exactly that. That fact that it tastes like dessert, despite being incredibly good for you, is terrific, too.

Tips

Any nuts or seeds (such as cashews, hazelnuts, sunflower seeds or pepitas) may be used in place of the almonds.

If the coconut oil is completely solid, warm it slightly in the microwave or by placing the jar or container in a hot water bath for easier measuring.

An equal amount of olive oil or melted unsalted butter may be used in place of the coconut oil.

Variation

Chocolate Teff Granola:
Increase the oats to 3¹⁄₂ cups (875 mL) and replace the buckwheat with 1 cup (250 mL) teff.

- Preheat oven to 350°F (180°C)
- Large rimmed baking sheet, lined with parchment paper

3 cups	certified GF large-flake (old-fashioned) rolled oats	750 mL
1¹⁄₂ cups	buckwheat groats	375 mL
1 cup	chopped almonds	250 mL
¹⁄₂ cup	virgin coconut oil (see tips, at left)	125 mL
²⁄₃ cup	fine crystal cane sugar or packed light brown sugar	150 mL
¹⁄₂ cup	unsweetened natural cocoa powder	125 mL
¹⁄₂ tsp	fine sea salt	2 mL

1. In a large bowl, combine oats, buckwheat and almonds.

2. In a small saucepan, melt coconut oil over low heat. Add sugar, cocoa powder and salt. Bring to a simmer over medium heat, stirring constantly, until sugar is melted.

3. Pour the cocoa mixture over the oat mixture and stir until well coated. Spread mixture evenly in a very compact layer on prepared baking sheet. Very firmly push and press the mixture down with a spatula to compact it (this will help create the clusters).

4. Bake in preheated oven for 20 minutes. Using spatula, carefully break apart into 7 or 8 chunks; very firmly compact the smaller clusters with spatula. Bake for 10 to 12 minutes or until fragrant. Let cool completely on pan.

5. Transfer granola to an airtight container. Store at room temperature for up to 2 weeks.

Cardamom Amaranth Granola

**Makes about
4½ cups (1.125 L)**

Tiny amaranth seeds are
a fantastic addition to
granola, adding a delicate
crispiness to hearty oats.
Fragrant cardamom and
coconut oil take this
breakfast cereal over
the top.

Tips

You can replace the amaranth
with an equal amount of
quinoa, rinsed, millet or teff.

Try adding 1 cup (250 mL)
chopped dried fruit (such
as apricots) to the cooled
granola.

An equal amount of olive oil
or melted unsalted butter
may be used in place of the
coconut oil.

- Preheat oven to 300°F (150°C)
- Large rimmed baking sheet, lined with parchment paper

3 cups	certified GF large-flake (old-fashioned) rolled oats	750 mL
1½ cups	unsweetened flaked coconut	375 mL
1 cup	amaranth	250 mL
½ cup	warmed virgin coconut oil	125 mL
½ cup	liquid honey, maple syrup or brown rice syrup	125 mL
1½ tsp	ground cardamom or ginger	7 mL
½ tsp	fine sea salt	2 mL

1. In a large bowl, combine oats, coconut and amaranth.

2. In a medium bowl, whisk together coconut oil, honey, cardamom and salt until well blended.

3. Add the honey mixture to the oat mixture and stir until well coated. Spread mixture evenly on prepared baking sheet.

4. Bake in preheated oven for 20 to 25 minutes or until oats are golden brown. Let cool completely on pan.

5. Transfer granola to an airtight container. Store at room temperature for up to 2 weeks.

Any Grain Muesli

Oats are the traditional grain of choice in muesli, the healthful fruit-and-cereal concoction developed by Swiss nutritionist Dr. Bircher-Benner more than a century ago. But cooked ancient grains are such a delicious variation, you may never go back to oats.

Tips

For the whole grains, try amaranth, millet, quinoa or sorghum. Information on cooking these grains can be found on pages 8–17.

For the fresh fruit, try mangos, pear, kiwi, strawberries and/or blueberries.

An equal amount of plain non-dairy yogurt (such as coconut yogurt) can be used in place of the yogurt.

Variation

Vanilla Maple Muesli: Replace the honey with an equal amount of pure maple syrup, and replace the orange zest with 1 tsp (5 mL) GF vanilla extract.

2 cups	plain yogurt	500 mL
¼ cup	liquid honey	60 mL
2 tsp	finely grated orange or lemon zest	10 mL
1½ cups	cooked certified GF whole grains, cooled	375 mL
3 cups	chopped fresh fruit or berries	750 mL
1½ cups	shredded peeled tart-sweet apples (such as Braeburn or Gala)	375 mL
1 cup	chopped toasted or raw nuts or seeds	250 mL

1. In a large bowl, whisk together yogurt, honey and orange zest. Stir in grains; gently fold in chopped fruit, apples and nuts.

2. Serve immediately or cover and refrigerate for up to 48 hours.

No-Cook Maple Buckwheat Porridge

The beauty of no-cook porridge is just that: no cooking! Here, the rich, full flavor of buckwheat is enhanced with maple syrup and cinnamon for a perfect year-round breakfast.

Tips

If using non-dairy milk, try coconut, almond, rice or hemp.

You can use an equal amount of fine crystal cane sugar, packed light brown sugar or liquid honey in place of the maple syrup.

Storage Tip

Store the porridge in an airtight container in the refrigerator for up to 2 days.

- Food processor or blender

1 cup	buckwheat groats	250 mL
1½ cups	water	375 mL
1 tbsp	ground flax seeds (flaxseed meal)	15 mL
1 tsp	ground cinnamon	5 mL
¼ tsp	fine sea salt	1 mL
⅔ cup	milk or plain non-dairy milk	150 mL
2 tbsp	pure maple syrup	30 mL
1 tsp	GF vanilla extract	5 mL

Suggested Accompaniments

Pure maple syrup
Milk or plain non-dairy milk
Chopped fresh fruit or berries

1. In a medium bowl, combine buckwheat and water. Cover and refrigerate for 8 hours or overnight. Drain.

2. In food processor, combine drained buckwheat, flax seeds, cinnamon, salt, milk, maple syrup and vanilla; process until semi-smooth.

3. Divide into two bowls and serve with any of the suggested accompaniments, as desired.

Toasted Teff Porridge

Teff porridge may require a few more minutes than packets of instant hot cereal, but it's worth the wait. Moreover, it's mostly unattended time, so you can go about your morning routine — returning once or twice for a brief stir — while your breakfast simmers.

Tip

If using non-dairy milk, try almond, rice, coconut or hemp.

Variations

Toasted Amaranth Porridge: Use an equal amount of amaranth in place of the teff and decrease the amount of water to 1 cup (250 mL). Increase the simmering time to 20 to 25 minutes.

Toasted Quinoa Porridge: Use an equal amount of quinoa, rinsed, and decrease the amount of water to 1 cup (250 mL). Increase the simmering time to 20 to 25 minutes.

1/2 cup	teff	125 mL
1/8 tsp	fine sea salt	0.5 mL
1 1/4 cups	milk or plain non-dairy milk, divided	300 mL
1 1/4 cups	water	300 mL
1 tsp	GF vanilla extract	5 mL

Suggested Accompaniments

Agave nectar, liquid honey, brown rice syrup or pure maple syrup
Fresh or dried fruit

1. In a small saucepan, toast teff over medium heat, stirring, for 2 to 3 minutes or until fragrant. Add salt, 1 cup (250 mL) of the milk, and water; bring to a boil. Reduce heat to low, cover and simmer, stirring occasionally, for 15 to 20 minutes or until liquid is absorbed. Stir in vanilla.

2. Serve drizzled with the remaining milk and any of the suggested accompaniments, as desired.

Carrot Cake Baked Amaranth

Hello, autumn. Here, carrots, raisins and fall spices merge effortlessly with amaranth for a warming breakfast that epitomizes cozy.

Tip
If using non-dairy milk, try almond, rice or hemp.

Storage Tip
Let cool completely, cover and refrigerate for up to 2 days. Warm in the microwave.

Variation
Carrot Cake Quinoa: Replace the amaranth with an equal amount of quinoa, rinsed.

- Preheat oven to 375°F (190°C)
- 9-inch (23 cm) square glass baking dish, sprayed with nonstick cooking spray

1 tbsp	unsalted butter or virgin coconut oil	15 mL
1 cup	amaranth	250 mL
1/4 cup	fine crystal cane sugar or packed dark brown sugar	60 mL
2 1/2 tsp	pumpkin pie spice	12 mL
1/2 tsp	fine sea salt	2 mL
2 1/2 cups	milk or plain non-dairy milk	625 mL
1 1/4 cups	finely shredded carrots	300 mL
1/2 cup	raisins	125 mL
1 tsp	GF vanilla extract	5 mL

Suggested Accompaniments
Pure maple syrup or liquid honey
Milk or plain non-dairy milk
Whipped cream cheese

1. In a medium saucepan, melt butter over medium heat. Add amaranth and cook, stirring, for 2 to 3 minutes or until fragrant and golden. Whisk in sugar, pumpkin pie spice, salt, milk, carrots, raisins and vanilla. Pour into prepared baking dish and cover tightly with foil.

2. Bake in preheated oven for 35 minutes. Transfer to a wire rack and carefully remove foil (steam will be released). Stir and let stand for 5 minutes.

3. Spoon into bowls and serve with any of the suggested accompaniments, as desired.

Beets, Grains and Greens Hash

Who says hash needs potatoes? No one who eats this dish will. The fresh spinach and nutty grains balance the earthy sweetness of the beets.

Tips

For the grains, try amaranth, millet, quinoa, rice or sorghum. Information on cooking these grains can be found on pages 8–17.

You can replace the canned beets with 1½ cups (375 mL) freshly cooked (steamed, boiled or roasted) diced beets.

To poach the eggs, pour enough water into a medium skillet to reach a depth of 1½ inches (4 cm). Add ½ tsp (2 mL) fine sea salt and bring to a simmer over medium heat. Crack each egg into a separate custard cup. Gently slide one egg at a time into the simmering water and simmer for 2 to 3 minutes or until egg whites are set (the yolks will be only partially cooked); cook longer for more firmly set yolks. Using a slotted spoon, carefully transfer eggs to hash.

2	slices bacon, chopped	2
1 cup	chopped onion	250 mL
1½ cups	hot cooked certified GF whole grains	375 mL
1	can (15 oz/425 mL) whole beets, drained and diced	1
½ cup	ready-to-use GF vegetable or chicken broth	125 mL
6 cups	packed baby spinach leaves	1.5 L
2	large eggs, poached (see tip, at left)	2

1. In a large skillet, cook bacon over medium-high heat until crisp. Using a slotted spoon, transfer bacon to a plate lined with paper towels. Drain off all but 1 tsp (5 mL) fat from skillet.

2. Add onion to the skillet and cook, stirring, for 5 to 6 minutes or until softened. Add grains, beets and broth; reduce heat to medium and cook, stirring up bottom crust two to three times, for 10 to 12 minutes or until warmed through and browned. Add spinach on top, cover and cook for 1 minute, until wilted. Stir spinach into hash.

3. Divide hash between two plates. Top each with a poached egg and sprinkle with bacon.

Southwestern Hominy Hash

The toasty corn flavor of hominy is a welcome way to start the day, especially in this Southwestern-style hash. You can keep it simple or go fancy, depending on how rushed or relaxed the morning.

Tips

An equal amount of millet or amaranth can be used in place of the quinoa.

A green bell pepper can be used in place of the red bell pepper.

1 tbsp	olive oil	15 mL
1	large red bell pepper, chopped	1
1½ cups	chopped green onions, white and green parts separated	375 mL
2	cloves garlic, minced	2
1 cup	quinoa, rinsed	250 mL
2½ tsp	chili powder	12 mL
2¼ cups	ready-to-use GF vegetable or chicken broth	550 mL
1	can (14 to 15 oz/398 to 425 mL) golden hominy, rinsed and drained	1
	Fine sea salt and cracked black pepper	

Suggested Accompaniments

Chopped fresh cilantro or flat-leaf (Italian) parsley
Chopped fresh chives or green onions
Crumbled queso fresco
Poached eggs
Plain Greek yogurt
Salsa

1. In a large saucepan, heat oil over medium-high heat. Add red pepper and white part of green onions; cook, stirring, for 6 to 8 minutes or until red pepper is softened. Add garlic, quinoa and chili powder; cook, stirring, for 1 minute.

2. Stir in broth and bring to a boil. Reduce heat to medium-low, cover and simmer, without stirring, for 12 minutes. Uncover and fluff hash with a spatula.

3. Stir in hominy and green part of green onions; cook, stirring, for 2 to 3 minutes or until liquid is absorbed and quinoa is tender and slightly browned. Cover and let stand for 5 minutes. Season to taste with salt and pepper. Serve warm with any of the suggested accompaniments, as desired.

Sorghum, Sage and Apple Breakfast Patties

Makes 4 servings (about 12 patties)

Homemade breakfast patties may sound like something best left to a skilled butcher. But if you swap out the meat for whole grains and produce, you can make your own with minimal fuss. Best yet, you'll know exactly what went into these patties: no mystery ingredients or preservatives, just premium, power-packed ingredients.

Storage Tip

Store the cooled patties in an airtight container in the refrigerator for up to 2 days. Alternatively, wrap them in foil, place them in an airtight container and freeze for up to 1 month. Thaw in the refrigerator for 3 to 4 hours.

- Food processor
- Large baking sheet

2 tbsp	olive oil, divided	30 mL
1	tart-sweet apple (such as Gala, Braeburn or Golden Delicious), peeled and chopped	1
½ cup	chopped green onions	125 mL
1 cup	minced shiitake or button mushrooms	250 mL
1½ cups	cooked sorghum (see page 17), cooled	375 mL
1 cup	certified GF large-flake (old-fashioned) rolled oats	250 mL
⅔ cup	toasted pecan halves (see page 26)	150 mL
1 tsp	dried rubbed sage	5 mL
1 tsp	fine sea salt	5 mL
¼ tsp	freshly cracked black pepper	1 mL
1	large egg, lightly beaten	1

1. In a large nonstick skillet, heat half the oil over medium-high heat. Add apple and green onions; cook, stirring, for 4 to 5 minutes or until apple is just softened. Transfer to food processor and let cool for at least 5 minutes. Wipe out skillet.

2. Add remaining oil to skillet and heat over medium-high heat. Add mushrooms and cook, stirring, for 4 to 5 minutes or until softened. Add to the apple mixture and let cool for 5 minutes.

3. To the apple mixture, add sorghum, oats, pecans, sage, salt and pepper. Process, using on/off pulses, until mixture is blended but still somewhat chunky.

4. Transfer to a large bowl and stir in egg until blended. Cover and refrigerate for at least 1 hour, until chilled, or for up to 1 day.

5. Preheat oven to 350°F (180°C). Line baking sheet with parchment paper.

6. Using a ¼-cup (60 mL) measure, scoop portions of sorghum mixture onto prepared baking sheet. Use a spatula to flatten each scoop into a 2-inch (5 cm) patty.

7. Bake for 18 to 23 minutes or until golden brown and hot in the center.

Whole-Grain Pancake and Waffle Mix

Ready your griddle or waffle maker. This easy-to-assemble, gluten-free mix will keep for up to a month, but you'll want to make a batch of these hearty, delicious pancakes or waffles as soon as possible.

Tip

For the non-dairy milk, try hemp, almond, soy or rice milk.

1½ cups	finely ground cornmeal	375 mL
1 cup	sorghum, millet, amaranth or quinoa flour	250 mL
½ cup	tapioca starch	125 mL
½ cup	certified GF quick-cooking rolled oats	125 mL
½ cup	ground flax seeds (flaxseed meal)	125 mL
2 tbsp	fine crystal cane sugar	30 mL
2 tbsp	GF baking powder	30 mL
1 tsp	fine sea salt	5 mL
¾ tsp	baking soda	3 mL

1. In a large bowl, whisk together cornmeal, sorghum flour, tapioca starch, oats, flax seeds, sugar, baking powder, salt and baking soda.

2. Transfer to a large airtight container and store in the refrigerator for up to 1 month.

To Prepare Pancakes

Makes 6 pancakes

1 cup	Whole-Grain Pancake and Waffle Mix	250 mL
1	large egg	1
⅔ cup	milk or plain non-dairy milk	150 mL
2 tsp	vegetable oil or unsalted butter, melted	10 mL
	Nonstick cooking spray	

1. In a medium bowl, combine pancake mix, egg, milk and oil until blended. Let stand for 1 minute.

2. Heat a griddle or skillet over medium heat. Spray with cooking spray. For each pancake, pour about ¼ cup (60 mL) batter onto griddle. Cook until bubbles appear on top. Turn pancake over and cook for about 1 minute or until golden brown. Repeat with the remaining batter, spraying griddle and adjusting heat as necessary between batches.

Storage Tip

Let pancakes or waffles cool completely on a wire rack, then wrap individually in plastic wrap and store in an airtight container in the refrigerator for up to 3 days or in the freezer for up to 1 month. Reheat in the microwave on High for 45 seconds, until warmed through (no need to thaw), or toast in the toaster oven for 1 to 2 minutes or until toasted and warmed through.

To Prepare Waffles

Makes 4 small waffles

- Preheat waffle maker to medium-high

1 cup	Whole-Grain Pancake and Waffle Mix	250 mL
1	large egg	1
$2/3$ cup	milk or plain non-dairy milk	150 mL
2 tsp	vegetable oil or unsalted butter, melted	10 mL
	Nonstick cooking spray	

1. In a medium bowl, combine pancake mix, egg, milk and oil until blended.

2. Spray preheated waffle maker with cooking spray. For each waffle, pour about $1/3$ cup (75 mL) batter into waffle maker. Cook according to manufacturer's instructions until golden brown.

Teff, Oatmeal and Molasses Pancakes

It's hard to beat a warm bowl of oatmeal on a chilly morning, but these cinnamon-scented, teff-enhanced pancakes manage the feat.

1 cup	certified GF quick-cooking rolled oats	250 mL
2 cups	buttermilk, divided	500 mL
1/2 cup	teff flour	125 mL
1/4 cup	millet flour	60 mL
2 tsp	GF baking powder	10 mL
1 tsp	ground cinnamon	5 mL
3/4 tsp	baking soda	3 mL
1/2 tsp	fine sea salt	2 mL
1	large egg	1
2 tbsp	vegetable oil	30 mL
1 tbsp	dark (cooking) molasses	15 mL
	Nonstick cooking spray	

Tips

An equal amount of liquid honey, brown rice syrup, pure maple syrup or agave nectar may be used in place of the molasses.

Non-dairy buttermilk (see page 29) can be used in place of the buttermilk.

Sorghum flour, amaranth flour or brown rice flour can be used in place of the millet flour.

Storage Tip

Let pancakes cool completely on a wire rack, then wrap individually in plastic wrap and store in an airtight container in the refrigerator for up to 3 days or in the freezer for up to 1 month. Reheat in the microwave on High for 45 seconds, until warmed through (no need to thaw), or toast in the toaster oven for 1 to 2 minutes or until toasted and warmed through.

1. In a small bowl, combine oats and half the buttermilk. Let stand for 10 minutes.

2. In a large bowl, whisk together teff flour, millet flour, baking powder, cinnamon, baking soda and salt. Add oat mixture, the remaining buttermilk, egg, oil and molasses, stirring until blended.

3. Heat a griddle or skillet over medium heat. Spray with cooking spray. For each pancake, pour about 1/4 cup (60 mL) batter onto griddle. Cook until bubbles appear on top. Turn pancake over and cook for about 1 minute or until just set. Repeat with the remaining batter, spraying griddle and adjusting heat as necessary between batches.

Fluffy Lemon Chia Seed Pancakes

**Makes
12 pancakes**

Cottage cheese in the batter makes these lemony pancakes light and fluffy, with a flavor reminiscent of cheesecake — a wonderful breakfast surprise! Chia seeds give them a cheerful polka-dotted appearance and a subtle crunch.

Tips
You can use 1½ tsp (7 mL) lemon extract in place of the lemon zest.

An equal amount of poppy seeds can be used in place of the chia seeds.

Storage Tip
Let pancakes cool completely on a wire rack, then wrap individually in plastic wrap and store in an airtight container in the refrigerator for up to 2 days or in the freezer for up to 1 month. Reheat in the microwave on High for 45 seconds, until warmed through (no need to thaw), or toast in the toaster oven for 1 to 2 minutes or until toasted and warmed through.

⅔ cup	millet or sorghum flour	150 mL
⅓ cup	tapioca starch	75 mL
½ tsp	baking soda	2 mL
¼ tsp	fine sea salt	1 mL
2 tbsp	fine crystal cane sugar	30 mL
1½ tbsp	chia seeds	22 mL
4	large eggs	4
1 cup	cottage cheese	250 mL
½ cup	milk	125 mL
2 tbsp	melted virgin coconut oil or unsalted butter	30 mL
1 tbsp	finely grated lemon zest	15 mL
	Nonstick cooking spray	

1. In a large bowl, whisk together millet flour, tapioca starch, baking soda and salt.

2. In a medium bowl, whisk together sugar, chia seeds, eggs, cottage cheese, milk, coconut oil and lemon zest until blended.

3. Add the egg mixture to the flour mixture and stir until just blended.

4. Heat a griddle or skillet over medium heat. Spray with cooking spray. For each pancake, pour about ¼ cup (60 mL) batter onto griddle. Cook until bubbles appear on top. Turn pancake over and cook for about 1 minute or until golden brown. Repeat with the remaining batter, spraying griddle and adjusting heat as necessary between batches.

Variation
Fluffy Banana Pancakes: Replace the milk with an equal amount of mashed very ripe banana. Omit the lemon zest and chia seeds. Add 1 tsp (5 mL) ground cinnamon and 1 tsp (5 mL) GF vanilla extract with the coconut oil.

Baked Blueberry Sorghum Pancake

Makes 4 servings

Looking for a weekend breakfast that's equal parts easy and amazing? Say hello to this blueberry oven pancake. Sorghum flour, a great match for jammy blueberries, keeps it especially light and tender.

Tips

A 9-inch (23 cm) square metal baking pan can be used in place of the skillet.

Non-dairy buttermilk (see page 29) can be used in place of the buttermilk.

Storage Tip

Let pancake cool completely in pan on a wire rack. Cut into pieces, remove from pan, then wrap pieces individually in plastic wrap and store in an airtight container in the refrigerator for up to 2 days or in the freezer for up to 1 month. Reheat in the microwave on High for 45 seconds, until warmed through (no need to thaw), or toast in the toaster oven for 1 to 2 minutes or until toasted and warmed through.

Variations

Sorghum Buttermilk Pancake: Omit the blueberries.

Chocolate Chip Sorghum Pancake: Use $1/2$ cup (125 mL) GF semisweet chocolate chips in place of the blueberries.

- 9-inch (23 cm) cast-iron skillet

$2/3$ cup	sorghum flour	150 mL
$1/3$ cup	tapioca starch	75 mL
$1 1/2$ tsp	GF baking powder	7 mL
$1/4$ tsp	baking soda	1 mL
$1/2$ tsp	fine sea salt	2 mL
$3 1/2$ tbsp	fine crystal cane sugar, divided	52 mL
1	large egg	1
$3/4$ cup	buttermilk	175 mL
4 tbsp	unsalted butter, melted, divided	60 mL
1 cup	blueberries	250 mL
	Pure maple syrup (optional)	

1. Place cast-iron skillet in oven. Preheat oven to 350°F (180°C).

2. In a large bowl, whisk together sorghum flour, tapioca starch, baking powder, baking soda and salt.

3. In a medium bowl, whisk together 3 tbsp (45 mL) sugar, egg, buttermilk and 2 tbsp (30 mL) butter.

4. Add the egg mixture to the flour mixture and stir until just blended.

5. Remove skillet from oven. Add the remaining butter, swirling to coat. Add batter and spread evenly with spatula. Sprinkle with blueberries and the remaining sugar. Return skillet to oven and bake for 22 to 27 minutes or until just set at center. Let stand for 5 minutes. Cut into wedges and serve with maple syrup, if using.

Dutch Puff with Raspberry Chia Jam

A Dutch puff, also known as a German pancake, Bismarck or Dutch baby, is a puffy oven pancake with a buttery, creamy middle and crispy, golden-brown edges. Millet or sorghum flour creates an especially crispy, light pancake that's made all the more delicious by a no-cook raspberry chia jam.

Tips

An equal amount of virgin coconut oil can be used in place of the butter.

For the non-dairy milk, try hemp, almond, soy or rice milk.

Variation

Sugar and Spice Teff Dutch Puff: Replace the millet flour with an equal amount of teff flour. Add 1 1/2 tsp (7 mL) pumpkin pie spice or ground cinnamon with the salt. Serve sprinkled with turbinado sugar or fine crystal cane sugar.

- Large ovenproof skillet

Raspberry Chia Jam

1 1/2 cups	fresh or thawed frozen raspberries	375 mL
1 1/2 tbsp	chia seeds	22 mL
1 tbsp	liquid honey	15 mL

Dutch Puff

3	large eggs, at room temperature	3
1/3 cup	millet or sorghum flour	75 mL
1/3 cup	potato starch	75 mL
1/8 tsp	fine sea salt	0.5 mL
3/4 cup	milk or plain non-dairy milk, at room temperature	175 mL
1/4 tsp	GF vanilla extract	1 mL
2 tbsp	unsalted butter	30 mL

1. *Jam:* In a medium bowl, crush raspberries with a fork. Stir in chia seeds and honey. Let stand for at least 30 minutes to thicken.

2. *Dutch Puff:* Meanwhile, place skillet in oven. Preheat oven to 450°F (230°C).

3. In a large bowl, using an electric mixer, beat eggs on high speed for 1 to 2 minutes or until frothy. Add millet flour, potato starch, salt, milk and vanilla; beat on medium-high speed for about 1 minute, stopping once to scrape down bottom and sides of bowl with a spatula, until smooth (batter will be thin).

4. Remove skillet from oven. Add butter and melt, swirling to coat. Add batter and immediately return skillet to oven. Bake for 19 to 24 minutes or until puffed and golden brown. Serve with jam.

French Crêpes

I've never met a crêpe I didn't love, and this version is no exception. The absence of gluten in the batter renders crêpes that are especially light and tender, perfect for any and all fillings you can dream up.

Tips

A regular nonstick skillet works just as well as any crêpe pan or specialty crêpe griddle.

For the non-dairy milk, try hemp, almond, soy or rice milk.

An equal amount of vegetable oil can be used in place of the butter.

Refrigerating the batter before use allows the bubbles that form during blending to subside, making the crêpes less likely to tear during cooking. The batter will keep for up to 48 hours.

- Blender or food processor

3	large eggs	3
1 cup	milk or plain non-dairy milk	250 mL
3 tbsp	unsalted butter, melted and cooled	45 mL
1/4 tsp	fine sea salt	1 mL
1/3 cup	millet flour	75 mL
1/3 cup	sorghum flour	75 mL
1/3 cup	potato starch	75 mL
	Nonstick cooking spray	

1. In blender, combine eggs, milk, butter and salt. Add millet flour, sorghum flour and potato starch; blend until smooth. Transfer to a bowl, cover and refrigerate for 1 hour.

2. Heat a large nonstick skillet over medium-high heat. Remove from heat and lightly coat pan with cooking spray. Whisk the batter slightly. For each crêpe, pour about 1/4 cup (60 mL) batter into pan, quickly tilting in all directions to cover bottom of pan. Cook for about 45 seconds or until just golden at the edges. With a spatula, carefully lift edge of crêpe to test for doneness. The crêpe is ready to turn when it is golden brown on the bottom and can be shaken loose from the pan. Turn crêpe over and cook for about 15 to 30 seconds or until golden brown.

3. Transfer crêpe to an unfolded kitchen towel to cool completely. Repeat with the remaining batter, spraying skillet and adjusting heat as necessary between crêpes, and stacking cooled crêpes between sheets of waxed paper to prevent sticking.

Storage Tip

Refrigerate crêpes between sheets of waxed paper, tightly covered in plastic wrap, for up to 2 days or freeze, enclosed in a sealable plastic bag, for up to 1 month.

Variation

Breton Buckwheat Gallettes: Omit the millet flour and 1 of the eggs. Add $\frac{1}{2}$ cup (125 mL) buckwheat flour, reduce the sorghum flour to $\frac{1}{4}$ cup (60 mL) and reduce the potato starch to $\frac{1}{4}$ cup (60 mL).

Crêpe Filling Ideas

- Lemon juice and a drizzle of honey
- A thin spread of nut or seed butter and all-fruit jam
- Greek yogurt and fresh fruit or jam
- Ricotta or cottage cheese and a drizzle of honey or agave nectar
- grated GF bittersweet chocolate and toasted nuts
- Thinly sliced ham and shredded Gruyère or Swiss cheese
- Sautéed spinach and freshly grated Parmesan cheese
- Shredded sharp (old) Cheddar cheese and thinly sliced or grated tart-sweet apples
- Thinly sliced pears and a drizzle of pure maple syrup
- Scrambled eggs or egg whites, or scrambled tofu

Salted Caramel Banana Waffles

Makes 10 waffles

Despite the decadent name, these blissful waffles have just the right level of sweetness.

Storage Tip

Let waffles cool completely on a wire rack, then wrap individually in plastic wrap and store in an airtight container in the refrigerator for up to 2 days or in the freezer for up to 1 month. Reheat in the microwave on High for 45 seconds, until warmed through (no need to thaw), or toast in the toaster oven for 1 to 2 minutes or until toasted and warmed through.

• Preheat waffle maker to medium-high

1¼ cups	millet flour	300 mL
½ cup	potato starch	125 mL
¼ cup	ground flax seeds (flaxseed meal)	60 mL
1½ tsp	GF baking powder	7 mL
½ tsp	fine sea salt	2 mL
3½ tbsp	packed dark brown sugar	52 mL
2	large eggs	2
1 cup	milk	250 mL
3 tbsp	unsalted butter, melted	45 mL
2 tsp	GF vanilla extract	10 mL
¾ cup	mashed ripe bananas	175 mL
	Nonstick cooking spray	

1. In a large bowl, whisk together millet flour, potato starch, flax seeds, baking powder and salt.

2. In a medium bowl, whisk together brown sugar, eggs, milk, butter and vanilla. Stir in bananas.

3. Add the egg mixture to the flour mixture and stir until just blended.

4. Spray preheated waffle maker with cooking spray. For each waffle, pour about ⅓ cup (75 mL) batter into waffle maker. Cook according to manufacturer's instructions until golden brown.

Double Chocolate Quinoa Waffles

These waffles are every bit as easy to make as regular ones, and yes, you really can eat them for breakfast!

Tip
Non-dairy buttermilk (see page 29) can be used in place of the buttermilk.

Storage Tip
Let waffles cool completely on a wire rack, then wrap individually in plastic wrap and store in an airtight container in the refrigerator for up to 2 days or in the freezer for up to 1 month. Reheat in the microwave on High for 45 seconds, until warmed through (no need to thaw), or toast in the toaster oven for 1 to 2 minutes or until toasted and warmed through.

• Preheat waffle maker to medium-high

1 1/4 cups	quinoa flour	300 mL
1/4 cup	unsweetened natural cocoa powder	60 mL
1 tsp	GF baking powder	5 mL
1/2 tsp	baking soda	2 mL
1/4 tsp	fine sea salt	1 mL
1/4 cup	fine crystal cane sugar	60 mL
1	large egg	1
1 cup	buttermilk	250 mL
1/2 cup	pumpkin purée (not pie filling)	125 mL
2 tbsp	unsalted butter, melted, or vegetable oil	30 mL
1 tsp	GF vanilla extract	5 mL
1/2 cup	miniature GF semisweet chocolate chips	125 mL
	Nonstick cooking spray	

1. In a large bowl, whisk together quinoa flour, cocoa powder, baking powder, baking soda and salt.

2. In a medium bowl, whisk together sugar, egg, buttermilk, pumpkin, butter and vanilla.

3. Add the egg mixture to the flour mixture and stir until just blended.

4. Spray preheated waffle maker with cooking spray. For each waffle, pour about 1/3 cup (75 mL) batter into waffle maker and sprinkle with 2 tsp (10 mL) chocolate chips. Cook according to manufacturer's instructions until set.

Zucchini, Parmesan and Amaranth Omelet

Makes 1 serving

Toss aside heavy, greasy hot breakfasts and welcome this appealing alternative, a fresh yet filling mix of zucchini, tender amaranth and fresh basil.

Tips

Cooked millet or quinoa, cooled, can be used in place of the amaranth. Information on cooking these grains can be found on pages 11–15.

If you don't have fresh basil on hand, you can use 1 tsp (5 mL) dried basil.

2	large eggs	2
1 tbsp	chopped fresh basil	15 mL
Pinch	fine sea salt	Pinch
1/3 cup	cooked amaranth (page 8), cooled	75 mL
2 tsp	olive oil or unsalted butter	10 mL
1/2 cup	grated zucchini	125 mL
2 tbsp	freshly grated Parmesan cheese	30 mL
	Nonstick cooking spray	

1. In a small bowl, beat eggs, basil and salt until blended. Stir in amaranth. Set aside.

2. In a small skillet, heat oil over medium heat. Add zucchini and cook, stirring, for 2 minutes or until softened.

3. Pour in egg mixture and sprinkle with cheese. Cook, without stirring, for 2 to 4 minutes or until eggs are set. Remove from heat and invert onto a plate. Spray skillet with cooking spray and return omelet, browned side up, to skillet. Cook for 1 minute. Invert onto plate and serve.

Kale and Millet Tortilla Española

Makes 6 servings

This riff on the classic Spanish tortilla replaces the traditional potatoes with a mix of millet and kale. The result is an ideal way to jump-start your morning.

Tip
Cooked amaranth, quinoa or brown rice, cooled, can be used in place of the millet. Information on cooking these grains can be found on pages 8–16.

- Preheat broiler, with rack set 4 to 6 inches (10 to 15 cm) from heat source
- Large ovenproof skillet

6	large eggs	6
1 tsp	fine sea salt	5 mL
1 tsp	hot smoked paprika	5 mL
3 tbsp	olive oil	45 mL
1	onion, chopped	1
3 cups	coarsely chopped kale, tough stems and center ribs removed	750 mL
1½ cups	cooked millet (see page 11), cooled	375 mL

1. In a medium bowl, whisk together eggs, salt and paprika. Set aside.

2. In ovenproof skillet, heat oil over medium-high heat. Add onion and cook, stirring, for 4 minutes. Add kale and cook, stirring occasionally, for 4 to 5 minutes or until vegetables are softened.

3. Add egg mixture and millet, gently shaking pan to distribute eggs. Reduce heat to medium and cook for about 8 minutes, gently shaking pan every minute, until eggs are almost set.

4. Place skillet under preheated broiler and broil for 1 to 2 minutes or until lightly browned. Slide tortilla out of the pan onto a cutting board and cut into wedges.

Mushroom and Sorghum Frittata

Makes 4 servings

A frittata — an Italian omelet in which the filling ingredients are mixed with the beaten eggs and the mixture is baked or broiled until set — is a great way to express your creativity. Use this recipe as a template and then vary it according to the whole grains, vegetables, herbs and cheeses you have on hand.

Tips

Cooked amaranth, millet, quinoa or brown rice can be used in place of the sorghum. Information on cooking these grains can be found on pages 8–16.

Don't relegate this frittata to weekends; make it ahead, let it cool, then store it in the refrigerator for weekday frittata squares on the go.

- Preheat oven to 350°F (180°C)
- 8-inch (20 cm) square glass baking dish, sprayed with nonstick cooking spray

6	large eggs	6
1 tsp	dried thyme	5 mL
½ tsp	fine sea salt	2 mL
¼ tsp	freshly ground black pepper	1 mL
1 tbsp	olive oil or unsalted butter	15 mL
12 oz	sliced mushrooms	375 g
1 cup	chopped green onions	250 mL
1¼ cups	cooked sorghum (see page 17), cooled	300 mL
1 cup	shredded Gruyère or Swiss cheese	250 mL

1. In a large bowl, beat eggs, thyme, salt and pepper until blended. Set aside.

2. In a large skillet, heat oil over medium-high heat. Add mushrooms and green onions; cook, stirring, for 4 to 6 minutes or until softened. Stir in sorghum and cook, stirring, for 1 minute.

3. Spread sorghum mixture in prepared baking dish and pour egg mixture over top. Sprinkle with cheese.

4. Bake in preheated oven for 23 to 28 minutes or until golden and set. Let cool in dish on a wire rack for at least 10 minutes before cutting. Serve warm or let cool completely.

Roasted Pepper Breakfast Bake

Squares of this vegetable- and protein-rich breakfast bake are equally well suited for eating on the run or gathering around the kitchen table on a lazy weekend morning.

Tips

Information on cooking the whole grains named in this recipe can be found on pages 8–16.

Crumbled feta cheese can be used in place of the goat cheese.

Storage Tip

Cut into squares and let cool completely. Wrap the squares tightly in plastic wrap and store in the refrigerator for up to 3 days. The squares are delicious cold, but you can also microwave them for 20 to 30 seconds to warm them up.

- Preheat oven to 350°F (180°C)
- Blender
- 9-inch (23 cm) square glass baking dish, sprayed with nonstick cooking spray

6	large eggs	6
2 cups	cottage cheese	500 mL
1	jar (12 oz/341 mL) roasted red bell peppers, drained and chopped	1
1¼ cups	cooked amaranth, millet, quinoa or brown rice, cooled	300 mL
1 cup	crumbled goat cheese	250 mL
1 tsp	dried basil	5 mL
¼ tsp	fine sea salt	1 mL
⅛ tsp	freshly ground black pepper	0.5 mL

1. In blender, combine eggs and cottage cheese; purée until smooth.

2. Transfer purée to a medium bowl and stir in roasted peppers, amaranth, goat cheese, basil, salt and pepper. Spread evenly in prepared baking dish.

3. Bake in preheated oven for 35 to 40 minutes or until golden brown and set. Let cool in dish on a wire rack for 15 minutes. Cut into squares and serve warm or let cool completely and serve at room temperature.

Ginger Peach Baked Millet

Although this is a sensational way to use fresh peaches, you do not have to wait for the summer harvest to make this baked breakfast: frozen peaches work beautifully.

Tips

An equal amount of amaranth, quinoa, rinsed, or teff can be used in place of the millet.

If using non-dairy milk, try soy, almond, rice or hemp.

- Preheat oven to 400°F (200°C)
- 8-inch (20 cm) square glass baking dish, sprayed with nonstick cooking spray

1 cup	millet	250 mL
2 tsp	ground ginger	10 mL
½ tsp	fine sea salt	2 mL
2 cups	milk or plain non-dairy milk	500 mL
2	large eggs	2
½ cup	mashed very ripe banana	125 mL
¼ cup	liquid honey	60 mL
1 tsp	GF vanilla extract	5 mL
2½ cups	diced fresh or thawed frozen peaches	625 mL
1 tbsp	turbinado sugar	15 mL

Suggested Accompaniments

Warm or cold milk or plain non-dairy milk
Pure maple syrup or liquid honey

1. In a medium saucepan, combine millet, ginger, salt and milk. Bring to a boil over medium-high heat. Reduce heat to low, cover and simmer for 15 minutes.

2. Meanwhile, in a small bowl, whisk together eggs, banana, honey and vanilla until blended.

3. Add the egg mixture to the millet mixture and stir until just blended. Gently fold in peaches. Spread evenly in prepared baking dish and sprinkle with sugar.

4. Bake in preheated oven for 20 to 25 minutes or until set at the center and golden. Let cool in dish on a wire rack for 5 minutes. Serve warm with any of the suggested accompaniments, as desired.

Baked Banana Berry Oatmeal

Makes 8 servings

Any morning that starts with this banana- and berry-loaded oatmeal is a great morning. Consider this a starting point and try countless other combinations of fruits, spices and sweeteners — even chocolate chips!

Tips

If using non-dairy milk, try almond, rice or hemp.

Other fruits, such as diced apples, pears, peaches or more berries, may be used in place of the bananas.

For the berries, try blueberries or raspberries.

For the nuts or seeds, try walnuts, pecans, hazelnuts, green pumpkin seeds (pepitas), sunflower seeds or hemp hearts.

Storage Tip

Let dish cool completely, then wrap individual portions in plastic wrap and store in an airtight container in the refrigerator for up to 3 days or in the freezer for up to 1 month. Enjoy cold, or reheat in the microwave on High for 30-second intervals until warm.

- Preheat oven to 375°F (190°C)
- 8-inch (20 cm) square glass baking dish, sprayed with nonstick cooking spray

2 cups	certified GF large-flake (old-fashioned) rolled oats	500 mL
1/3 cup	fine crystal cane sugar or packed light brown sugar	75 mL
1 1/2 tsp	GF baking powder	7 mL
1 tsp	ground cinnamon	5 mL
1/2 tsp	fine sea salt	2 mL
2	large eggs, lightly beaten	2
1 3/4 cups	milk or plain non-dairy milk	425 mL
2 tsp	GF vanilla extract	10 mL
2	bananas, diced	2
3/4 cup	fresh berries	175 mL
1/3 cup	chopped toasted nuts (see page 26) or toasted seeds (see page 27)	75 mL

1. In a large bowl, combine oats, sugar, baking powder, cinnamon and salt.

2. In a small bowl, whisk together eggs, milk and vanilla.

3. Pour the egg mixture over the oat mixture and stir until combined. Stir in bananas. Pour into prepared baking dish, spreading evenly. Sprinkle with berries and nuts.

4. Bake in preheated oven for 35 to 45 minutes or until set at the center and golden. Let cool in dish on a wire rack for 20 minutes. Cut into servings and serve warm.

Coconut Custard with Chia and Mango

Go ahead, have dessert for breakfast. This decadent-tasting custard is, in fact, just what you need to start the day: vitamin C–rich mango, fiber-loaded chia seeds and protein-packed eggs. Best yet, you can make the custards ahead of time, then grab and go in the morning.

Tips

The custard will continue to firm up as it cools.

Other fruits and berries, including dried fruit, may be used in place of the mango. Try an equal amount of blueberries, raspberries or diced banana, or ¾ cup (175 mL) raisins, dried cranberries or chopped dried apricots.

Storage Tip

Let custard cool completely, then wrap in plastic wrap and store in the refrigerator for up to 3 days.

- Preheat oven to 375°F (190°C)
- Six ¾-cup (175 mL) ramekins, sprayed with nonstick cooking spray

3	large eggs	3
1¼ cups	well-stirred coconut milk (full-fat)	300 mL
⅓ cup	liquid honey	75 mL
¼ tsp	fine sea salt	1 mL
¼ cup	chia seeds	60 mL
1½ cups	chopped fresh or thawed frozen mango	375 mL

1. In a large bowl, whisk together eggs, coconut milk, honey and salt until blended. Stir in chia seeds. Pour into prepared ramekins and sprinkle evenly with mango.

2. Bake in preheated oven for 18 to 23 minutes or until set at the center and golden. Let cool on a wire rack for 20 minutes. Wrap in plastic wrap and refrigerate until firm.

Blueberry Hazelnut Coffee Cake

This not-too-sweet coffee cake is an ode to Portland, Oregon, where hazelnuts, blueberries and weekend brunches reign supreme. With this cake, you can celebrate and savor all three, anytime, anywhere.

Tips

Other berries, such as raspberries, blackberries or cranberries, can be used in place of the blueberries. If using cranberries, increase the amount of cane sugar to ¾ cup (175 mL).

Other nuts or seeds, such as pecans, almonds or green pumpkin seeds (pepitas), can be substituted for the hazelnuts.

To make this cake dairy-free, use non-dairy buttermilk (see page 29) in place of the buttermilk and vegetable oil in place of the butter.

Storage Tip

Store the cooled coffee cake tightly covered or in an airtight container in the refrigerator for up to 3 days.

- Preheat oven to 350°F (180°C)
- 9-inch (23 cm) square metal baking pan, sprayed with nonstick cooking spray

Filling

⅔ cup	chopped toasted hazelnuts (see page 26)	150 mL
¼ cup	packed dark brown sugar	60 mL
1½ tsp	ground cinnamon	7 mL

Cake

1½ cups	amaranth flour	375 mL
½ cup	potato starch	125 mL
1 tsp	GF baking powder	5 mL
1 tsp	baking soda	5 mL
¾ tsp	fine sea salt	3 mL
⅔ cup	fine crystal cane sugar	150 mL
2	large eggs	2
½ cup	unsalted butter, melted	125 mL
2 tsp	GF vanilla extract	10 mL
1⅓ cups	buttermilk	325 mL
1½ cups	blueberries	375 mL

1. *Filling:* In a small bowl, combine hazelnuts, brown sugar and cinnamon.

2. *Cake:* In a large bowl, whisk together amaranth flour, potato starch, baking powder, baking soda and salt.

3. In a medium bowl, whisk together sugar, eggs, butter and vanilla until well blended. Whisk in buttermilk until blended.

4. Add the egg mixture to the flour mixture and stir until just blended. Gently fold in blueberries.

5. Spread half the batter evenly in prepared pan and sprinkle with filling. Dollop the remaining batter on top of the filling (it need not cover the filling completely).

6. Bake in preheated oven for 28 to 33 minutes or until a toothpick inserted in the center comes out clean. Let cool completely in pan on a wire rack.

Baked Millet, Apple and Raisin Breakfast "Cupcakes"

Part muffin, part cereal and 100% delicious, these portable millet "cupcakes" are the new definition of fast food.

Tips

An equal amount of olive oil or melted unsalted butter can be used in place of the coconut oil.

An equal amount of amaranth or quinoa, rinsed, can be used in place of the millet.

Storage Tip

Store the cooled "cupcakes" in an airtight container in the refrigerator for up to 5 days or in the freezer for up to 3 months. Let thaw at room temperature for 1 to 2 hours before serving.

- 12-cup muffin pan, greased

1½ cups	unsweetened apple juice	375 mL
2	large tart-sweet apples (such as Gala, Braeburn or Golden Delicious), peeled and shredded	2
1 cup	millet	250 mL
¾ cup	raisins or other chopped dried fruit	175 mL
¼ tsp	fine sea salt	1 mL
2 tbsp	warmed virgin coconut oil	30 mL
½ cup	chopped toasted nuts or seeds (optional)	125 mL

1. In a medium saucepan, bring apple juice to a boil over medium-high heat. Reduce heat to medium-low and stir in apples, millet, raisins, salt and coconut oil; cover and simmer for 5 minutes. Remove from heat and let stand for 15 minutes. Uncover and stir in nuts, if using.

2. Meanwhile, preheat oven to 350°F (180°C).

3. Divide millet mixture equally among prepared muffin cups.

4. Bake for 25 to 30 minutes or until tops are pale golden and slightly puffed. Let cool in pan on a wire rack for 15 minutes, then transfer to the rack to cool completely.

Lemony Zucchini Mini Muffins

Makes 3 dozen mini muffins

Fresh zucchini finds citrusy expression in these moist grab-and-go mini muffins.

Tip

If using non-dairy milk, try almond, rice or hemp.

Storage Tip

Store the cooled muffins in an airtight container in the refrigerator for up to 5 days.

- Preheat oven to 400°F (200°C)
- Three 12-cup mini muffin pans, sprayed with nonstick cooking spray

1 cup	quinoa flour	250 mL
2/3 cup	certified GF quick-cooking rolled oats	150 mL
1 1/2 tsp	GF baking powder	7 mL
1/2 tsp	baking soda	2 mL
1/4 tsp	fine sea salt	1 mL
1/2 cup	fine crystal cane sugar	125 mL
1	large egg	1
1/2 cup	milk or plain non-dairy milk	125 mL
2 tsp	finely grated lemon zest	10 mL
1 tbsp	freshly squeezed lemon juice	15 mL
2 tbsp	olive oil	30 mL
2 tbsp	liquid honey	30 mL
1 1/3 cups	shredded zucchini	325 mL

1. In a large bowl, whisk together quinoa flour, oats, baking powder, baking soda and salt.

2. In a medium bowl, whisk together sugar, egg, milk, lemon zest, lemon juice, oil and honey until well blended.

3. Add the egg mixture to the flour mixture and stir until just blended. Gently fold in zucchini.

4. Divide batter equally among prepared muffin cups.

5. Bake in preheated oven for 10 to 12 minutes or until a toothpick inserted in the center comes out clean. Let cool in pans on a wire rack for 5 minutes, then transfer to the rack to cool completely.

Strawberry Breakfast Bars

Oats and millet are perfect foods for the beginning of the day: high in protein, they also contain essential fats and are rich in minerals, including zinc, calcium, magnesium and iron. Vitamin C assists in the absorption of iron, so add some orange juice in a travel mug for an ideal meal on the go.

Tip

Lining a pan with foil is easy. Begin by turning the pan upside down. Tear off a piece of foil longer than the pan, then mold the foil over the pan. Remove the foil and set it aside. Flip the pan over and gently fit the shaped foil into the pan, allowing the foil to hang over the sides (the overhang ends will work as "handles" when you remove the contents of the pan).

Storage Tip

Wrap bars individually and refrigerate for up to 2 weeks.

- Preheat oven to 350°F (180°C)
- Food processor
- 8-inch (20 cm) square metal baking pan, lined with foil (see tip, at left) and sprayed with nonstick cooking spray

¾ cup	certified GF large flake (old-fashioned) rolled oats	175 mL
⅔ cup	millet flour	150 mL
⅓ cup	packed light brown sugar	75 mL
3 tbsp	ground flax seeds (flaxseed meal)	45 mL
⅛ tsp	fine sea salt	0.5 mL
7 tbsp	cold virgin coconut oil, cut into small pieces	105 mL
¾ cup	all-fruit strawberry jam	175 mL

1. In food processor, combine oats, millet flour, brown sugar, flax seeds and salt; pulse until blended. Add coconut oil and process, using on/off pulses, until mixture resembles coarse, damp crumbs.

2. Press half the oat mixture firmly into prepared pan. Spread jam over oat mixture. Sprinkle the remaining oat mixture on top, gently pressing it into jam.

3. Bake in preheated oven for 30 to 35 minutes or until golden brown. Let cool completely in pan on a wire rack. Using foil liner, lift loaf from pan and place on a cutting board; using a spatula, lift loaf off foil and discard foil. Cut loaf into 12 bars.

Cinnamon Raisin Breakfast Squares

Makes 16 squares

Breakfast bars don't have to come in packages, nor taste like cardboard. A perfect example: these yummy homemade cinnamon breakfast squares, plump with raisins and rich with ancient grains.

Tip

Cooked buckwheat, millet, quinoa or brown rice, cooled, can be used in place of the amaranth. Information on cooking these grains can be found on pages 9–16.

Storage Tip

Wrap bars individually and refrigerate for up to 2 weeks.

- Food processor
- 9-inch (23 cm) square metal baking pan, lined with foil (see tip, page 70)

1 cup	cooked amaranth (see page 8), cooled	250 mL
1 tsp	ground cinnamon	5 mL
1/4 tsp	fine sea salt	1 mL
1 cup	unsweetened nut or seed butter	250 mL
1/4 cup	liquid honey or brown rice syrup	60 mL
1 tsp	GF vanilla extract	5 mL
2 cups	certified GF large-flake (old-fashioned) rolled oats	500 mL
1 cup	raisins	250 mL

1. In food processor, combine amaranth, cinnamon, salt, nut butter, honey and vanilla; process until blended. Scrape into a large bowl and stir in oats and raisins until combined.

2. Press mixture into prepared pan and refrigerate for at least 1 hour, until firm. Using foil liner, lift loaf from pan and invert onto a cutting board; peel off foil and cut into 16 squares.

Mocha Java Teff Pucks

Here's a portable, whole-grain, double-chocolate breakfast that includes a dose of coffee, too. Plus, it comes together in short order. If you're wondering about the "puck" title, don't worry: it's an entirely positive eponym: it simply refers to the diminutive, low, round shape.

Tips

If using non-dairy milk, try coconut, almond, rice or hemp.

You can substitute 4 tsp (20 mL) instant coffee powder for the espresso powder.

Storage Tip

Store the cooled pucks tightly covered or in an airtight container in the refrigerator for up to 3 days. Serve cold or at room temperature.

- Preheat oven to 350°F (180°C)
- Blender
- 12-cup muffin pan, 10 cups lined with paper liners.

1 cup	teff	250 mL
1¾ cups	water	425 mL
1 cup	pitted soft dates (such as Medjool)	250 mL
⅓ cup	unsweetened natural cocoa powder	75 mL
2 tsp	instant espresso powder	10 mL
½ tsp	fine sea salt	2 mL
2 cups	milk or plain non-dairy milk	500 mL
1 tsp	GF vanilla extract	5 mL
½ cup	ground flax seeds (flaxseed meal)	125 mL
⅓ cup	miniature GF semisweet chocolate chips	75 mL

1. In a small saucepan, combine teff and water. Bring to a boil over medium-high heat. Reduce heat to low, cover and simmer, stirring occasionally, for 12 to 15 minutes or until water is absorbed. Remove from heat and let stand for 5 minutes. Fluff teff with a fork.

2. In blender, combine dates, cocoa, espresso powder, salt, milk and vanilla; purée until smooth.

3. Transfer date mixture to a large bowl and stir in cooked teff, flax seeds and chocolate chips.

4. Divide batter equally among prepared muffin cups.

5. Bake in preheated oven for 23 to 28 minutes or until firmly set. Let cool completely in pan on a wire rack.

Rise and Shine Biscotti

Cookies for breakfast? That's a good thing when the cookies in question are crunchy, faintly sweet, Italian-style biscotti packed with whole grains (millet and oats), protein (eggs, chia seeds and sunflower seeds) and antioxidants (tart-sweet cranberries). Go ahead, have two!

Tips

Raisins, dried cherries or chopped dried apricots can be used in place of the dried cranberries.

The biscotti will continue to harden as they cool after the second bake.

Storage Tip

Store the cooled biscotti in an airtight container at room temperature for up to 1 week or in the freezer for up to 3 months.

- Preheat oven to 300°F (150°C)
- Food processor
- Large rimmed baking sheet, lined with parchment paper

1½ cups	certified GF large-flake (old-fashioned) rolled oats, divided	375 mL
¾ cup	millet or sorghum flour	175 mL
¼ cup	potato starch	60 mL
1 tsp	GF baking powder	5 mL
½ tsp	baking soda	2 mL
¼ tsp	fine sea salt	1 mL
⅔ cup	dried cranberries	150 mL
½ cup	toasted sunflower seeds (see page 27)	125 mL
3 tbsp	chia seeds	45 mL
⅓ cup	fine crystal cane sugar or packed light brown sugar	75 mL
2	large eggs	2
⅓ cup	liquid honey	75 mL
1 tbsp	finely grated orange zest	15 mL

1. In food processor, pulse ¾ cup (175 mL) of the oats until they resemble fine flour.

2. Transfer ground oats to a medium bowl and whisk in the remaining oats, millet flour, potato starch, baking powder, baking soda and salt. Stir in cranberries, sunflower seeds and chia seeds.

3. In a large bowl, whisk together sugar, eggs, honey and orange zest until blended. Gradually add the flour mixture, stirring until just blended. Divide dough in half.

4. Place dough halves on prepared baking sheet and, using moistened hands, shape into two parallel 12- by 2-inch (30 by 5 cm) rectangles, spaced about 3 inches (7.5 cm) apart.

5. Bake in preheated oven for 30 to 35 minutes or until set at the center and golden. Remove from oven, leaving oven on, and let cool on pan on a wire rack for 15 minutes.

6. Cut rectangles crosswise into ½-inch (1 cm) slices. Place slices, cut side down, on baking sheet. Bake for 8 to 10 minutes or until edges are golden. Let cool on pan for 1 minute, then transfer to wire racks to cool completely.

Amaranth Apricot Breakfast Cookies

Makes 30 large cookies

Packed with protein, calcium and fiber, amaranth is a superb way to start your day. These cookies make eating it easy and delicious.

Tip

Cooked millet or quinoa, cooled, can be used in place of the amaranth. Information on cooking these grains can be found on pages 11–15.

Storage Tip

Store the cooled cookies in an airtight container in the refrigerator for up to 5 days or in the freezer for up to 3 months.

- Preheat oven to 350°F (180°C)
- Large baking sheets, lined with parchment paper

⅓ cup	packed light brown sugar	75 mL
½ tsp	fine sea salt	2 mL
2	large eggs	2
¾ cup	unsweetened applesauce	175 mL
¼ cup	melted virgin coconut oil	60 mL
1 tsp	GF vanilla extract	5 mL
1⅔ cups	certified GF quick-cooking rolled oats	400 mL
1½ cups	cooked amaranth (see page 8), cooled	375 mL
½ cup	chopped dried apricots	125 mL

1. In a large bowl, whisk together brown sugar, salt, eggs, applesauce, coconut oil and vanilla. Stir in oats, amaranth and apricots until just blended. Let stand for 10 minutes.

2. Drop batter by 2 tbsp (30 mL) onto prepared baking sheets, spacing cookies 2 inches (5 cm) apart.

3. Bake, one sheet at a time, in preheated oven for 12 to 15 minutes or until just set at the center. Let cool on pan on a wire rack for 5 minutes, then transfer to the rack to cool completely.

Banana Breakfast Cookies

You know those spotted bananas on your countertop? They're ready for a love match with oats. Add a short list of pantry ingredients and in a matter of minutes you have scrumptious cookies that are frugal, vegan and gluten-free. Eat them for breakfast or dessert, or as a snack, to fuel up before a workout or to refuel after a workout — or even for dinner on one of those days when you need cookies for dinner.

Tip

Bananas are very ripe (and are both sweeter and softer) when their peels are mostly brown or heavily spotted.

Storage Tip

Store the cooled cookies in an airtight container in the refrigerator for up to 5 days or in the freezer for up to 3 months.

- Preheat oven to 350°F (180°C)
- Large rimmed baking sheets, lined with parchment paper

2 cups	certified GF large-flake (old-fashioned) or quick-cooking rolled oats	500 mL
1/2 tsp	fine sea salt	2 mL
2	large very ripe bananas, mashed	2
1 cup	unsweetened creamy nut or seed butter	250 mL
2 tbsp	pure maple syrup or liquid honey	30 mL
3/4 cup	miniature GF semisweet chocolate chips or chopped dried fruit (optional)	175 mL

1. In a large bowl, whisk together oats and salt.

2. In a small saucepan, combine bananas, nut butter and maple syrup. Heat over low heat, stirring until melted and smooth.

3. Add the banana mixture to the oat mixture, stirring until blended. Fold in chocolate chips, if using.

4. Drop batter by 2 tbsp (30 mL) onto prepared baking sheets, spacing cookies 2 inches (5 cm) apart.

5. Bake, one sheet at a time, in preheated oven for 9 to 11 minutes or until just set at the center. Let cool on pan on a wire rack for 2 minutes, then transfer to the rack to cool completely.

Peanut Butter Chocolate Chip Breakfast Cookies

Makes 30 cookies

Not too sweet, yet utterly addictive, these breakfast cookies will keep you satisfied for hours.

Tip

Any unsweetened nut or seed butter (such as cashew butter, almond butter, sunflower seed butter or tahini) may be used in place of the peanut butter.

Storage Tip

Store the cooled cookies in an airtight container in the refrigerator for up to 5 days or in the freezer for up to 3 months.

- Preheat oven to 350°F (180°C)
- Large baking sheets, lined with parchment paper

1$\frac{1}{2}$ cups	certified GF quick-cooking rolled oats	375 mL
1 cup	amaranth flour	250 mL
$\frac{1}{2}$ tsp	GF baking powder	2 mL
$\frac{1}{2}$ tsp	baking soda	2 mL
$\frac{1}{2}$ tsp	fine sea salt	2 mL
2	large eggs, lightly beaten	2
$\frac{1}{2}$ cup	unsweetened peanut butter	125 mL
$\frac{1}{4}$ cup	liquid honey, pure maple syrup or brown rice syrup	60 mL
3 tbsp	melted virgin coconut oil	45 mL
1 tsp	GF vanilla extract	5 mL
$\frac{2}{3}$ cup	GF semisweet chocolate chips	150 mL

1. In a large bowl, whisk together oats, amaranth flour, baking powder, baking soda and salt. Stir in eggs, peanut butter, honey, coconut oil and vanilla until just blended. Gently fold in chocolate chips.

2. Drop batter by 2 tbsp (30 mL) onto prepared baking sheets, spacing cookies 2 inches (5 cm) apart. With a metal spatula, flatten each mound to $\frac{1}{2}$-inch (1 cm) thickness.

3. Bake, one sheet at a time, in preheated oven for 12 to 15 minutes or until just set at the center. Let cool on pan on a wire rack for 5 minutes, then transfer to the rack to cool completely.

Sweet Potato and Pecan Breakfast Cookies

Sweet potatoes and pecans are available year-round in my adopted state of Texas, so I've worked them into a host of recipes, ranging from snacks to sides to main dishes. Here, they shine in moist and flavorful breakfast cookies.

Tip

An equal amount of quinoa flour, amaranth flour, millet flour or sorghum flour can be used in place of the buckwheat flour.

Storage Tip

Store the cooled cookies in an airtight container in the refrigerator for up to 5 days or in the freezer for up to 3 months.

- Preheat oven to 375°F (190°C)
- Large baking sheets, lined with parchment paper

1½ cups	certified GF large-flake (old-fashioned) rolled oats	375 mL
⅔ cup	buckwheat flour	150 mL
⅓ cup	tapioca starch	75 mL
¼ cup	ground flax seeds (flaxseed meal)	60 mL
2 tsp	ground cinnamon	10 mL
1 tsp	baking soda	5 mL
¼ tsp	fine sea salt	1 mL
2	large eggs, lightly beaten	2
½ cup	unsweetened applesauce	125 mL
½ cup	dark (cooking) molasses	125 mL
⅓ cup	melted virgin coconut oil	75 mL
1½ cups	finely shredded sweet potato	375 mL
¾ cup	chopped toasted pecans (see page 26)	175 mL

1. In a large bowl, whisk together oats, buckwheat flour, tapioca starch, flax seeds, cinnamon, baking soda and salt. Stir in eggs, applesauce, molasses and coconut oil until just blended. Gently fold in sweet potato and pecans.

2. Drop batter by 2 tbsp (30 mL) onto prepared baking sheets, spacing cookies 2 inches (5 cm) apart.

3. Bake, one sheet at a time, in preheated oven for 12 to 15 minutes or until just set at the center. Let cool on pan on a wire rack for 5 minutes, then transfer to the rack to cool completely.

Maple Ancient Grain Crunch

This crispy, crunchy, faintly sweet topping is terrific on countless breakfast dishes, from hot porridge to yogurt to fresh fruit.

Tip

An equal amount of liquid honey, brown rice syrup or agave nectar can be used in place of the maple syrup.

- Preheat oven to 375°F (190°C)
- Rimmed baking sheet, lined with parchment paper

⅓ cup	quinoa, rinsed	75 mL
⅓ cup	millet	75 mL
¼ cup	teff	60 mL
¼ cup	amaranth	60 mL
⅛ tsp	fine sea salt	0.5 mL
1½ tbsp	melted virgin coconut oil	22 mL
1½ tbsp	pure maple syrup	22 mL

1. In a small bowl, combine quinoa, millet, teff, amaranth, salt, coconut oil and maple syrup. Spread evenly on prepared baking sheet.

2. Bake in preheated oven for 11 to 13 minutes, stirring occasionally, until quinoa is crisp. Transfer to a large plate and let cool completely.

3. Transfer quinoa crunch to an airtight container and store at room temperature for up to 1 month.

Yogurt with Popped Amaranth and Fruit

Honey-sweetened yogurt brings out the natural, delicious goodness of whole grains and fruit in this make-ahead breakfast.

Tips

Plain non-dairy yogurt can be used in place of the Greek yogurt.

An equal amount of pure maple syrup, brown rice syrup or agave nectar can be used in place of the honey.

1 cup	popped amaranth (see page 9)	250 mL
⅛ tsp	fine sea salt	0.5 mL
3 tbsp	liquid honey, divided	45 mL
1 cup	plain Greek yogurt	250 mL
1½ cups	assorted diced seasonal fruit or berries	375 mL

1. In a small bowl, combine amaranth, salt and 2 tbsp (30 mL) of the honey.

2. Divide yogurt between two small bowls. Drizzle with the remaining honey. Top each with half the fruit and half the amaranth mixture.

Blueberry Lime Millet Shake

Forget sugar-laden drinks from the smoothie shop; this luscious, fruit-sweetened shake is tart-sweet bliss in a glass.

- Blender

½ cup	cooked millet (see page 11), chilled	125 mL
1½ cups	frozen blueberries	375 mL
1 cup	unsweetened apple juice	250 mL
1 tbsp	freshly squeezed lime juice	15 mL

1. In blender, purée millet, blueberries, apple juice and lime juice until smooth. Pour into two glasses and serve immediately.

Mango Quinoa Shake

Cooked quinoa lends creaminess, without dairy, to this super-fruity tropical shake.

Tip
An equal amount of frozen pineapple chunks or diced frozen peaches can be used in place of the mango.

- Blender

½ cup	cooked quinoa (see page 15), chilled	125 mL
1½ cups	diced frozen mango	375 mL
½ cup	sliced frozen ripe banana	125 mL
1½ cups	orange juice	375 mL

1. In blender, purée quinoa, mango, banana and orange juice until smooth. Pour into two glasses and serve immediately.

Peachy Chia Smoothie

This vibrant blend of peaches, chia and pineapple juice will wake you up and energize you like no cup of coffee can.

- Blender

1¼ cups	frozen sliced or diced peaches	300 mL
2 tbsp	chia seeds	30 mL
1 tbsp	minced gingerroot	15 mL
1 cup	pineapple juice	250 mL

1. In blender, purée peaches, chia seeds, ginger and pineapple juice until smooth. Pour into two glasses and serve immediately.

Coconut, Cardamom and Chia Smoothie

Even with no added sweeteners, this rich and creamy smoothie is as satisfying for dessert as it is for breakfast.

Variation

Replace the coconut milk with 1 cup (250 mL) plain cultured soy or rice yogurt plus ½ cup (125 mL) plain non-dairy milk (such as soy, almond, rice or hemp).

• Blender

1 cup	sliced frozen ripe banana	250 mL
¼ cup	pitted Medjool or other soft dates, roughly chopped	60 mL
2 tbsp	chia seeds	30 mL
¼ tsp	ground cardamom or cinnamon	1 mL
1 cup	well-stirred coconut milk (full-fat), chilled	250 mL
½ cup	ice water	125 mL

1. In blender, purée banana, dates, chia seeds, cinnamon, coconut milk and ice water until smooth. Pour into two glasses and serve immediately.

Emerald Smoothie

Sometimes it's easy being green. Even the picky eaters in the house will love this delicious smoothie (though you may have to blindfold them for the first few sips).

• Blender

⅓ cup	cooked quinoa (see page 15), chilled	75 mL
2 cups	loosely packed spinach leaves or trimmed kale leaves	500 mL
1 cup	green grapes	250 mL
¾ cup	sliced frozen ripe banana	175 mL
½ cup	chopped kiwifruit	125 mL
1 cup	orange juice	250 mL

1. In blender, purée quinoa, spinach, grapes, banana, kiwi and orange juice until smooth. Pour into two glasses and serve immediately.

Soups, Stews and Chilis

continued…

Amaranth Beet Soup

The beets give this soup its gorgeous ruby hue, while amaranth adds balance and a mellow undercurrent of flavor.

Tips

If you prefer a rustic texture, do not purée the soup.

When puréeing soup in a food processor or blender, fill the bowl no more than halfway full at a time.

Storage Tip

Store the cooled soup (without any accompaniments) in an airtight container in the refrigerator for up to 2 days or in the freezer for up to 6 months. Thaw overnight in the refrigerator or in the microwave using the Defrost function. Warm soup in a medium saucepan over medium-low heat.

- Food processor, blender or immersion blender

1 tbsp	olive oil	15 mL
2 cups	chopped onions	500 mL
6	cloves garlic, minced	6
4 cups	chopped peeled beets	1 L
1/3 cup	amaranth	75 mL
	Fine sea salt	
1 tsp	garam masala	5 mL
6 cups	water	1.5 L
	Freshly ground black pepper	

Suggested Accompaniments
Plain yogurt
Chopped fresh mint or chives

1. In a large pot, heat oil over medium-high heat. Add onions and cook, stirring, for 6 to 8 minutes or until softened. Add garlic and cook, stirring, for 30 seconds.

2. Stir in beets, amaranth, $1/2$ tsp (2 mL) salt, garam masala and water; bring to a boil. Reduce heat to low, cover and simmer for 25 to 30 minutes or until beets are very tender.

3. Working in batches, transfer soup to food processor (or use immersion blender in pot) and purée until smooth. Return soup to pot (if necessary) and warm over low heat, stirring occasionally, for 4 to 5 minutes or until heated through. Season to taste with salt and pepper. Serve with any of the suggested accompaniments, as desired.

Broccoli, Leek and Sage Bisque

Makes 4 servings

This creamy soup gets its luxurious texture from rolled oats — which break down and become creamy — and a quick whirl in the food processor.

Tips

For best results, use a vegetable peeler to peel the thick outer layer off the broccoli stems before chopping.

For the non-dairy milk, try hemp, rice or almond milk.

When puréeing soup in a food processor or blender, fill the bowl no more than halfway full at a time.

Storage Tip

Store the cooled soup in an airtight container in the refrigerator for up to 2 days or in the freezer for up to 6 months. Thaw overnight in the refrigerator or in the microwave using the Defrost function. Warm soup in a medium saucepan over medium-low heat.

- Food processor, blender or immersion blender

1 tbsp	unsalted butter or olive oil	15 mL
2 cups	chopped leeks (white and pale green parts only)	500 mL
2 tsp	dried rubbed sage	10 mL
1/4 tsp	freshly ground black pepper	1 mL
1 1/2 lbs	broccoli, coarsely chopped (both florets and peeled stems)	750 g
1 cup	certified GF large-flake (old-fashioned) rolled oats	250 mL
4 cups	ready-to-use GF vegetable broth	1 L
1 1/2 cups	water	375 mL
1 cup	milk or plain non-dairy milk	250 mL

1. In a large saucepan, melt butter over medium-high heat. Add leeks and cook, stirring, for 5 to 6 minutes or until softened. Add sage and pepper; cook, stirring, for 30 seconds.

2. Stir in broccoli, oats, broth and water; bring to a boil. Reduce heat and simmer, stirring occasionally, for 15 to 18 minutes or until broccoli is tender.

3. Working in batches, transfer soup to food processor (or use immersion blender in pan) and purée until smooth. Return soup to pan (if necessary) and whisk in milk. Warm over medium heat, stirring, for 2 to 3 minutes or until heated through.

Gingery Quinoa Soup with Miso and Cabbage

Ginger, garlic and miso give this streamlined soup kick, while quinoa and vegetables make it filling enough for main-dish fare.

Tip
An equal amount of millet or amaranth can be used in place of the quinoa.

Storage Tip
Store the cooled soup in an airtight container in the refrigerator for up to 2 days or in the freezer for up to 6 months. Thaw overnight in the refrigerator or in the microwave using the Defrost function. Warm soup in a medium saucepan over medium-low heat.

2	cloves garlic, minced	2
2 tbsp	minced gingerroot	30 mL
1 cup	quinoa, rinsed	250 mL
3 cups	ready-to-use GF vegetable or chicken broth	750 mL
3 cups	water	750 mL
3 tbsp	GF miso paste	45 mL
4 cups	shredded savoy cabbage	1 L
1 cup	frozen petite peas	250 mL
1/3 cup	thinly sliced green onions	75 mL
1 tbsp	unseasoned rice vinegar or cider vinegar	15 mL
	Fine sea salt and freshly cracked black pepper	
	Asian chili sauce (such as Sriracha)	

1. In a large pot, combine garlic, ginger, quinoa, broth, water and miso. Bring to a boil over medium-high heat. Reduce heat to low, cover and simmer, stirring occasionally, for 15 minutes.

2. Stir in cabbage and peas; simmer, uncovered, for 3 to 5 minutes or until quinoa is tender and cabbage is wilted. Stir in green onions and vinegar. Season to taste with salt and pepper. Serve drizzled with chili sauce.

Lemon and Mint Carrot Soup

This vibrant orange soup is a springtime celebration, with grassy flavors of carrots and millet complemented by the bright duo of lemon and mint.

Tip

When puréeing soup in a food processor or blender, fill the bowl no more than halfway full at a time.

Storage Tip

Store the cooled soup (without the mint) in an airtight container in the refrigerator for up to 2 days or in the freezer for up to 6 months. Thaw overnight in the refrigerator or in the microwave using the Defrost function. Warm soup in a medium saucepan over medium-low heat.

- Food processor, blender or immersion blender

1 tbsp	olive oil	15 mL
1½ cups	chopped onions	375 mL
2 tbsp	minced gingerroot	30 mL
1¼ lbs	carrots, chopped (about 3 cups/750 mL)	625 g
½ cup	millet	125 mL
6 cups	ready-to-use GF chicken or vegetable broth	1.5 L
2 tsp	finely grated lemon zest	10 mL
2 tbsp	freshly squeezed lemon juice	30 mL
1 tbsp	liquid honey	15 mL
	Fine sea salt and freshly ground black pepper	
½ cup	packed fresh mint leaves, minced	125 mL

1. In a large pot, heat oil over medium-high heat. Add onions and ginger; cook, stirring, for 5 to 6 minutes or until onions are softened.

2. Stir in carrots, millet and broth; bring to a boil. Reduce heat and simmer, stirring occasionally, for 25 to 30 minutes or until carrots and millet are very soft.

3. Working in batches, transfer soup to food processor (or use immersion blender in pot) and purée until smooth. Return soup to pot (if necessary) and whisk in lemon zest, lemon juice and honey. Warm over medium heat, stirring, for 1 minute. Season to taste with salt and pepper. Stir in mint.

Cauliflower, Sharp Cheddar and Amaranth Soup

Since cheese is a natural with cauliflower, combining the two with the nutty goodness of amaranth makes delicious sense.

Tips

In a pinch, you can use two 12-oz (375 g) bags of frozen cauliflower florets, thawed and drained of excess liquid, in place of the fresh cauliflower. Reduce the cauliflower cooking time in step 1 to 5 to 6 minutes, and reduce the simmering time in step 2 to 20 to 25 minutes.

An equal amount of quinoa, rinsed, or millet can be used in place of the amaranth.

When puréeing soup in a food processor or blender, fill the bowl no more than halfway full at a time.

Storage Tip

Store the cooled soup (without the chives) in an airtight container in the refrigerator for up to 2 days or in the freezer for up to 6 months. Thaw overnight in the refrigerator or in the microwave using the Defrost function. Warm soup in a medium saucepan over medium-low heat.

• Food processor, blender or immersion blender

1 tbsp	unsalted butter or olive oil	15 mL
1½ cups	chopped onions	375 mL
4 cups	cauliflower florets (about 1 medium head)	1 L
1½ tsp	ground coriander	7 mL
	Fine sea salt	
⅓ cup	amaranth	75 mL
6 cups	water	1.5 L
1½ cups	shredded sharp (old) white Cheddar cheese	375 mL
	Freshly ground black pepper	
¼ cup	chopped fresh chives	60 mL

1. In a large pot, melt butter over medium-high heat. Add onions and cook, stirring, for 5 to 6 minutes or until softened. Add cauliflower, coriander and 1½ tsp (7 mL) salt; cook, stirring, for 6 to 8 minutes or until cauliflower is browned.

2. Stir in amaranth and water; bring to a boil. Reduce heat and simmer, stirring occasionally, for 25 to 30 minutes or until cauliflower is very soft.

3. Working in batches, transfer soup to food processor (or use immersion blender in pot) and purée until smooth. Return soup to pot (if necessary) and stir in cheese. Warm over medium heat, stirring, for 1 to 2 minutes or until cheese is melted. Season to taste with salt and pepper. Serve sprinkled with chives.

Hominy, Corn and Amaranth Soup

Hominy is corn that has been dried, then soaked in an alkaline solution. It is an essential ingredient in corn tortillas, and when you bite into one of the plump, chewy kernels, you will instantly recognize the dried corn flavor. A classic ingredient in Mexican soups, it is highlighted here with the sweetness of fresh corn and the earthiness of amaranth.

Tip

The specified amount of chipotle chile powder will create a medium spiciness. Feel free to add less or more to suit your taste.

Storage Tip

Store the cooled soup (without the cilantro garnish or any accompaniments) in an airtight container in the refrigerator for up to 2 days or in the freezer for up to 6 months. Thaw overnight in the refrigerator or in the microwave using the Defrost function. Warm soup in a medium saucepan over medium-low heat.

Variation

Amaranth and Black Bean Soup: Replace the hominy with 2 cans (each 14 to 19 oz/398 to 540 mL) black beans, drained and rinsed.

1 tbsp	olive oil	15 mL
2 tsp	ground cumin	10 mL
1 tsp	chipotle chile powder	5 mL
1¼ cups	fresh or frozen corn kernels	300 mL
¾ cup	amaranth	175 mL
2	cans (each 14 to 15 oz/398 to 425 mL) hominy, drained and rinsed	2
4 cups	ready-to-use GF chicken or vegetable broth	1 L
1	can (28 oz/796 mL) crushed tomatoes	1
1 cup	packed fresh cilantro leaves	250 mL
1 tbsp	freshly squeezed lime juice	15 mL
	Fine sea salt and freshly ground black pepper	

Suggested Accompaniments

Diced firm-ripe Hass avocado
Crumbled queso fresco
Thinly sliced radishes

1. In a large pot, heat oil over medium-high heat. Add cumin and chipotle chile powder; cook, stirring, for 30 to 60 seconds or until fragrant.

2. Stir in corn, amaranth, hominy and broth; bring to a boil. Reduce heat to low, cover and simmer, stirring occasionally, for 15 to 20 minutes or until amaranth is very tender.

3. Stir in tomatoes and simmer, uncovered, for 5 minutes. Stir in half the cilantro and lime juice. Season to taste with salt and pepper. Serve sprinkled with the remaining cilantro and with any of the suggested accompaniments, as desired.

Quinoa and Eggplant Parmesan Soup

Makes 6 servings

Baking eggplant makes it super-tender and creamy with almost no effort. Here, it is combined with marinara sauce and quinoa for an easy, soup-style version of eggplant Parmesan.

Storage Tip

Store the cooled soup (without the cheese or basil) in an airtight container in the refrigerator for up to 2 days or in the freezer for up to 6 months. Thaw overnight in the refrigerator or in the microwave using the Defrost function. Warm soup in a medium saucepan over medium-low heat.

- Preheat oven to 450°F (230°C)
- Large rimmed baking sheet, oiled

2 lbs	eggplant (about 1 large or 2 medium), halved lengthwise	1 kg
2 tbsp	olive oil	30 mL
1½ cups	chopped onions	375 mL
3	cloves garlic, minced	3
½ cup	quinoa, rinsed	125 mL
5 cups	water	1.25 L
1	jar (26 oz/700 mL) GF marinara sauce	1
	Fine sea salt and freshly cracked black pepper	
¾ cup	freshly grated Parmesan cheese	175 mL
½ cup	packed fresh basil leaves, thinly sliced	125 mL

1. Place eggplant cut side down on prepared baking sheet. Roast in preheated oven for 40 to 45 minutes or until very tender and lightly browned on top and bottom. Let cool slightly.

2. Meanwhile, in a large pot, heat oil over medium-high heat. Add onions and cook, stirring, for 5 to 6 minutes or until softened. Add garlic and cook, stirring, for 30 seconds.

3. Stir in quinoa and water; bring to a boil. Reduce heat to low, cover and simmer for 15 to 20 minutes or until quinoa is very tender.

4. Scoop eggplant flesh from skins, discard skins and coarsely chop eggplant. Add eggplant and marinara sauce to the pot, cover and simmer, stirring occasionally, for 10 minutes. Season to taste with salt and pepper. Serve sprinkled with cheese and basil.

Kale, Oats and Ale Soup

Kale, oats and ale are a trifecta of complementary flavors. Steel-cut oats may sound like a less-than-usual addition to soup, but they add toasty flavor, creaminess and heartiness in one fell swoop.

Storage Tip

Store the cooled soup in an airtight container in the refrigerator for up to 2 days or in the freezer for up to 6 months. Thaw overnight in the refrigerator or in the microwave using the Defrost function. Warm soup in a medium saucepan over medium-low heat.

1 tbsp	olive oil	15 mL
2 cups	chopped onions	500 mL
½ tsp	ground allspice	2 mL
	Freshly ground black pepper	
1 cup	certified GF steel-cut oats	250 mL
1	bottle (12 oz/341 mL) GF lager-style beer	1
6 cups	ready-to-use GF beef or vegetable broth	1.5 L
6 cups	chopped kale (tough stems and center ribs removed)	1.5 L
1 tbsp	cider vinegar	15 mL
	Fine sea salt	

1. In a large saucepan, heat oil over medium-high heat. Add onions and cook, stirring, for 6 to 8 minutes or until very soft but not browned. Add allspice and ¼ tsp (1 mL) pepper; cook, stirring, for 30 seconds.

2. Stir in oats, beer and broth; bring to a boil. Reduce heat to medium-low, cover, leaving lid ajar, and simmer, stirring occasionally, for 15 minutes. Stir in kale, cover, leaving lid ajar, and simmer, stirring occasionally, for 5 to 10 minutes or until kale is wilted and oats are tender but not falling apart. Stir in vinegar. Season to taste with salt and pepper.

Scottish Leek and Steel-Cut Oats Soup

Creamy and comforting, but not too heavy or rich, this soup is velvety bliss. A long simmer coaxes out the sweetness of the leeks.

Tips

You can use 1 cup (250 mL) large-flake (old-fashioned) rolled oats in place of the steel-cut oats. Reduce the cooking time in step 2 to 10 to 15 minutes. The soup will have a creamier, more bisque-like texture.

An equal amount of millet can be used in place of the oats. Reduce the cooking time in step 2 to 25 to 30 minutes.

If using non-dairy milk, try rice, hemp, almond or soy. Avoid coconut milk, as the flavor will overpower the soup.

Storage Tip

Store the cooled soup (without the chives) in an airtight container in the refrigerator for up to 2 days or in the freezer for up to 6 months. Thaw overnight in the refrigerator or in the microwave using the Defrost function. Warm soup in a medium saucepan over medium-low heat.

1 tbsp	unsalted butter	15 mL
1½ cups	thinly sliced halved leeks (white and pale green parts only)	375 mL
¼ tsp	ground nutmeg	1 mL
½ cup	certified GF steel-cut oats	125 mL
4 cups	ready-to-use GF chicken or vegetable broth	1 L
1½ cups	milk or plain non-dairy milk	375 mL
	Fine sea salt and freshly ground black pepper	
2 tbsp	minced fresh chives (optional)	30 mL

1. In a large saucepan, melt butter over medium heat. Add leeks and cook, stirring, for 12 to 15 minutes or until very soft but not browned. Add nutmeg and cook, stirring, for 30 seconds.

2. Stir in oats and broth; bring to a boil. Reduce heat to low, cover and simmer, stirring occasionally, for 45 to 50 minutes.

3. Stir in milk, cover and simmer for 3 to 5 minutes or until warmed through. Season to taste with salt and pepper. Serve sprinkled with chives, if desired.

Miso, Mushroom and Buckwheat Soup

The rich, umami flavor of miso imparts a nutty, slightly sweet flavor to the soup that marries all of the elements into a cohesive, complementary whole.

Tips

Shiitake mushroom stems are often tough and dry. If that is the case, remove them before slicing the caps. But don't toss the stems out: freeze them for when you're making vegetable stock, as they add tremendous depth of flavor.

An equal amount of quinoa, rinsed, or amaranth can be used in place of the buckwheat.

Storage Tip

Store the cooled soup (without the green onions) in an airtight container in the refrigerator for up to 2 days or in the freezer for up to 6 months. Thaw overnight in the refrigerator or in the microwave using the Defrost function. Warm soup in a medium saucepan over medium-low heat.

1 tbsp	olive oil	15 mL
8 oz	shiitake or button mushrooms (stems removed if necessary), sliced	250 g
1 cup	chopped onions	250 mL
2	cloves garlic, minced	2
1½ tbsp	minced gingerroot	22 mL
⅔ cup	buckwheat groats	150 mL
6 cups	ready-to-use GF vegetable broth	1.5 L
3 tbsp	GF miso paste	45 mL
	Fine sea salt and freshly ground black pepper	
⅓ cup	thinly sliced green onions	75 mL

1. In a large saucepan, heat oil over medium-high heat. Add mushrooms and onions; cook, stirring, for 6 to 8 minutes or until slightly softened. Add garlic and ginger; cook, stirring, for 1 minute.

2. Stir in buckwheat, broth and miso; bring to a boil, stirring often. Reduce heat to medium, cover, leaving lid ajar, and simmer, stirring occasionally, for 15 to 20 minutes or until buckwheat is tender. Season to taste with salt and pepper. Serve sprinkled with green onions.

Parsnip, Millet and Ale Bisque

Makes 6 servings

This robust and sophisticated soup places the otherwise humble parsnip front and center. Millet accentuates the natural creaminess of the parsnips, while beer and spices add piquant contrast.

Tip

An equal amount of dry white wine, or additional broth, can be used in place of the beer.

Storage Tip

Store the cooled soup (without any accompaniments) in an airtight container in the refrigerator for up to 2 days or in the freezer for up to 6 months. Thaw overnight in the refrigerator or in the microwave using the Defrost function. Warm soup in a medium saucepan over medium-low heat.

2 tbsp	unsalted butter or olive oil	30 mL
4 cups	chopped parsnips	1 L
1½ cups	chopped onions	375 mL
¾ cup	millet	175 mL
½ tsp	ground nutmeg	2 mL
¼ tsp	cayenne pepper	1 mL
6 cups	ready-to-use GF vegetable or chicken broth	1.5 L
1	bottle (12 oz/341 mL) GF beer	1
	Fine sea salt and freshly ground black pepper	

Suggested Accompaniments

Chopped fresh chives or flat-leaf (Italian) parsley
Crumbled blue cheese

1. In a large pot, melt butter over medium-high heat. Add parsnips and onions; cook, stirring, for 7 to 9 minutes or until slightly softened. Add millet, nutmeg and cayenne; cook, stirring, for 1 minute.

2. Stir in broth and bring to a boil. Reduce heat and simmer, stirring occasionally, for 30 to 35 minutes or until millet is creamy and vegetables are very tender.

3. Using a potato masher in the pot, coarsely mash vegetables. Stir in beer and simmer, stirring occasionally, for 10 minutes. Season to taste with salt and black pepper. Serve with any of the suggested accompaniments, as desired.

Brown Rice and Kaddu Masala Soup

Makes 6 servings

Spices, coconut milk and lemon form a perfect trio of Indian flavor in this streamlined soup. Pumpkin (*kaddu* in Hindi) and brown rice make it more than hearty enough for a main dish.

Tips

Brown basmati rice or other long-grain brown rice can be used in place of the medium-grain brown rice.

An equal amount of quinoa, rinsed, or millet can be used in place of the rice. Reduce the cooking time in step 1 to 15 to 20 minutes.

If 15-oz (425 mL) cans of pumpkin aren't available, purchase one 28-oz (796 mL) can and measure out 1¾ cups (425 mL). Refrigerate extra pumpkin in an airtight container for up to 1 week.

Storage Tip

Store the cooled soup (without the mint garnish) in an airtight container in the refrigerator for up to 2 days or in the freezer for up to 6 months. Thaw overnight in the refrigerator or in the microwave using the Defrost function. Warm soup in a medium saucepan over medium-low heat.

⅔ cup	medium-grain brown rice	150 mL
2 tbsp	fine crystal cane sugar or packed light brown sugar	30 mL
4 cups	ready-to-use GF vegetable or chicken broth	1 L
2 tsp	garam masala	10 mL
1 tsp	ground cumin	5 mL
1 tsp	ground ginger	5 mL
½ cup	packed fresh mint or cilantro leaves, chopped, divided	125 mL
1	can (15 oz/425 mL) pumpkin purée (not pie filling)	1
1 cup	well-stirred coconut milk (full-fat)	250 mL
1½ tbsp	freshly squeezed lemon juice	22 mL
	Fine sea salt and freshly ground black pepper	

1. In a large pot, whisk together rice, sugar, broth, garam masala, cumin and ginger. Bring to a boil over medium-high heat. Reduce heat and simmer, stirring occasionally, for 45 to 55 minutes or until rice is tender.

2. Whisk in half the mint, pumpkin, coconut milk and lemon juice; simmer, stirring once or twice, for 5 minutes. Season to taste with salt and pepper. Serve sprinkled with the remaining mint.

Variations

Chicken Masala Soup: For a heartier soup, add 2 cups (500 mL) shredded or diced cooked chicken breast with the pumpkin.

Shrimp Masala Soup: Add 12 oz (375 g) cooked small or medium shrimp with the pumpkin.

Russian Butternut Squash and Buckwheat Soup

Buckwheat is a fundamental grain in Russian cuisine and is used to make countless dishes, from porridge to breads to pancakes. Here, it provides an earthy backdrop to a silken butternut squash soup.

Tip

When puréeing soup in a food processor or blender, fill the bowl no more than halfway full at a time.

Storage Tip

Store the cooled soup (without any accompaniments) in an airtight container in the refrigerator for up to 2 days or in the freezer for up to 6 months. Thaw overnight in the refrigerator or in the microwave using the Defrost function. Warm soup in a medium saucepan over medium-low heat.

• Food processor, blender or immersion blender

1 tbsp	unsalted butter	15 mL
1 1/4 cups	minced onions	300 mL
1 1/2 tsp	ground allspice	7 mL
1/2 tsp	ground cloves	2 mL
	Freshly ground black pepper	
8 cups	diced peeled butternut squash (about 3 lbs/1.5 kg)	2 L
1/3 cup	buckwheat groats	75 mL
8 cups	ready-to-use GF chicken or vegetable broth	2 L
	Fine sea salt	

Suggested Accompaniments

Plain yogurt
Minced fresh chives

1. In a large pot, melt butter over medium-high heat. Add onions and cook, stirring, for 5 to 6 minutes or until softened. Add allspice, cloves and 1/2 tsp (2 mL) pepper; cook, stirring, for 1 minute.

2. Stir in squash, buckwheat and broth; bring to a boil. Reduce heat to low, cover and simmer, stirring occasionally, for 30 to 35 minutes or until squash and buckwheat are very tender.

3. Working in batches, transfer soup to food processor (or use immersion blender in pot) and purée until smooth. Return soup to pot (if necessary) and warm over medium heat, stirring, for 1 minute. Season to taste with salt and pepper. Serve with the suggested accompaniments, as desired.

Sweet Potato and Apple Bisque

This silken bisque has just the right balance of sweet, savory and spicy.

Tip

When puréeing soup in a food processor or blender, fill the bowl no more than halfway full at a time.

Storage Tip

Store the cooled soup (without any accompaniments) in an airtight container in the refrigerator for up to 2 days or in the freezer for up to 6 months. Thaw overnight in the refrigerator or in the microwave using the Defrost function. Warm soup in a medium saucepan over medium-low heat.

• Food processor, blender or immersion blender

4	cloves garlic, peeled	4
1	large tart apple (such as Granny Smith), peeled and chopped	1
1½ lbs	sweet potatoes, peeled and shredded	750 g
⅓ cup	buckwheat groats	75 mL
1½ tsp	dried rubbed sage	7 mL
¼ tsp	cayenne pepper	1 mL
7 cups	ready-to-use GF chicken or vegetable broth	1.75 L
2 tsp	cider vinegar	10 mL

Suggested Accompaniments

Finely diced tart apple

Chopped fresh flat-leaf (Italian) parsley

1. In a large pot, combine garlic, apple, sweet potatoes, buckwheat, sage, cayenne and broth. Bring to a boil over medium-high heat. Reduce heat and simmer, stirring occasionally, for 25 to 30 minutes or until buckwheat is very soft.

2. Working in batches, transfer soup to food processor (or use immersion blender in pot) and purée until smooth. Return soup to pot (if necessary) and whisk in vinegar. Warm over medium heat, stirring, for 1 minute. Serve with the suggested accompaniments, as desired.

Clockwise from top right: Ancient Grains Granola (page 40),
Chocolate Buckwheat Granola (page 41) and
Cardamom Amaranth Granola (page 42)

Fluffy Lemon Chia Seed
Pancakes (page 53)

Blueberry Hazelnut Coffee Cake (page 67)

Baked Millet, Apple and Raisin
Breakfast "Cupcakes" (page 68)

Tomatillo, Black Bean
and Amaranth Soup (page 108)

Hot-and-Sour Shrimp and
Amaranth Soup (page 112)

Chorizo, Kale and Teff Soup (page 118)

Peruvian Quinoa and Sweet Potato Sopa

This minimalist soup is far more than the sum of its parts. Sweet potatoes, corn and quinoa, iconic Peruvian ingredients, offer hearty depth of flavor despite a short simmer time, making this an ideal weeknight soup when the weather turns cold.

Tips

An equal amount of amaranth can be used in place of the quinoa.

When puréeing soup in a food processor or blender, fill the bowl no more than halfway full at a time.

An immersion blender may be used to partially purée the soup (instead of transferring half of it to a food processor). Pulse the immersion blender in the soup 5 to 6 times.

Storage Tip

Store the cooled soup (without the green part of green onions) in an airtight container in the refrigerator for up to 2 days or in the freezer for up to 6 months. Thaw overnight in the refrigerator or in the microwave using the Defrost function. Warm soup in a medium saucepan over medium-low heat.

- Food processor or blender

1 tbsp	olive oil	15 mL
4	green onions, thinly sliced, green and white parts separated	4
1½ tsp	ground cumin	7 mL
¼ tsp	cayenne pepper	1 mL
1	medium-large sweet potato, peeled and finely diced	1
4 cups	fresh or frozen corn kernels	1 L
⅔ cup	quinoa, rinsed	150 mL
6 cups	ready-to-use GF vegetable or chicken broth	1.5 L
	Fine sea salt and freshly cracked black pepper	

1. In a large pot, heat oil over medium-high heat. Add white part of green onions and cook, stirring, for 2 to 3 minutes or until softened. Add cumin and cayenne; cook, stirring, for 30 seconds.

2. Stir in sweet potato, corn, quinoa and broth; bring to a boil. Reduce heat and simmer, stirring occasionally, for 15 to 20 minutes or until sweet potato and quinoa are very tender.

3. Working in batches, transfer half the soup to food processor and purée until smooth. Return puréed soup to pot. Season soup to taste with salt and black pepper. Simmer, stirring occasionally, for 2 to 3 minutes to warm through. Serve sprinkled with green part of green onions.

Pepper Pot Teff Soup

This Jamaican dish has many guises and can be made with meats as well as fish and seafood. It dates back to the Arawak Indians, who prepared a stew that was kept going on the fire, with new ingredients added every day.

Storage Tip

Store the cooled soup in an airtight container in the refrigerator for up to 2 days or in the freezer for up to 6 months. Thaw overnight in the refrigerator or in the microwave using the Defrost function. Warm soup in a medium saucepan over medium-low heat.

Variation

Shrimp Pepper Pot Soup: Add 12 oz (375 g) fresh or thawed frozen medium shrimp, peeled and deveined, with the coconut milk. Simmer for 3 to 5 minutes or until shrimp are pink, firm and opaque.

1	large sweet potato (about 1 lb/500 g), peeled and cut into 1/2-inch (1 cm) cubes	1
2 cups	fresh or frozen sliced okra	500 mL
1 1/4 tsp	ground allspice	6 mL
3/4 tsp	dried thyme	3 mL
2	cans (each 10 oz/284 mL) diced tomatoes with chiles, with juice	2
5 cups	ready-to-use GF vegetable or chicken broth	1.25 L
6 cups	chopped kale or collard greens (tough stems and center ribs removed)	1.5 L
1/2 cup	teff	125 mL
1 cup	well-stirred coconut milk (full-fat)	250 mL
1 tbsp	freshly squeezed lime juice	15 mL
	Fine sea salt and hot pepper sauce	

1. In a large pot, combine sweet potato, okra, allspice, thyme, tomatoes and broth. Bring to a boil over medium-high heat. Reduce heat to low, cover and simmer for 10 minutes.

2. Stir in kale and teff; cover and simmer, stirring occasionally, for 20 to 25 minutes or until sweet potatoes and kale are very tender and teff has thickened the soup.

3. Stir in coconut milk and lime juice; simmer, uncovered, for 2 to 3 minutes or until heated through. Season to taste with salt and hot pepper sauce.

Spanish Tomato Soup

Millet stands in for the typical bread in this Spanish-inspired soup.

Tips

When puréeing soup in a food processor or blender, fill the bowl no more than halfway full at a time.

Canned tomatoes vary in their sweetness, so taste the finished soup for sweetness — you may want to add a bit of liquid honey or another sweetener to balance the acidity of the tomatoes.

Storage Tip

Store the cooled soup in an airtight container in the refrigerator for up to 2 days or in the freezer for up to 6 months. Thaw overnight in the refrigerator or in the microwave using the Defrost function. Warm soup in a medium saucepan over medium-low heat.

- Food processor, blender or immersion blender

2 tbsp	olive oil	30 mL
1	red bell pepper, chopped	1
1¼ cups	chopped onions	300 mL
3	cloves garlic, chopped	3
1 tsp	hot or sweet smoked paprika	5 mL
1 tsp	ground cumin	5 mL
⅔ cup	millet	150 mL
1	can (28 oz/796 mL) crushed tomatoes	1
5½ cups	ready-to-use GF chicken or vegetable broth	1.375 L
	Fine sea salt and freshly ground black pepper	

1. In a large saucepan, heat oil over medium-high heat. Add red pepper and onions; cook, stirring, for 6 to 8 minutes or until softened. Add garlic, paprika and cumin; cook, stirring, for 30 seconds.

2. Stir in millet, tomatoes and broth; bring to a boil. Reduce heat and simmer, stirring occasionally, for 30 to 35 minutes or until millet is very plump and soft.

3. Working in batches, transfer soup to food processor (or use immersion blender in pan) and purée until smooth. Return soup to pan (if necessary) and warm over medium heat, stirring, for 1 minute. Season to taste with salt and pepper.

Rustic Buckwheat Soup

Here, an assortment of vegetables from your refrigerator, along with buckwheat from the pantry, is transformed into a rustic, yet boast-worthy soup.

Tip

An immersion blender may be used to partially purée the soup (instead of transferring half of it to a food processor). Pulse the immersion blender in the soup 5 to 6 times.

Storage Tip

Store the cooled soup (without the cheese) in an airtight container in the refrigerator for up to 2 days or in the freezer for up to 6 months. Thaw overnight in the refrigerator or in the microwave using the Defrost function. Warm soup in a medium saucepan over medium-low heat.

- Food processor or blender

4	cloves garlic, minced	4
2 cups	chopped onions	500 mL
2 cups	chopped carrots	500 mL
1 cup	chopped celery	250 mL
1 cup	buckwheat groats	250 mL
2 tsp	minced fresh rosemary	10 mL
1	can (28 oz/796 mL) crushed tomatoes	1
8 cups	ready-to-use GF chicken or vegetable broth	2 L
2 tbsp	balsamic vinegar	30 mL
	Fine sea salt and freshly cracked black pepper	
	Freshly grated Parmesan cheese (optional)	

1. In a large pot, combine garlic, onions, carrots, celery, rosemary, buckwheat, tomatoes and broth. Bring to a boil over medium-high heat. Reduce heat to low, cover and simmer, stirring occasionally, for 40 to 45 minutes or until buckwheat and vegetables are very tender.

2. Working in batches, transfer half the soup to food processor and purée until smooth. Return puréed soup to pot and stir in vinegar. Warm over medium heat, stirring, for 1 minute. Season to taste with salt and pepper. Serve sprinkled with cheese, if desired.

Mujaddara (Lebanese Lentil, Rice and Spinach Soup)

This soup is based on mujaddara, a blend of lentils and grains, which is a staple dish throughout the Arabic world. My interpretation is based on Lebanese variations, where greens, fresh herbs and lemon are common additions.

Tips

Other varieties of long-grain brown rice can be used in place of the brown basmati rice.

An equal amount of quinoa, rinsed, can be used in place of the rice. Omit step 2 and add the quinoa, salt and pepper with the lentils.

Brown lentils can be used in place of the green lentils. Reduce the cooking time in step 3 to 25 to 30 minutes.

Storage Tip

Store the cooled soup (without the yogurt) in an airtight container in the refrigerator for up to 2 days or in the freezer for up to 6 months. Thaw overnight in the refrigerator or in the microwave using the Defrost function. Warm soup in a medium saucepan over medium-low heat.

1 tbsp	olive oil	15 mL
2 cups	chopped onions	500 mL
5	cloves garlic, chopped	5
1 tbsp	ground cumin	15 mL
3/4 cup	brown basmati rice	175 mL
	Fine sea salt and freshly ground black pepper	
10 cups	water	2.5 L
1 cup	dried green lentils, rinsed	250 mL
6 cups	packed spinach leaves, trimmed and roughly torn	1.5 L
1/3 cup	packed fresh mint leaves, chopped	75 mL
2 tsp	finely grated lemon zest	10 mL
1 tbsp	freshly squeezed lemon juice	15 mL
	Plain Greek yogurt	

1. In a large pot, heat oil over medium-high heat. Add onions and cook, stirring, for 6 to 8 minutes or until softened. Add garlic and cumin; cook, stirring, for 1 minute.

2. Stir in rice, 2 tsp (10 mL) salt, 1 tsp (5 mL) pepper and water; bring to a boil. Reduce heat to low, cover, leaving lid ajar, and simmer for 25 minutes.

3. Stir in lentils, cover, leaving lid ajar, and simmer, stirring occasionally, for 30 to 35 minutes or until lentils and rice are very tender.

4. Stir in spinach, mint, lemon zest and lemon juice; cook, stirring once or twice, for 1 to 2 minutes or until spinach is wilted. Season to taste with salt and pepper. Serve with dollops of yogurt.

Greek Greens, Rice and Black-Eyed Pea Soup

Makes 8 servings

Black-eyed peas — *mavromatika* — are common fare in Greek cuisine. Here, they join brown rice and Swiss chard in a fennel-scented broth that is equally simple and special.

Tips

Brown basmati rice or medium-grain brown rice can be used in place of the long-grain brown rice.

An equal amount of quinoa, rinsed, or millet can be used in place of the rice. Decrease the cooking time in step 2 to 15 minutes.

Storage Tip

Store the cooled soup in an airtight container in the refrigerator for up to 2 days or in the freezer for up to 6 months. Thaw overnight in the refrigerator or in the microwave using the Defrost function. Warm soup in a medium saucepan over medium-low heat.

1 tbsp	olive oil	15 mL
2 cups	chopped onions	500 mL
1 tbsp	fennel seeds, crushed	15 mL
¾ cup	long-grain brown rice	175 mL
1	can (14 to 15 oz/398 to 425 mL) diced tomatoes, with juice	1
6 cups	ready-to-use GF chicken or vegetable broth	1.5 L
2	cans (each 14 to 19 oz/398 to 540 mL) black-eyed peas, drained and rinsed	2
8 cups	packed chopped Swiss chard (tough stems removed)	2 L
1 tbsp	red wine vinegar	15 mL
	Fine sea salt and freshly ground black pepper	

1. In a large pot, heat oil over medium-high heat. Add onions and cook, stirring, for 6 to 8 minutes or until softened. Add fennel seeds and cook, stirring, for 30 seconds.

2. Stir in rice, tomatoes and broth; bring to a boil. Reduce heat to low, cover and simmer, stirring occasionally, for 45 minutes.

3. Stir in peas, Swiss chard and vinegar; cover and simmer for 8 to 10 minutes or until Swiss chard is wilted and rice is very tender. Season to taste with salt and pepper.

Split Pea Soup with Chia Chutney

A bowl of golden sunshine on a cold day, this exotic take on split pea soup is the antidote to mid-winter blues.

Tips

Dried yellow lentils or green split peas may be used in place of the yellow split peas.

The soup can be made ahead, but the chutney should be prepared shortly before eating.

Storage Tip

Store the cooled soup (without the chutney) in an airtight container in the refrigerator for up to 3 days or in the freezer for up to 6 months. Thaw overnight in the refrigerator or in the microwave using the Defrost function. Warm soup in a medium saucepan over medium-low heat.

- Food processor, blender or immersion blender

Chia Chutney

1	1-inch (2.5 cm) piece gingerroot, roughly chopped	1
1½ cups	packed fresh cilantro leaves	375 mL
2 tbsp	freshly squeezed lime juice	30 mL
1 tbsp	toasted sesame oil	15 mL
2 tsp	liquid honey or agave nectar	10 mL
1 tbsp	chia seeds	15 mL

Soup

1 tbsp	olive oil	15 mL
2 cups	chopped onions	500 mL
2 cups	chopped carrots	500 mL
2 tsp	ground turmeric	10 mL
1½ tsp	ground coriander	7 mL
2 cups	dried yellow split peas, rinsed	500 mL
	Fine sea salt	
8 cups	water	2 L
	Freshly ground black pepper	

1. *Chutney:* In food processor, combine ginger, cilantro, lime juice, sesame oil and honey; pulse until finely chopped. Transfer to a small bowl and stir in chia seeds. Let stand while you prepare the soup.

2. *Soup:* In a large pot, heat oil over medium-high heat. Add onions and carrots; cook, stirring, for 6 to 8 minutes or until softened. Add turmeric and coriander; cook, stirring, for 30 seconds.

3. Stir in peas, 1¼ tsp (6 mL) salt and water; bring to a boil. Reduce heat to low, cover and simmer, stirring occasionally, for 35 to 40 minutes or until peas are very tender.

4. Working in batches, transfer soup to food processor (or use immersion blender in pot) and purée until smooth. Return soup to pot (if necessary) and warm over medium heat for 2 to 3 minutes or until heated through. Season to taste with salt and pepper.

5. Serve soup topped with chutney.

Tuscan Swiss Chard and Sorghum Soup

Plump sorghum grains contrast beautifully with nutty chickpeas, fragrant rosemary and earthy Swiss chard in this wholesome, immensely satisfying soup.

Storage Tip

Store the cooled soup in an airtight container in the refrigerator for up to 2 days or in the freezer for up to 6 months. Thaw overnight in the refrigerator or in the microwave using the Defrost function. Warm soup in a medium saucepan over medium-low heat.

2 tsp	olive oil	10 mL
2 cups	chopped onions	500 mL
4	cloves garlic, minced	4
2 tsp	minced fresh rosemary	10 mL
¾ cup	sorghum	175 mL
	Fine sea salt	
8 cups	water	2 L
6 cups	packed chopped Swiss chard (tough stems removed)	1.5 L
1	can (14 to 19 oz/398 to 540 mL) chickpeas, drained and rinsed	1
1 tbsp	red wine vinegar	15 mL
	Freshly ground black pepper	

1. In a large pot, heat oil over medium-high heat. Add onions and cook, stirring, for 6 to 8 minutes or until softened. Add garlic and rosemary; cook, stirring, for 1 minute.

2. Stir in sorghum, 1½ tsp (7 mL) salt and water; bring to a boil. Reduce heat to low, cover, leaving lid ajar, and simmer, stirring occasionally, for 55 to 60 minutes or until sorghum is tender.

3. Stir in Swiss chard and chickpeas; cover and simmer for 5 to 8 minutes or until Swiss chard is wilted. Stir in vinegar. Season to taste with salt and pepper.

West African Teff, Tsire and Chickpea Soup

When cooked until tender, teff grains yield a rich and nutty soup base. The malty flavor of the grain is accented by tsire, a West African seasoning made of ground peanuts and spices. Tsire is often used to coat meat before cooking, but it also adds a unique flavor to stews and vegetable dishes. Here, I've captured that flavor with common pantry items: peanut butter, chili powder and pumpkin pie spice, to delicious effect.

Tip

If you have a peanut allergy, substitute another nut or seed butter, such as cashew, almond, sunflower or tahini. Alternatively, simply omit the peanut butter.

Storage Tip

Store the cooled soup in an airtight container in the refrigerator for up to 2 days or in the freezer for up to 6 months. Thaw overnight in the refrigerator or in the microwave using the Defrost function. Warm soup in a medium saucepan over medium-low heat.

1 tbsp	olive oil	15 mL
2 cups	chopped onions	500 mL
1 tbsp	chili powder	15 mL
2 tsp	pumpkin pie spice	10 mL
1/3 cup	teff	75 mL
2	cans (each 14 to 19 oz/398 to 540 mL) chickpeas, drained and rinsed	2
1	can (14 to 15 oz/398 to 425 mL) crushed tomatoes	1
6 cups	ready-to-use GF chicken or vegetable broth	1.5 L
1 cup	packed fresh cilantro leaves, chopped	250 mL
3 tbsp	unsweetened creamy peanut butter	45 mL
3 tbsp	freshly squeezed lemon juice	45 mL
	Fine sea salt and freshly ground black pepper	

1. In a large pot, heat oil over medium-high heat. Add onions and cook, stirring, for 6 to 8 minutes or until softened. Add chili powder and pumpkin pie spice; cook, stirring, for 1 minute.

2. Stir in teff, chickpeas, tomatoes and broth; bring to a boil. Reduce heat to medium-low, cover, leaving lid ajar, and simmer, stirring occasionally, for 15 to 20 minutes or until teff is very tender. Stir in cilantro, peanut butter and lemon juice until combined. Season to taste with salt and pepper.

Berbere-Spiced Teff, White Bean and Collard Greens Soup

A celebration of Ethiopian ingredients, this spicy, warming soup is a welcome departure from run-of-the-mill vegetable soups. Great Northern beans are a good substitution for the white peas used in many of the country's dishes, but you can use other white beans in their place.

Storage Tip

Store the cooled soup in an airtight container in the refrigerator for up to 2 days or in the freezer for up to 6 months. Thaw overnight in the refrigerator or in the microwave using the Defrost function. Warm soup in a medium saucepan over medium-low heat.

1 tbsp	olive oil	15 mL
1	red bell pepper, chopped	1
2 cups	chopped onions	500 mL
4	cloves garlic, minced	4
1½ tbsp	chili powder	22 mL
2 tsp	ground ginger	10 mL
¼ tsp	cayenne pepper	1 mL
4 cups	chopped collard greens (tough stems and center ribs removed)	1 L
¾ cup	teff	175 mL
1	can (28 oz/796 mL) diced tomatoes, with juice	1
6 cups	ready-to-use GF vegetable or chicken broth	1.5 L
1	can (14 to 19 oz/398 to 540 mL) Great Northern beans, drained and rinsed	1
	Fine sea salt and freshly ground black pepper	
	Red wine vinegar	

1. In a large pot, heat oil over medium-high heat. Add red pepper and onions; cook, stirring, for 6 to 8 minutes or until softened. Add garlic, chili powder, ginger and cayenne; cook, stirring, for 30 seconds.

2. Stir in collard greens, teff, tomatoes and broth; bring to a boil. Reduce heat to low, cover and simmer, stirring occasionally, for 15 to 20 minutes or until teff is very tender. Stir in beans, cover and simmer for 5 minutes to blend the flavors. Season to taste with salt, black pepper and vinegar.

Bok Choy, Black Bean and Quinoa Soup

Lightly simmered bok choy, with its almost bitter leaves and sweet, succulent stems, offers a fine balance of flavor and texture in this easily assembled soup. Ginger, tamari and toasted sesame oil enrich the quick mushroom broth; quinoa makes the soup hearty enough for a main dish.

Tips

You can use 1 tbsp (15 mL) ground ginger in place of the fresh ginger.

Shiitake mushroom stems are often tough and dry. If that is the case, remove them before slicing the caps. But don't toss the stems out: freeze them for when you're making vegetable stock, as they add tremendous depth of flavor.

Storage Tip

Store the cooled soup in an airtight container in the refrigerator for up to 2 days. Warm in a medium saucepan over medium-low heat.

3	cloves garlic, minced	3
2 tbsp	minced gingerroot	30 mL
⅔ cup	red or white quinoa, rinsed	150 mL
4 cups	ready-to-use GF vegetable or chicken broth	1 L
4 cups	water	1 L
3 tbsp	GF tamari or soy sauce	45 mL
1 tbsp	toasted sesame oil	15 mL
12 oz	shiitake or cremini mushrooms (stems removed if necessary), sliced	375 g
1	can (14 to 15 oz/398 to 425 mL) black beans, drained and rinsed	1
6 cups	sliced bok choy	1.5 L
2 tbsp	unseasoned rice vinegar	30 mL
	Fine sea salt and freshly ground black pepper	

1. In a large pot, combine garlic, ginger, quinoa, broth, water, tamari and sesame oil. Bring to a boil over medium-high heat. Reduce heat to low, cover and simmer for 15 to 20 minutes or until quinoa is very tender.

2. Stir in mushrooms and beans; simmer, stirring occasionally, for 5 minutes or until mushrooms are tender.

3. Stir in bok choy and vinegar; simmer for 3 to 4 minutes or until bok choy is wilted. Season to taste with salt and pepper.

Tomatillo, Black Bean and Amaranth Soup

Puréed tomatillos add sweetness and a citrusy tang, smoky chipotles contribute a bit of heat, and black beans and amaranth lend depth and protein, making this a stick-to-the-ribs bowl of soup, despite the abundance of fresh, bright flavor.

Tips

The specified amount of chipotle chile powder will create a medium spiciness. Feel free to add less or more to suit your taste.

An equal amount of quinoa, rinsed, can be used in place of the amaranth.

Storage Tip

Store the cooled soup (without the cilantro, queso fresco or lime wedges) in an airtight container in the refrigerator for up to 2 days or in the freezer for up to 6 months. Thaw overnight in the refrigerator or in the microwave using the Defrost function. Warm soup in a medium saucepan over medium-low heat.

- Food processor

2	cans (each 12 oz/340 mL) whole tomatillos, with juice	2
1 tbsp	olive oil	15 mL
4	cloves garlic, minced	4
1 tsp	chipotle chile powder	5 mL
¾ cup	amaranth	175 mL
2	cans (each 14 to 19 oz/398 to 540 mL) black beans, drained and rinsed	2
3 cups	ready-to-use GF vegetable or chicken broth	750 mL
1 cup	packed fresh cilantro leaves, chopped	250 mL
2 tbsp	freshly squeezed lime juice	30 mL
	Crumbled queso fresco (optional)	
	Lime wedges (optional)	

1. In food processor, purée tomatillos and their juice. Set aside.

2. In a large pot, heat oil over medium-high heat. Add garlic and chipotle chile powder; cook, stirring, for 1 minute. Stir in tomatillo purée; cook, stirring for 2 minutes.

3. Stir in amaranth, beans and broth; bring to a boil. Reduce heat to low, cover and simmer, stirring occasionally, for 15 to 20 minutes or until amaranth is very tender. Stir in cilantro and lime juice. Serve sprinkled with queso fresco (if using), with lime wedges on the side, if desired.

Gallo Pinto Soup with Quinoa

Gallo pinto, a hearty concoction of beans, rice and spices, is a staple dish in Costa Rica and Nicaragua. Here, it is transformed into a streamlined soup with quinoa in place of the rice.

Tips

To make the soup vegan, simply omit the bacon and use vegetable broth instead of chicken broth. Sauté the bell pepper and green onions in 1 tbsp (15 mL) olive oil or virgin coconut oil.

An equal amount of amaranth can be used in place of the quinoa.

Storage Tip

Store the cooled soup (without the cilantro, green part of green onions or bacon) in an airtight container in the refrigerator for up to 2 days or in the freezer for up to 6 months. Thaw overnight in the refrigerator or in the microwave using the Defrost function. Warm soup in a medium saucepan over medium-low heat.

3	slices bacon, chopped	3
1	large red bell pepper, chopped	1
4	green onions, chopped, white and green parts separated	4
1 tsp	ground cumin	5 mL
1 tsp	ground coriander	5 mL
¾ cup	quinoa, rinsed	175 mL
1	can (14 to 19 oz/398 to 540 mL) red or black beans, drained and rinsed	2
6 cups	ready-to-use GF chicken or vegetable broth	1.5 L
1 cup	packed fresh cilantro leaves, chopped Fine sea salt and freshly ground black pepper	250 mL

1. In a large pot, cook bacon over medium-high heat until crisp. Using a slotted spoon, transfer bacon to a plate lined with paper towels. Drain off all but 1 tbsp (15 mL) fat.

2. Add red pepper and white part of green onions to the pot. Cook, stirring, for 5 to 6 minutes or until pepper is slightly softened. Add cumin and coriander; cook, stirring, for 30 seconds.

3. Stir in quinoa, beans and broth; bring to a boil. Reduce heat to low, cover and simmer for 15 to 20 minutes or until quinoa is very tender. Stir in cilantro and green part of green onions. Season to taste with salt and pepper. Serve sprinkled with bacon.

Variations

Coconut Gallo Pinto Soup: Reduce the broth to 5 cups (1.25 L). Add 1 cup (250 mL) well-stirred coconut milk (full-fat) after the quinoa is cooked and simmer for 1 to 2 minutes to heat through.

Traditional Gallo Pinto Soup: Replace the quinoa with an equal amount of medium- or long-grain brown rice. Increase the cooking time in step 3 to 45 to 55 minutes, adding the beans during the last 10 to 15 minutes of cooking time.

Edamame and Millet Soup with Avocado

Makes 4 servings

Tender grains of millet, buttery chunks of avocado and a hit of heat from fresh ginger and hot sauce make this soup a warming and vibrant balm in the depths of winter.

Storage Tip

Prepare the soup through step 2 and store the cooled soup in an airtight container in the refrigerator for up to 2 days or in the freezer for up to 6 months. Thaw overnight in the refrigerator or in the microwave using the Defrost function. Warm soup in a medium saucepan over medium-low heat.

1 tbsp	toasted sesame oil	15 mL
4	green onions, chopped, white and green parts separated	4
2 tbsp	minced gingerroot	30 mL
¾ cup	millet	175 mL
6 cups	ready-to-use GF vegetable or chicken broth	1.5 L
2 cups	frozen shelled edamame (about 12 oz/375 g)	500 mL
	GF soy sauce	
1	large firm-ripe Hass avocado, diced	1
	Asian chili sauce (such as Sriracha)	

1. In a large saucepan, heat oil over medium-high heat. Add white part of green onions and ginger; cook, stirring occasionally, for 2 to 3 minutes or until softened.

2. Stir in millet and broth; bring to a boil. Reduce heat and simmer for 15 minutes. Stir in edamame; simmer for 7 to 9 minutes or until edamame are tender. Season to taste with soy sauce.

3. Divide green part of green onions among four bowls. Ladle soup into the bowls and top with avocado. Drizzle with chili sauce.

Green Minestrone with Quinoa

A mélange of green vegetables and a swirl of verdant pesto give this minestrone a distinct summery vibe.

Storage Tip

Prepare the soup through step 4 and store the cooled soup in an airtight container in the refrigerator for up to 2 days or in the freezer for up to 6 months. Thaw overnight in the refrigerator or in the microwave using the Defrost function. Warm soup in a medium saucepan over medium-low heat.

2 tsp	olive oil	10 mL
1½ cups	chopped onions	375 mL
	Freshly cracked black pepper	
2	zucchini, halved lengthwise, then thinly sliced	2
4 cups	ready-to-use GF vegetable or chicken broth	1 L
4 cups	water	1 L
12 oz	green beans, trimmed and cut into thirds (about 1½ cups/375 mL)	375 g
1½ cups	frozen shelled edamame or baby lima beans	375 mL
⅔ cup	quinoa, rinsed	150 mL
4 cups	shredded savoy cabbage	1 L
	Fine sea salt	
½ cup	basil pesto	125 mL
⅓ cup	freshly grated Parmesan cheese	75 mL

1. In a large pot, heat oil over medium-high heat. Add onions and ¼ tsp (1 mL) pepper; cook, stirring, for 5 to 6 minutes or until softened.

2. Stir in zucchini, broth and water; bring to a boil. Reduce heat and simmer, stirring occasionally, for 15 minutes.

3. Stir in green beans, edamame and quinoa; cover and simmer over low heat, stirring occasionally, for 15 to 20 minutes or until edamame and quinoa are very tender.

4. Stir in cabbage, cover and simmer for 2 to 3 minutes or until cabbage is wilted. Season to taste with salt and pepper.

5. Ladle soup into bowls. Swirl spoonfuls of pesto in each bowl and sprinkle with cheese.

Hot-and-Sour Shrimp and Amaranth Soup

Here, a fragrant broth combines with shrimp, delicate grains and strong herbs to make one very special soup.

Tip

An equal amount of quinoa, rinsed, or millet can be used in place of the amaranth.

Storage Tip

Store the cooled soup (without the mint, cilantro or green onions) in an airtight container in the refrigerator for up to 2 days. Warm soup in a medium saucepan over medium-low heat. Serve as directed.

2 tbsp	finely grated gingerroot	30 mL
1 tbsp	fine crystal cane sugar or packed light brown sugar	15 mL
2	bottles (each 8 oz/227 mL) clam juice	2
4 cups	water	1 L
1 tbsp	Asian chili sauce (such as Sriracha)	15 mL
1 cup	amaranth	250 mL
1 lb	fresh or thawed frozen large shrimp, peeled and deveined	500 g
2 tbsp	freshly squeezed lime juice	30 mL
	Fine sea salt and freshly ground black pepper	
½ cup	packed fresh mint leaves, torn	125 mL
½ cup	packed fresh cilantro leaves	125 mL
¼ cup	thinly sliced green onions	60 mL

1. In a large saucepan, combine ginger, sugar, clam juice, water and chili sauce. Bring to a boil over medium-high heat. Stir in amaranth, reduce heat to low, cover and simmer, stirring once or twice, for 15 to 20 minutes or until amaranth is very tender.

2. Stir in shrimp and simmer, uncovered, for 3 to 5 minutes or until shrimp are pink, firm and opaque. Stir in lime juice. Season to taste with salt and pepper. Serve sprinkled with mint, cilantro and green onions.

Shrimp Scampi Quinoa Soup

Don't be misled by its plain-looking appearance: this soup version of shrimp scampi is thoroughly satisfying and delicious.

Storage Tip

Store the cooled soup in an airtight container in the refrigerator for up to 24 hours. Warm in a medium saucepan over medium-low heat.

1 lb	fresh or thawed frozen medium shrimp, peeled and deveined	500 g
	Fine sea salt and freshly ground black pepper	
2 tbsp	unsalted butter	30 mL
6	cloves garlic, minced, divided	6
1 tsp	dried thyme	5 mL
¾ cup	quinoa, rinsed	175 mL
6 cups	ready-to-use GF chicken or vegetable broth	1.5 L
1 cup	packed fresh flat-leaf (Italian) parsley leaves, chopped	250 mL
⅓ cup	packed fresh basil leaves, thinly sliced	75 mL
2 tsp	finely grated lemon zest	10 mL
1 tbsp	freshly squeezed lemon juice	15 mL

1. Season shrimp with salt and pepper. In a large saucepan, melt butter over medium-high heat. Add shrimp and half the garlic; cook, stirring, for 1 to 2 minutes or until shrimp are no longer translucent. Add the remaining garlic and thyme; cook, stirring, for 30 seconds.

2. Stir in quinoa and broth; bring to a boil. Reduce heat to low, cover and simmer, stirring occasionally, for 15 to 20 minutes or until quinoa is very tender. Stir in parsley, basil, lemon zest and lemon juice. Season to taste with salt and pepper.

3. Divide shrimp among four bowls and ladle soup over top.

Lime, Coconut and Millet Chicken Soup

If ever there was a soup to counter the mid-winter blues, this is it. Warming and filling, yet also bright with citrus flavor and creamy coconut, it's a passport to a sunny, tropical day.

Tips

Shiitake mushroom stems are often tough and dry. If that is the case, remove them before slicing the caps. But don't toss the stems out: freeze them for when you're making vegetable stock, as they add tremendous depth of flavor.

An equal amount of quinoa, rinsed, or amaranth can be used in place of the millet.

Storage Tip

Store the cooled soup (without the cilantro) in an airtight container in the refrigerator for up to 2 days or in the freezer for up to 6 months. Thaw overnight in the refrigerator or in the microwave using the Defrost function. Warm soup in a medium saucepan over medium-low heat.

2 tsp	olive oil	10 mL
12 oz	shiitake or cremini mushrooms (stems removed if necessary), sliced	375 g
1 cup	finely chopped onions	250 mL
2 tbsp	minced gingerroot	30 mL
¾ cup	millet	175 mL
1 tbsp	packed light brown sugar	15 mL
3½ cups	ready-to-use GF chicken or vegetable broth	875 mL
2 cups	diced or shredded cooked chicken breasts	500 mL
1	can (14 oz/400 mL) coconut milk (full-fat), well stirred	1
¼ cup	freshly squeezed lime juice	60 mL
3 tbsp	GF soy sauce or Asian fish sauce	45 mL
½ cup	packed fresh cilantro leaves, roughly chopped	125 mL

1. In a large pot, heat oil over medium-high heat. Add mushrooms, onions and ginger; cook, stirring, for 6 to 8 minutes or until softened.

2. Stir in millet, brown sugar and broth; bring to a boil. Reduce heat to low, cover and simmer, stirring occasionally, for 15 to 20 minutes or until millet is tender.

3. Stir in chicken, coconut milk, lime juice and soy sauce; simmer, uncovered, for 5 minutes to heat through and blend the flavors. Serve sprinkled with cilantro.

Summer Chicken, Corn and Quinoa Soup

Presenting a sensational summer soup — in more ways than one: first, it's a salute to the flavors of summer, featuring corn, zucchini and basil pesto; second, it's ready in no time, so you can enjoy every moment of summer fun and relaxation.

Storage Tip

Store the cooled soup (without the cheese) in an airtight container in the refrigerator for up to 2 days. Warm in a medium saucepan over medium-low heat.

1/2 cup	quinoa, rinsed	125 mL
4 cups	ready-to-use GF chicken or vegetable broth	1 L
1	zucchini, diced	1
1	can (28 oz/796 mL) diced tomatoes (preferably fire-roasted), with juice	1
2 cups	diced or shredded cooked chicken breasts	500 mL
2 cups	fresh or thawed frozen corn kernels	500 mL
1/4 cup	basil pesto	60 mL
2 tsp	finely grated lemon zest	10 mL
2 tbsp	freshly squeezed lemon juice	30 mL
	Fine sea salt and freshly ground black pepper	
	Freshly grated Parmesan cheese (optional)	

1. In a large saucepan, combine quinoa and broth. Bring to a boil over medium-high heat. Reduce heat to low, cover and simmer for 10 minutes. Stir in zucchini, cover and simmer for 5 to 10 minutes or until quinoa is very tender.

2. Stir in tomatoes, cover and simmer for 5 minutes. Stir in chicken, corn, pesto, lemon zest and lemon juice; cover and simmer for 1 to 2 minutes or until chicken is heated through. Season to taste with salt and pepper. Serve sprinkled with cheese, if desired.

Pork, Bok Choy and Millet Hot Pot

This speedy Szechuan-inspired soup will please everyone at the supper table.

Tips

Shiitake mushroom stems are often tough and dry. If that is the case, remove them before slicing the caps. But don't toss the stems out: freeze them for when you're making vegetable stock, as they add tremendous depth of flavor.

An equal amount of quinoa, rinsed, or amaranth can be used in place of the millet.

Storage Tip

Store the cooled soup in an airtight container in the refrigerator for up to 2 days. Warm in a medium saucepan over medium-low heat.

12 oz	lean ground pork	375 g
2 tbsp	minced gingerroot, divided	30 mL
1 tsp	freshly ground black pepper, divided	5 mL
2 tbsp	GF tamari or soy sauce, divided	30 mL
6 cups	ready-to-use GF chicken or vegetable broth	1.5 L
8 oz	shiitake or button mushrooms (stems removed if necessary), sliced	250 g
¾ cup	millet	175 mL
3	green onions, thinly sliced	3
6 cups	sliced bok choy	1.5 L
2 tsp	unseasoned rice vinegar or cider vinegar	10 mL

1. In a large pot, cook pork, half the ginger, half the pepper and half the tamari over medium-high heat, breaking pork up with the back of a spoon, for 5 to 6 minutes or until pork is no longer pink. Using a slotted spoon, transfer pork mixture to a plate. Drain off any fat.

2. Add the remaining ginger, the remaining pepper, broth and the remaining tamari to the pot. Bring to a boil. Stir in mushrooms and millet; reduce heat to low, cover and simmer, stirring occasionally, for 15 to 20 minutes or until millet is tender.

3. Return pork mixture to the pot and stir in green onions, bok choy and vinegar; simmer, uncovered, for 2 minutes or until bok choy is lightly wilted. Serve immediately.

Sausage, Millet and Swiss Chard Soup

Makes 6 servings

Here, the combination of fresh greens, sausage and tender millet creates a comforting, warming soup.

Tip

An equal amount of quinoa, rinsed, can be used in place of the millet.

Storage Tip

Store the cooled soup (without the cheese) in an airtight container in the refrigerator for up to 2 days or in the freezer for up to 6 months. Thaw overnight in the refrigerator or in the microwave using the Defrost function. Warm soup in a medium saucepan over medium-low heat.

1 lb	GF Italian pork or turkey sausage (bulk or casings removed)	500 g
1½ cups	chopped onions	375 mL
4	cloves garlic, minced	4
¾ cup	millet	175 mL
1 cup	dry red wine	250 mL
	Fine sea salt	
5 cups	water	1.25 L
6 cups	packed chopped Swiss chard (tough stems removed)	1.5 L
1	can (28 oz/796 mL) crushed tomatoes	1
	Freshly ground black pepper	
½ cup	freshly grated Parmesan cheese	125 mL

1. In a large pot, cook sausage over medium-high heat, breaking it up with a spoon, for 6 to 8 minutes or until no longer pink. Using a slotted spoon, transfer sausage to a plate lined with paper towels. Drain off all but 2 tsp (10 mL) fat from pot.

2. Add onions to the pot and cook, stirring, for 5 to 6 minutes or until softened. Add garlic and cook, stirring, for 30 seconds. Add millet and wine; cook, stirring, for 1 minute.

3. Stir in ½ tsp (2 mL) salt and water; bring to a boil. Reduce heat to low, cover and simmer, stirring occasionally, for 15 to 20 minutes or until millet is tender.

4. Return sausage to the pot and stir in Swiss chard and tomatoes; cover and simmer, stirring occasionally, for 4 to 5 minutes or until Swiss chard is tender. Season to taste with salt and pepper. Serve sprinkled with cheese.

Chorizo, Kale and Teff Soup

The first few spoonfuls of this meaty soup, enriched with potatoes, teff and kale, will have you dreaming of the warm sunshine of Spain and Portugal.

Storage Tip

Store the cooled soup in an airtight container in the refrigerator for up to 2 days or in the freezer for up to 6 months. Thaw overnight in the refrigerator or in the microwave using the Defrost function. Warm soup in a medium saucepan over medium-low heat.

1 tbsp	olive oil	15 mL
12 oz	GF cured chorizo or other smoked sausage, diced	375 g
2 cups	chopped onions	500 mL
4	cloves garlic, minced	4
6 cups	chopped kale (tough stems and center ribs removed)	1.5 L
3 cups	diced peeled potatoes	750 mL
1/3 cup	teff	75 mL
8 cups	ready-to-use GF vegetable or chicken broth	2 L
1	can (28 oz/796 mL) crushed tomatoes	1
	Fine sea salt and freshly ground black pepper	

1. In a large pot, heat oil over medium-high heat. Add chorizo and cook, stirring, for 3 to 4 minutes or until browned. Using a slotted spoon, transfer chorizo to a plate lined with paper towels.

2. Add onions to the pot and cook, stirring, for 6 to 8 minutes or until softened. Add garlic and kale; cook, stirring, for 1 minute.

3. Stir in potatoes, teff and broth; bring to a boil. Reduce heat to medium-low, cover, leaving lid ajar, and simmer, stirring occasionally, for 15 to 20 minutes or until potatoes and teff are very tender. Use a wooden spoon to coarsely break up about half of the potatoes.

4. Return chorizo to the pot and stir in tomatoes; simmer, uncovered, stirring occasionally, for 5 to 10 minutes or until soup is slightly thickened. Season to taste with salt and pepper.

Sorghum, Ham and Leek Minestrone

Here, chewy pearls of sorghum, smoky ham and leeks add up to a stick-to-the-ribs, home-style soup.

Tip

If using the larger 19-oz (540 mL) cans of beans, you may want to add up to $\frac{1}{2}$ cup (125 mL) extra broth to thin the soup.

Storage Tip

Store the cooled soup (without the parsley or cheese) in an airtight container in the refrigerator for up to 2 days or in the freezer for up to 6 months. Thaw overnight in the refrigerator or in the microwave using the Defrost function. Warm soup in a medium saucepan over medium-low heat.

2 tbsp	olive oil	30 mL
2 cups	chopped leeks (white and green parts only)	500 mL
3	cloves garlic, minced	3
2$\frac{1}{2}$ tsp	chopped fresh rosemary	12 mL
2	cans (each 14 to 19 oz/398 to 540 mL) cannellini (white kidney) beans, drained and rinsed	2
2 cups	cooked sorghum (see page 17)	500 mL
1$\frac{1}{2}$ cups	diced smoked ham	375 mL
1	can (28 oz/796 mL) diced tomatoes, with juice	1
6 cups	ready-to-use GF chicken or vegetable broth	1.5 L
$\frac{3}{4}$ cup	packed fresh flat-leaf (Italian) parsley leaves, chopped	175 mL
	Fine sea salt and freshly ground black pepper	
$\frac{1}{4}$ cup	freshly grated Parmesan cheese	60 mL

1. In a large pot, heat oil over medium-high heat. Add leeks and cook, stirring, for 6 to 8 minutes or until softened. Add garlic and rosemary; cook, stirring, for 30 seconds.

2. In a small bowl, coarsely mash 1 cup (250 mL) of the beans with a fork. Stir mashed beans, whole beans, sorghum, ham, tomatoes and broth into the pot; bring to a boil. Reduce heat to low, cover and simmer, stirring occasionally, for 5 to 10 minutes to heat through and blend the flavors. Remove from heat and let stand for 5 minutes. Stir in parsley. Season to taste with salt and pepper. Serve sprinkled with cheese.

Lemony Brussels Sprouts and Quinoa Soup

Brussels sprouts deserve more than side-dish status. Highlight them in this straightforward soup dotted with quinoa and smoky bits of bacon and brightened with a splash of lemon.

Storage Tip

Store the cooled soup (without the bacon) in an airtight container in the refrigerator for up to 2 days or in the freezer for up to 6 months. Thaw overnight in the refrigerator or in the microwave using the Defrost function. Warm soup in a medium saucepan over medium-low heat.

3	slices bacon, finely chopped	3
2 cups	finely chopped onions	500 mL
1 cup	finely chopped celery	250 mL
1/2 cup	quinoa, rinsed	125 mL
6 cups	ready-to-use GF vegetable or chicken broth	1.5 L
1 lb	Brussels sprouts, trimmed (see tip, page 142) and very thinly sliced crosswise	500 g
1/4 cup	freshly squeezed lemon juice	60 mL
	Fine sea salt and freshly ground black pepper	

1. In a large pot, cook bacon over medium-high heat until crisp. Using a slotted spoon, transfer bacon to a plate lined with paper towels. Drain off all but 1 tbsp (15 mL) fat.

2. Add onions and celery to the pot. Cook, stirring occasionally, for 6 to 8 minutes or until softened.

3. Stir in quinoa and broth; bring to a boil. Reduce heat to low, cover and simmer, stirring occasionally, for 15 to 20 minutes or until quinoa is very tender.

4. Stir in Brussels sprouts and simmer, stirring, for 1 to 2 minutes or until wilted but still bright green. Stir in lemon juice. Season to taste with salt and pepper. Serve sprinkled with bacon.

Irish Bacon, Cabbage and Millet Soup

Makes 6 servings

Cabbage plus bacon is a classic Irish duo, but the addition of millet in lieu of the standard white potatoes makes this soup fresh and new.

Storage Tip

Store the cooled soup (without the bacon) in an airtight container in the refrigerator for up to 2 days or in the freezer for up to 6 months. Thaw overnight in the refrigerator or in the microwave using the Defrost function. Warm soup in a medium saucepan over medium-low heat.

6	thick slices bacon, chopped	6
2 cups	chopped onions	500 mL
1½ cups	diced carrots	375 mL
3	cloves garlic, minced	3
1 cup	millet	250 mL
8 cups	ready-to-use GF vegetable or chicken broth	2 L
8 cups	sliced savoy cabbage (about 1 small head)	2 L
	Fine sea salt and freshly cracked black pepper	

1. In a large pot, cook bacon over medium-high heat until crisp. Using a slotted spoon, transfer bacon to a plate lined with paper towels. Drain off all but 1 tbsp (15 mL) fat from pot.

2. Add onions and carrots to the pot. Cook, stirring, for 6 to 8 minutes or until softened. Add garlic and cook, stirring, for 1 minute.

3. Stir in millet and broth; bring to a boil. Reduce heat to low, cover and simmer, stirring occasionally, for 20 to 25 minutes or until millet is very tender.

4. Stir in cabbage, cover and simmer, stirring once or twice, for 4 to 5 minutes or until cabbage is wilted. Season to taste with salt and pepper. Serve sprinkled with bacon.

Lowcountry Pumpkin Soup with Molasses, Teff and Bacon

This velvety pumpkin soup features key ingredients — molasses, cured pork, spices and buttermilk — from the southern coastal region of the United States known as the Lowcountry. The addition of teff thickens and enriches the soup, giving it all-day-on-the-stove texture and flavor.

Tips

If 15-oz (425 mL) cans of pumpkin purée aren't available, purchase two 28-oz (796 mL) cans and measure out 3½ cups (875 mL). Refrigerate extra pumpkin in an airtight container for up to 1 week.

An equal amount of liquid honey or pure maple syrup can be used in place of the molasses.

An equal amount of plain yogurt (not Greek yogurt) can be used in place of the buttermilk.

Storage Tip

Store the cooled soup (without the bacon or chives) in an airtight container in the refrigerator for up to 2 days or in the freezer for up to 6 months. Thaw overnight in the refrigerator or in the microwave using the Defrost function. Warm soup in a medium saucepan over medium-low heat.

3	slices bacon, chopped	3
⅓ cup	teff	75 mL
1 tsp	ground allspice	5 mL
¼ tsp	cayenne pepper	1 mL
2	cans (each 15 oz/425 mL) pumpkin purée (not pie filling)	2
5½ cups	ready-to-use GF chicken or vegetable broth	1.375 L
3 tbsp	dark (cooking) molasses	45 mL
1 cup	buttermilk	250 mL
	Fine sea salt and freshly cracked black pepper	
¼ cup	minced fresh chives	60 mL

1. In a large pot, cook bacon over medium-high heat until crisp. Using a slotted spoon, transfer bacon to a plate lined with paper towels. Drain off all but 1 tbsp (15 mL) fat.

2. Add teff, allspice, cayenne, pumpkin, broth and molasses to the pot. Bring to a boil over medium-high heat. Reduce heat to low, cover and simmer, stirring occasionally, for 15 to 20 minutes or until teff is very tender.

3. Reduce heat to low and whisk in buttermilk. Simmer, stirring occasionally, for 5 minutes (do not let boil). Season to taste with salt and black pepper. Serve sprinkled with bacon and chives.

Buckwheat, Butternut Squash and Mushroom Stew

Sweet cubes of golden butternut squash complement the earthy, umami flavors of mushrooms and buckwheat in this deeply flavored stew.

Tips

To save time, look for bags of diced peeled butternut squash in the produce section of the supermarket.

An equal amount of quinoa, rinsed, millet, teff or amaranth can be used in place of the buckwheat.

Storage Tip

Store the cooled soup in an airtight container in the refrigerator for up to 2 days or in the freezer for up to 6 months. Thaw overnight in the refrigerator or in the microwave using the Defrost function. Warm soup in a medium saucepan over medium-low heat.

2 tbsp	olive oil	30 mL
1 lb	cremini or button mushrooms, sliced	500 g
2 cups	diced peeled butternut squash	500 mL
1½ cups	thinly sliced leeks (white and pale green parts only)	375 mL
1 tsp	dried thyme	5 mL
1 tsp	dried rubbed sage	5 mL
½ cup	Marsala or sherry	125 mL
1 cup	buckwheat groats	250 mL
6 cups	ready-to-use GF vegetable or chicken broth	1.5 L
	Fine sea salt and freshly ground black pepper	

1. In a large saucepan, heat oil over medium-high heat. Add mushrooms, squash and leeks; cook, stirring, for 12 to 15 minutes or until squash is slightly softened. Add thyme, sage and Marsala; cook, stirring, for 2 minutes or until liquid has almost evaporated.

2. Stir in buckwheat and broth; bring to a boil. Reduce heat to medium-low, cover and simmer, stirring occasionally, for 15 to 20 minutes or until buckwheat and squash are tender. Season to taste with salt and pepper.

Sweet Potato and Peanut Stew with Quinoa

Makes 6 servings

Peanuts are a significant crop, as well as ingredient, in the American South. In addition to sweet dishes and desserts, they are often used to deepen the flavor and thicken soups and stews, as they do here.

Tips

Other roasted or toasted nuts or seeds, such as cashews, almonds or sunflower seeds, can be used in place of the peanuts.

Hot cooked amaranth or millet can be used in place of the quinoa. Information on cooking these grains can be found on pages 8–11.

Storage Tip

Store the cooled stew in an airtight container in the refrigerator for up to 3 days or in the freezer for up to 6 months. Thaw overnight in the refrigerator or in the microwave using the Defrost function. Warm stew in a medium saucepan over medium-low heat.

1 tbsp	olive oil	15 mL
1½ cups	chopped onions	375 mL
3	cloves garlic, finely chopped	3
4 cups	diced peeled sweet potatoes	1 L
1	can (28 oz/796 mL) diced tomatoes, with juice	1
4 cups	ready-to-use GF vegetable or chicken broth	1 L
6 cups	packed coarsely chopped Swiss chard (tough stems removed)	1.5 L
¾ cup	lightly salted roasted peanuts, chopped	175 mL
1 tbsp	freshly squeezed lemon juice	15 mL
	Fine sea salt and freshly ground black pepper	
4 cups	hot cooked quinoa (see page 15)	1 L

1. In a large pot, heat oil over medium-high heat. Add onions and cook, stirring, for 5 to 6 minutes or until softened. Add garlic and cook, stirring, for 30 seconds.

2. Stir in sweet potatoes, tomatoes and broth; bring to a boil. Reduce heat to low, cover and simmer, stirring occasionally, for 25 to 30 minutes or until sweet potatoes are tender.

3. Stir in Swiss chard and peanuts; cover and simmer for 5 minutes or until greens are wilted. Stir in lemon juice. Season to taste with salt and pepper.

4. Divide quinoa among six bowls and ladle stew over top.

Trinidadian Fish Stew with Millet

This is a stew with zing, guaranteed to add Caribbean verve to your dinner table with minimal effort.

Tip
For both convenience and frugality, consider using thawed frozen fish fillets in this stew.

Storage Tip
Store the cooled stew in an airtight container in the refrigerator for up to 24 hours. Warm in a medium saucepan over medium-low heat.

2 tbsp	virgin coconut oil	30 mL
3	cloves garlic, minced	3
1 tsp	dried thyme	5 mL
½ tsp	ground allspice	2 mL
½ tsp	hot pepper flakes	2 mL
1 tbsp	packed dark brown sugar or coconut sugar	15 mL
3 tbsp	dark rum	45 mL
1	can (28 oz/796 mL) crushed tomatoes	1
2 cups	ready-to-use GF vegetable or chicken broth	500 mL
1 lb	skinless cod, halibut or other white fish fillets, cut into 1-inch (2.5 mL) pieces	500 g
1 cup	packed fresh cilantro leaves	250 mL
1 tbsp	freshly squeezed lime juice	15 mL
	Fine sea salt and freshly ground black pepper	
4 cups	hot cooked millet (see page 11)	1 L

1. In a large saucepan, melt oil over medium-low heat. Add garlic, thyme, allspice and hot pepper flakes; increase heat to medium-high and cook, stirring, for 30 seconds. Add brown sugar and rum, scraping up any browned bits on bottom of pan.

2. Stir in tomatoes and broth; bring to a boil. Reduce heat to low. Stir in cod, cover and simmer for about 5 minutes or until fish is opaque and flakes easily when tested with a fork. Stir in cilantro and lime juice. Season to taste with salt and black pepper.

3. Divide millet among four bowls and ladle stew over top.

Sicilian Seafood and Quinoa Stew

Aromatic Sicilian ingredients — capers, garlic and coriander — plus a hint of sweetness from the raisins give this healthy Mediterranean stew its gusto.

Tip

For both convenience and frugality, consider using thawed frozen fish fillets and shrimp in this stew.

Storage Tip

Store the cooled stew (without the parsley) in an airtight container in the refrigerator for up to 24 hours. Warm in a medium saucepan over medium-low heat.

1 tbsp	olive oil	15 mL
1 cup	chopped onions	250 mL
3	cloves garlic, minced	3
2 tbsp	golden or dark raisins, chopped	30 mL
1 tbsp	drained capers, minced	15 mL
1 tsp	ground coriander	5 mL
2/3 cup	quinoa, rinsed	150 mL
4 cups	ready-to-use GF chicken or vegetable broth	1 L
1	can (14 to 15 oz/398 to 425 mL) crushed tomatoes	1
12 oz	skinless cod or halibut fillets, cut into 1-inch (2.5 cm) pieces	375 g
8 oz	fresh or thawed frozen medium shrimp, peeled and deveined	250 g
1 cup	packed fresh flat-leaf (Italian) parsley leaves, roughly chopped	250 mL
1 tbsp	red wine vinegar	15 mL
	Fine sea salt and freshly ground black pepper	

1. In a large saucepan, heat oil over medium-high heat. Add onions and cook, stirring, for 5 to 6 minutes or until softened. Add garlic, raisins, capers and coriander; cook, stirring, for 30 seconds.

2. Stir in quinoa and broth; bring to a boil. Reduce heat to low, cover and simmer, stirring occasionally, for 15 minutes. Stir in tomatoes, cover and simmer for 5 minutes.

3. Stir in cod and shrimp; cover and simmer for about 5 minutes or until fish is opaque and flakes easily when tested with a fork and shrimp are pink, firm and opaque. Stir in parsley and vinegar. Season to taste with salt and pepper.

Persian Chicken, Chia and Black-Eyed Pea Stew

Makes 6 servings

Both chia seeds and black-eyed peas are prized in Persian cooking. Here, they combine in an aromatic stew that evokes *sabzi*, a dish whose name means a mix of greens and herbs. The vibrant flavors are an ideal mid-winter wake-up call.

Storage Tip

Store the cooled stew (without the parsley or green part of green onions) in an airtight container in the refrigerator for up to 2 days or in the freezer for up to 6 months. Thaw overnight in the refrigerator or in the microwave using the Defrost function. Warm stew in a medium saucepan over medium-low heat.

3 tbsp	chia seeds	45 mL
5 cups	ready-to-use GF chicken or vegetable broth	1.25 L
2 lbs	boneless skinless chicken thighs	1 kg
1 tbsp	olive oil	15 mL
2 cups	chopped green onions, white and green parts separated	500 mL
2 tsp	ground cinnamon	10 mL
½ tsp	ground nutmeg	2 mL
6 cups	packed spinach leaves, roughly torn	1.5 L
2	cans (each 14 to 19 oz/398 to 540 mL) black-eyed peas, drained and rinsed	2
1 tbsp	finely grated lemon zest	15 mL
3 tbsp	freshly squeezed lemon juice	45 mL
1 cup	packed fresh flat-leaf (Italian) parsley leaves, chopped	250 mL
	Fine sea salt and freshly ground black pepper	

1. Place chia seeds in a sealable plastic bag. Seal bag, pressing out air. Using a mallet or rolling pin, crush seeds.

2. In a large pot, bring broth to a boil over medium-high heat. Add chicken, reduce heat to low, cover and simmer for 15 to 20 minutes or until chicken is no longer pink inside. Transfer chicken to a plate. Pour broth into a large bowl and set aside. Wipe out pot. When cool enough to handle, shred chicken.

3. In the same pot, heat oil over medium-high heat. Add white part of green onions and cook, stirring, for 2 to 3 minutes or until softened. Add cinnamon and nutmeg; cook, stirring, for 30 seconds.

4. Add crushed chia seeds and the reserved broth; bring to a boil. Reduce heat and simmer for 5 minutes.

5. Return chicken and any accumulated juices to the pot and stir in spinach, black-eyed peas, lemon zest and lemon juice; simmer for 5 minutes to heat through and blend the flavors. Stir in parsley and green part of green onions. Season to taste with salt and pepper.

Greek Chickpea Chili

If you love Greek salads, as I do, then this chili, featuring many of the same flavors and vegetables, will be a welcome option for the cooler months of the year.

Tip

If you can only find larger 19-oz (540 mL) cans of chickpeas, you will need about 2¼ cans (4½ cups/1.125 L drained).

Storage Tip

Store the cooled chili (without the mint or any accompaniments) in an airtight container in the refrigerator for up to 2 days or in the freezer for up to 6 months. Thaw overnight in the refrigerator or in the microwave using the Defrost function. Warm chili in a medium saucepan over medium-low heat.

2 tsp	olive oil	10 mL
2	large red bell peppers, chopped	2
1½ cups	chopped onions	375 mL
4	cloves garlic, minced	4
1 tbsp	ground cumin	15 mL
2 tsp	ground coriander	10 mL
3	cans (each 14 to 15 oz/398 to 425 mL) chickpeas, drained and rinsed	3
1	can (28 oz/796 mL) crushed tomatoes	1
2 cups	ready-to-use GF vegetable or chicken broth	500 mL
2 cups	hot cooked millet (see page 11)	500 mL
2 tsp	finely grated lemon zest	10 mL
2 tbsp	freshly squeezed lemon juice	30 mL
	Fine sea salt and freshly ground black pepper	
½ cup	packed fresh mint leaves, roughly chopped	125 mL

Suggested Accompaniments

Plain Greek yogurt
Crumbled feta cheese
Chopped kalamata olives

1. In a large pot, heat oil over medium-high heat. Add red peppers and onions; cook, stirring, for 6 to 8 minutes or until softened. Add garlic, cumin and coriander; cook, stirring, for 2 minutes.

2. Stir in chickpeas, tomatoes and broth; bring to a boil. Reduce heat to medium-low, cover, leaving lid ajar, and simmer, stirring occasionally, for 20 minutes. Stir in millet, lemon zest and lemon juice; simmer, uncovered, for 5 minutes. Season to taste with salt and pepper. Serve sprinkled with mint and with any of the suggested accompaniments, as desired.

Garden Vegetable Quinoa Chili

Makes 8 servings

Both carnivores and vegetarians will clamor for seconds of this vegetable-loaded chili.

Tip

If using the larger 19-oz (540 mL) cans of beans, you may want to add up to 1/2 cup (125 mL) water to thin the chili.

Storage Tip

Store the cooled chili (without any accompaniments) in an airtight container in the refrigerator for up to 2 days or in the freezer for up to 6 months. Thaw overnight in the refrigerator or in the microwave using the Defrost function. Warm chili in a medium saucepan over medium-low heat.

1 1/2 tbsp	vegetable oil	22 mL
2	zucchini, diced	2
1	red bell pepper, chopped	1
1	green bell pepper, chopped	1
1 1/2 cups	chopped onions	375 mL
4	cloves garlic, minced	4
3 tbsp	chili powder	45 mL
1 1/2 tbsp	ground cumin	22 mL
1 tsp	hot pepper sauce	5 mL
2	cans (each 14 to 19 oz/398 to 540 mL) red kidney beans, drained and rinsed	2
1	can (14 to 19 oz/398 to 540 mL) black beans, drained and rinsed	1
1	can (28 oz/796 mL) crushed tomatoes	1
1	can (14 to 15 oz/398 to 425 mL) tomato sauce	1
1 1/2 cups	hot cooked quinoa (see page 15)	375 mL
	Fine sea salt and freshly ground black pepper	

Suggested Accompaniments

Plain Greek yogurt
Lime wedges
Fresh cilantro leaves
Chopped green onions
Chopped radishes

1. In a large pot, heat oil over medium-high heat. Add zucchini, red pepper, green pepper and onions; cook, stirring, for 8 to 10 minutes or until softened. Add garlic, chili powder, cumin and hot pepper sauce; cook, stirring, for 1 minute.

2. In a small bowl, coarsely mash half of the red beans with a fork. Stir mashed beans, whole red beans, black beans, tomatoes and tomato sauce into the pot; bring to a boil. Reduce heat and simmer, stirring often, for about 30 minutes to blend the flavors. Stir in quinoa. Season to taste with salt and pepper. Serve with any of the suggested accompaniments, as desired.

Tex-Mex Beef and Teff Chili

Teff grains sneak into this otherwise classic beef-and-beans chili, instantly deepening the flavor and thickening the dish, making it taste as if it has been simmering all day.

Tips

Regular canned diced tomatoes may be used in place of the tomatoes with chiles. You'll need about 3¾ cups (925 mL) tomatoes with juice for this recipe.

For variety, substitute lean ground turkey or extra-lean ground pork for the beef.

Storage Tip

Store the cooled chili (without any accompaniments) in an airtight container in the refrigerator for up to 2 days or in the freezer for up to 6 months. Thaw overnight in the refrigerator or in the microwave using the Defrost function. Warm chili in a medium saucepan over medium-low heat.

1 lb	extra-lean ground beef	500 g
1 tbsp	olive oil	15 mL
1	green bell pepper, chopped	1
1½ cups	chopped onions	375 mL
4	cloves garlic, minced	4
¼ cup	teff	60 mL
3 tbsp	chili powder	45 mL
1 tbsp	ground cumin	15 mL
1¼ cups	ready-to-use GF beef broth or water	300 mL
3	cans (each 10 oz/284 mL) diced tomatoes with chiles, with juice	3
2	cans (each 14 to 19 oz/398 to 540 mL) red kidney beans, drained and rinsed	2
2 tbsp	tomato paste	30 mL

Suggested Accompaniments

Fresh cilantro leaves
Chopped green onions
Plain Greek yogurt
Crumbled queso fresco
Chopped radishes

1. In a large pot, cook beef over medium-high heat, breaking it up with a spoon, for 5 to 6 minutes or until no longer pink. Using a slotted spoon, transfer beef to a plate. Drain off fat from pot.

2. In the same pot, heat oil over medium-high heat. Add green pepper and onions; cook, stirring, for 6 to 8 minutes or until softened. Add garlic, teff, chili powder and cumin; cook, stirring, for 1 minute.

3. Stir in broth and bring to a boil. Reduce heat to medium-low, cover, leaving lid ajar, and simmer, stirring occasionally, for 15 to 20 minutes or until teff is very tender and mixture has thickened.

4. Return beef to the pot and stir in tomatoes, beans and tomato paste; bring to a boil. Reduce heat to medium-low, cover, leaving lid ajar, and simmer, stirring occasionally, for 15 minutes or until slightly thickened. Serve with any of the suggested accompaniments, as desired.

Salads and Sides

continued...

Rainbow Chard, Chia and Apricot Salad

Makes 4 side-dish servings

On a busy weeknight, a simple yet satisfying salad to partner with grilled chicken or broiled salmon is better than money in the bank. The interest return soars when the salad is a nutritional powerhouse of antioxidants, fiber and protein.

Tips

Other dried fruit, such as golden raisins or dried cherries, may be used in place of the apricots.

Other varieties of Swiss chard may be used in place of the rainbow Swiss chard.

1 tbsp	chia seeds	15 mL
2 tbsp	extra virgin olive oil	30 mL
1½ tbsp	white wine vinegar	22 mL
1 tbsp	liquid honey	15 mL
	Fine sea salt and cracked black pepper	
1	large bunch rainbow Swiss chard, tough stems and center ribs removed, leaves thinly sliced crosswise (about 5 cups/1.25 L)	1
¼ cup	dried apricots, chopped	60 mL

1. In a small bowl, whisk together chia seeds, oil, vinegar and honey. Season to taste with salt and pepper. Let stand for 5 minutes to thicken slightly.

2. In a large bowl, combine Swiss chard and apricots. Add dressing and gently toss to coat. Let stand for 10 minutes to blend the flavors.

Bok Choy Chia Salad

This fresh, crunchy salad is staggeringly simple. A dressing of miso, chia and ginger brightens and boosts the fresh flavor of the bok choy.

1 tbsp	chia seeds	15 mL
2 tsp	minced gingerroot	10 mL
1 tsp	fine crystal cane sugar	5 mL
1½ tbsp	unseasoned rice vinegar	22 mL
1½ tbsp	extra virgin olive oil	22 mL
1 tbsp	GF white or yellow miso paste	15 mL
8 cups	sliced bok choy (about 1 large)	2 L

1. In a small bowl, whisk together chia seeds, ginger, sugar, vinegar, oil and miso. Let stand for 5 minutes to thicken slightly.

2. Place bok choy in a large bowl. Add dressing and gently toss to coat.

Baharat Carrot Salad

Baharat means "spice" in Arabic, and it refers to a multipurpose spice blend used throughout the Middle East. The blend varies by region, but black pepper, coriander and cumin are almost always present. Turkish blends often include dried mint; in this salad, I've added fresh mint instead.

Tip

Cilantro or flat-leaf (Italian) parsley can be used in place of the mint.

¾ tsp	freshly cracked black pepper	3 mL
¾ tsp	ground cumin	3 mL
½ tsp	ground coriander	2 mL
½ tsp	ground cinnamon	2 mL
¼ tsp	ground cardamom	1 mL
3 tbsp	extra virgin olive oil	45 mL
2 tbsp	freshly squeezed lemon juice	30 mL
2 tbsp	chia seeds	30 mL
4 cups	coarsely shredded carrots (about 1 lb/500 g)	1 L
	Fine sea salt	
¾ cup	packed fresh mint leaves, chopped	175 mL

1. In a small bowl, whisk together pepper, cumin, coriander, cinnamon, cardamom, oil and lemon juice. Stir in chia seeds. Let stand for 5 minutes to thicken slightly.

2. Place carrots in a large bowl. Add dressing and gently toss to coat. Season to taste with salt. Cover and refrigerate for at least 1 hour, until chilled, or for up to 4 hours.

3. Just before serving, add mint, gently tossing to combine.

Curried Amaranth Mango Salad

A bounty of tropical ingredients — coconut, mango, cilantro and lime — get even better when combined in this fresh-tasting amaranth salad.

Tips

To toast coconut, preheat oven to 300°F (150°C). Spread coconut in a thin, even layer on an ungreased baking sheet. Bake for 15 to 20 minutes, stirring every 5 minutes, until golden brown and fragrant. Transfer to a plate and let cool completely.

Cooked millet, quinoa, brown rice or sorghum, cooled, can be used in place of the amaranth. Information on cooking these grains can be found on pages 11–17.

3 cups	cooked amaranth (see page 8), cooled	750 mL
1	large firm-ripe mango, diced	1
1	small red bell pepper, chopped	1
2 tsp	curry powder	10 mL
2 tbsp	plain yogurt	30 mL
2 tbsp	freshly squeezed lime juice	30 mL
1 tbsp	vegetable oil	15 mL
1 tbsp	liquid honey	15 mL
	Fine sea salt and freshly cracked black pepper	
1 cup	packed fresh cilantro or flat-leaf (Italian) parsley leaves, chopped	250 mL
⅔ cup	unsweetened flaked coconut, toasted (see tip, at left)	150 mL
2 tbsp	toasted sesame seeds (see page 27)	30 mL

1. In a large bowl, combine amaranth, mango and red pepper.

2. In a small bowl, whisk together curry powder, yogurt, lime juice, oil and honey. Add to the amaranth mixture and gently toss to coat. Season to taste with salt and pepper. Cover and refrigerate for at least 1 hour, until chilled, or for up to 4 hours.

3. Just before serving, add cilantro and coconut, gently tossing to combine. Sprinkle with sesame seeds.

Southeast Asian Amaranth Salad

Makes 8 side-dish servings

This amaranth salad evokes the bright, fresh fruit and vegetable dishes served throughout Southeast Asia.

Tips

Cooked millet or quinoa, cooled, can be used in place of the amaranth. Information on cooking these grains can be found on pages 11–15.

If 15-oz (425 mL) cans of mandarin oranges aren't available, use two 10-oz (284 mL) cans. (If you prefer fewer oranges, use 1½ cans and reserve extras for another use.)

1½ cups	cooked amaranth (see page 8), cooled	375 mL
2 cups	chopped purple cabbage	500 mL
1½ cups	shredded peeled jicama	375 mL
1	can (15 oz/425 mL) mandarin oranges, drained and coarsely chopped	1
2 tsp	Chinese five-spice powder	10 mL
2 tsp	fine crystal cane sugar	10 mL
3 tbsp	unseasoned rice vinegar	45 mL
2 tbsp	extra virgin olive oil	30 mL
	Fine sea salt and freshly cracked black pepper	
½ cup	packed fresh cilantro or mint leaves, chopped	125 mL

1. In a large bowl, combine amaranth, cabbage, jicama and oranges.

2. In a small bowl, whisk together five-spice powder, sugar, vinegar and oil. Add to the amaranth mixture and gently toss to coat. Season to taste with salt and pepper. Cover and refrigerate for at least 30 minutes, until chilled, or for up to 4 hours.

3. Just before serving, add cilantro, gently tossing to combine.

Yucatán Amaranth and Pineapple Salad

Jewel red, yellow and green make this salad as painterly as it is utterly delicious. Tender, nutty grains of amaranth add a surprising pop of crunch and flavor.

Tips

A pineapple is ripe enough to eat when a leaf is easily pulled from the top. To prepare it, cut off the leafy top and a small layer of the base, then slice off the tough skin and "eyes." Cut the flesh into slices, then remove the chewy central core from each slice. Cut each slice into dice.

An equal amount of dried tart cherries or cranberries, chopped, can be used in place of the pomegranate seeds.

This salad is best served within 1 to 2 hours of being prepared.

1 cup	cooked amaranth (see page 8), cooled	250 mL
4 cups	fresh pineapple chunks (about 1 large pineapple)	1 L
3/4 cup	loosely packed mint leaves, chopped	175 mL
1/2 cup	pomegranate seeds	125 mL
1 tsp	ancho chile powder	5 mL
2 tsp	finely grated lime zest	10 mL
1 1/2 tbsp	freshly squeezed lime juice	22 mL
1 tbsp	liquid honey or fine crystal cane sugar	15 mL

1. In a large bowl, gently toss amaranth, pineapple, mint, pomegranate seeds, ancho chile powder, lime zest, lime juice and honey.

Amaranth Salad with Watermelon, Olives and Feta

The new classic combination of watermelon and feta is updated here with the ancient grain amaranth, for an enlightened summer salad.

Tips

Cooked millet, quinoa, brown rice or sorghum, cooled, can be used in place of the amaranth. Information on cooking these grains can be found on pages 11–17.

An equal amount of packed baby spinach leaves can be used in place of the arugula.

To make this salad dairy-free and vegan, simply omit the feta cheese. If you like, increase the olives to ³⁄₄ cup (175 mL).

3 tbsp	extra virgin olive oil	45 mL
1¹⁄₂ tbsp	white wine vinegar	22 mL
1	shallot, finely chopped	1
4 cups	cubed seedless watermelon (³⁄₄-inch/2 cm cubes)	1 L
2 cups	cooked amaranth (see page 8), cooled	500 mL
3 cups	packed baby arugula (about 2 oz/60 g)	750 mL
¹⁄₂ cup	pitted brine-cured olives (such as kalamata), quartered	125 mL
	Fine sea salt and freshly cracked black pepper	
¹⁄₂ cup	crumbled feta cheese	125 mL

1. In a large bowl, whisk together oil and vinegar. Add shallot and watermelon, gently tossing to coat. Refrigerate for 15 minutes.

2. Add amaranth, arugula and olives, gently tossing to coat. Season to taste with salt and pepper. Sprinkle with cheese.

Amaranth Tabbouleh with Fennel and Herbs

I've specified amaranth for the grain here, a departure from the traditional wheat bulgur, but you can use the ancient grain of your choice.

Tips

Cooked millet, quinoa, brown rice or sorghum, cooled, can be used in place of the amaranth. Information on cooking these grains can be found on pages 11–17.

An equal amount of red or green grapes, halved, can be used in place of the grape tomatoes.

3 cups	cooked amaranth (see page 8), cooled	750 mL
2 cups	grape or cherry tomatoes, halved	500 mL
1 cup	chopped fennel bulb, fronds reserved	250 mL
1 cup	packed fresh flat-leaf (Italian) parsley leaves, chopped	250 mL
1 cup	packed fresh mint leaves, chopped	250 mL
½ cup	chopped green onions	125 mL
⅓ cup	chopped reserved fennel fronds	75 mL
2 tsp	ground cumin	10 mL
1 tsp	ground coriander	5 mL
3 tbsp	freshly squeezed lemon juice	45 mL
3 tbsp	extra virgin olive oil	45 mL
	Fine sea salt and cracked black pepper	

1. In a large bowl, combine amaranth, tomatoes, fennel bulb, parsley, mint, green onions, fennel fronds, cumin, coriander, lemon juice and oil. Generously season to taste with salt and pepper. Refrigerate for at least 1 hour, until chilled, or for up to 4 hours.

Arugula, Amaranth and Goat Cheese Salad

Makes 4 side-dish servings

Toasted until they puff, green pumpkin seeds add a crunch to this bistro-inspired salad, and the tangy Dijon vinaigrette dressing is a breeze to make.

Tip

Cooked millet, quinoa or sorghum, cooled, can be used in place of the amaranth. Information on cooking these grains can be found on pages 11–17.

2 cups	cooked amaranth (see page 8), cooled	500 mL
4 cups	packed baby arugula (about 4 oz/125 g)	1 L
3 tbsp	extra virgin olive oil	45 mL
2 tsp	white wine vinegar	10 mL
1 tsp	Dijon mustard	5 mL
¾ tsp	dried thyme	3 mL
	Fine sea salt and freshly cracked black pepper	
2 oz	goat cheese, crumbled	60 g
3 tbsp	green pumpkin seeds (pepitas), toasted (see page 27)	45 mL

1. In a large bowl, combine amaranth and arugula.

2. In a small bowl, whisk together oil, vinegar, mustard and thyme. Add to the amaranth mixture and gently toss to coat. Season to taste with salt and pepper. Add cheese and pumpkin seeds, gently tossing to combine.

Amaranth, Avocado and Black-Eyed Pea Salad

Makes 8 side-dish or 4 main-dish servings

Beans are not the only legumes prized in Mexican cooking: a variety of peas, including black-eyed peas, are used in soups, stews, fillings and salsas. Here, they team up with a host of other Mexican ingredients in a quick-to-make, sensational salad.

Tip

To toast pumpkin seeds, spread them in a dry skillet and cook over low heat, stirring constantly, for 1 to 4 minutes or until seeds make a popping sound and are golden and fragrant. Immediately transfer seeds to a plate and let them cool completely before adding them to the recipe.

1 tsp	chipotle chile powder	5 mL
3 tbsp	extra virgin olive oil	45 mL
2 tsp	finely grated lemon zest	10 mL
2 tbsp	freshly squeezed lemon juice	30 mL
3 cups	cooked amaranth (see page 8), cooled	750 mL
1 cup	chopped red radishes	250 mL
1/2 cup	packed fresh cilantro leaves, chopped	125 mL
1	can (14 to 19 oz/398 to 540 mL) black-eyed peas, drained and rinsed	1
	Fine sea salt and hot pepper sauce	
1	large firm-ripe Hass avocado	1
1/2 cup	crumbled queso fresco or mild feta cheese	125 mL
1/4 cup	toasted green pumpkin seeds (pepitas)	60 mL

1. In a small bowl, whisk together chipotle chile powder, oil, lemon zest and lemon juice.

2. In a large bowl, combine amaranth, radishes, cilantro and peas. Add dressing and gently toss to coat. Season to taste with salt and hot pepper sauce. Cover and refrigerate for at least 30 minutes, until chilled, or for up to 4 hours.

3. Just before serving, dice avocado and gently stir into salad. Sprinkle with cheese and pumpkin seeds.

Brussels Sprouts, Avocado and Buckwheat Salad

Makes 6 side-dish servings

This flavorful salad showcases the contrasting textures of toothsome, crisp and creamy in a tangy lime dressing.

Tip

Trim the root end from the Brussels sprouts and cut off any loose, thick outer leaves, then rinse well to remove any grit that may have gathered under loose leaves.

• Steamer basket		
1½ lbs	Brussels sprouts, trimmed (see tip, at left)	750 g
	Ice water	
3 tbsp	extra virgin olive oil	45 mL
1½ tbsp	liquid honey	22 mL
2 tsp	finely grated lime zest	10 mL
1½ tbsp	freshly squeezed lime juice	22 mL
	Fine sea salt and freshly cracked black pepper	
2 cups	cooked buckwheat (see page 9), cooled	500 mL
1	large firm-ripe Hass avocado	1

1. Place Brussels sprouts in a steamer basket set over a large pot of boiling water. Cover and steam for 5 to 6 minutes or until tender-crisp but still bright green. Transfer to a large bowl of ice water to stop the cooking. Drain and pat dry with paper towels.

2. In a small bowl, whisk together oil, honey, lime zest and lime juice. Season to taste with salt and pepper.

3. Using a very sharp knife or a mandoline, thinly slice Brussels sprouts lengthwise. Transfer to a large bowl. Add buckwheat and dressing, gently tossing to coat. Cover and refrigerate for at least 30 minutes, until chilled, or for up to 2 hours.

4. Just before serving, dice avocado and gently stir into salad.

Roasted Cauliflower and Buckwheat Salad

Makes 6 side-dish servings

Roasted cauliflower and buckwheat get jazzed up with golden raisins, fresh parsley and a piquant caper dressing. The result is a noteworthy salad everyone will adore.

Tips

To mash garlic, working with one clove at a time, place the side of a chef's knife flat against the clove. Place the heel of your hand on the side of the knife and apply pressure so that the clove flattens slightly (this will loosen the peel). Remove and discard the peel, then roughly chop the garlic. Sprinkle a pinch of coarse salt over the garlic. Use the flat part of the knife as before to press the garlic against the cutting board. Repeat until the garlic turns into a fine paste. The mashed garlic is now ready for use in your favorite recipe.

Cooked millet, quinoa or sorghum, cooled, can be used in place of the buckwheat. Information on cooking these grains can be found on pages 11–17.

- Preheat oven to 450°F (230°C)
- Large rimmed baking sheet, lined with parchment paper or foil

4 cups	small cauliflower florets (about 1 medium head)	1 L
3 tbsp	extra virgin olive oil, divided	45 mL
2	cloves garlic, mashed (see tip, at left)	2
2 tbsp	drained capers, minced	30 mL
2 tbsp	freshly squeezed lemon juice	30 mL
2 cups	cooked buckwheat (see page 9), cooled	500 mL
¼ cup	golden raisins	60 mL
	Fine sea salt and freshly cracked black pepper	
1 cup	firmly packed fresh flat-leaf (Italian) parsley leaves, roughly chopped	250 mL

1. In a large bowl, toss cauliflower with 1 tbsp (15 mL) oil. Spread in a single layer on prepared baking sheet. Roast in preheated oven for 35 to 40 minutes, stirring once or twice, until tender and golden brown. Let cool slightly in pan on a wire rack.

2. In a small bowl, whisk together garlic, capers, the remaining oil and lemon juice.

3. In a large bowl, combine roasted cauliflower, buckwheat and raisins. Add dressing and gently toss to coat. Season to taste with salt and pepper. Let cool for 15 minutes.

4. Add parsley, gently tossing to combine. Serve immediately.

Avocado, Orange and Millet Salad

Makes 6 side-dish servings

Here, the smooth, mellow flavor of avocado finds perfect harmony with sunny oranges, mild millet and refreshing mint.

Tips

Avocados come in several varieties, but Hass are the most widely available. A Hass avocado — notable for its dark, bumpy skin and rich, buttery flesh — is ideal in this simple salad, but any other variety may be used in its place.

If 15-oz (425 mL) cans of mandarin oranges aren't available, use two 10-oz (284 mL) cans. (If you prefer fewer oranges, use 1½ cans and reserve extras for another use.)

An equal amount of cilantro or parsley leaves can be used in place of the mint.

Variations

Black Bean, Avocado and Millet Salad: Add a 14- to 19-oz (398 to 540 mL) can of black beans, drained and rinsed, with the avocado. This makes 4 main-dish servings.

Avocado, Jicama and Millet Salad: For added crunch, add 1 cup (250 mL) chopped peeled jicama with the avocado.

1 tbsp	chia seeds	15 mL
1 tsp	ground cumin	5 mL
3 tbsp	melted virgin coconut oil	45 mL
1½ tbsp	freshly squeezed lemon juice	22 mL
1 tbsp	liquid honey or agave nectar	15 mL
	Fine sea salt and freshly cracked black pepper	
2 cups	cooked millet (see page 11), cooled	500 mL
1	firm-ripe Hass avocado, diced	1
1	can (15 oz/425 mL) mandarin oranges, drained, coarsely chopped	1
½ cup	packed fresh mint leaves, roughly chopped	125 mL

1. In a small bowl, whisk together chia seeds, cumin, oil, lemon juice and honey. Season to taste with salt and pepper. Let stand for 5 minutes to thicken slightly.

2. In a large bowl, combine millet and dressing. Add avocado, oranges and mint, gently tossing to coat.

Garden Vegetable
Quinoa Chili (page 129)

Rainbow Chard, Chia
and Apricot Salad (page 133)

Amaranth Salad with Watermelon,
Olives and Feta (page 138)

Peach, Radicchio and Quinoa Salad (page 150)

Provençal Sorghum Salad (page 167)

Lowcountry Okra, Tomatoes and Black-Eyed Peas
with Creamy Millet (page 183)

Sorghum with Zucchini Chickpea Ragù (page 184)

Smoky Chipotle Quinoa Burgers (page 191)

Zucchini and Millet Salad

A trio of fresh, zesty ingredients — lemon, Parmesan cheese and hazelnuts — elevates modest millet and fresh zucchini with style.

Tips

This salad is also wonderful made with cooked amaranth or quinoa, cooled. Information on cooking these grains can be found on pages 8–15.

For the best flavor, use small to medium zucchini in this recipe, as they are sweeter when raw than larger ones.

3 tbsp	extra virgin olive oil	45 mL
1 tbsp	finely grated lemon zest	15 mL
2 tbsp	freshly squeezed lemon juice	30 mL
2 cups	cooked millet (see page 11), cooled	500 mL
3	small zucchini, diced	3
½ cup	freshly grated Parmesan cheese	125 mL
	Fine sea salt and freshly cracked black pepper	
¼ cup	chopped toasted hazelnuts (see page 26)	60 mL

1. In a small bowl, whisk together oil, lemon zest and lemon juice.

2. In a large bowl, combine millet, zucchini and cheese. Add dressing and gently toss to coat. Season to taste with salt and pepper. Sprinkle with hazelnuts.

Middle Eastern Millet Salad

Sweet dates, nutty chickpeas and an easy, Middle East–inspired dressing flatter the grassy flavors of millet in this simple salad.

Tips

Plump, tender Medjool dates are the most commonly available soft dates in the U.S. and Canada, but any other variety of soft, fresh dates may be used in their place.

You can quickly toast slivered almonds on the stovetop. Spread them in a dry medium skillet set over medium heat. Stir until the almonds are golden brown and fragrant. Immediately transfer to a plate to cool.

1 tsp	ground cardamom	5 mL
3 tbsp	extra virgin olive oil	45 mL
1 tbsp	finely grated lemon zest	15 mL
2 tbsp	freshly squeezed lemon juice	30 mL
1 tbsp	liquid honey	15 mL
	Fine sea salt and freshly ground black pepper	
3½ cups	cooked millet (see page 11), cooled	875 mL
1	can (14 to 19 oz/398 to 540 mL) chickpeas, drained and rinsed	1
⅔ cup	pitted soft dates (such as Medjool), chopped	150 mL
½ cup	slivered almonds, toasted (see tip, at left)	125 mL
1 cup	packed fresh cilantro leaves, roughly chopped	250 mL

1. In a small bowl, whisk together cardamom, oil, lemon zest, lemon juice and honey. Season to taste with salt and pepper.

2. In a large bowl, combine millet, chickpeas and dates. Add dressing and gently toss to coat. Add almonds and cilantro, gently tossing to combine.

White Bean, Radish and Millet Salad

A bright tarragon vinaigrette balances the sweetness of green onions, beans and radishes in this fresh, yet filling, spring salad.

Tip

If you don't have fresh tarragon on hand, you can use 1 tsp (5 mL) dried tarragon.

2 tsp	minced fresh tarragon	10 mL
3 tbsp	extra virgin olive oil	45 mL
1 tbsp	white wine vinegar	15 mL
	Fine sea salt and freshly cracked black pepper	
2 cups	cooked millet (see page 11), cooled	500 mL
1 cup	chopped red radishes	250 mL
¾ cup	packed fresh flat-leaf (Italian) parsley leaves, chopped	175 mL
½ cup	thinly sliced green onions	125 mL
1	can (14 to 19 oz/398 to 540 mL) white beans, drained and rinsed	1

1. In a small bowl, whisk together tarragon, oil and vinegar. Season to taste with salt and pepper.

2. In a large bowl, combine millet, radishes, parsley, green onions and beans. Add dressing and gently toss to coat.

Vietnamese Chicken and Millet Salad

Makes 4 main-dish servings

Mild millet and shredded chicken breast take beautifully to a robust, Vietnamese-inspired dressing and crisp-fresh fruits and vegetables.

Tips

Cooked amaranth, quinoa, brown rice or sorghum, cooled, can be used in place of the millet. Information on cooking these grains can be found on pages 8–17.

To make this dish vegetarian, simply omit the chicken. Try adding $2/3$ cup (150 mL) toasted or roasted nuts (such as peanuts or cashews) or seeds (such as green pumpkin seeds or sunflower seeds) to the salad for protein.

3 cups	cooked millet (see page 11), cooled	750 mL
2 cups	shredded cooked chicken breast	500 mL
2 cups	shredded purple cabbage	500 mL
1 cup	shredded carrots	250 mL
$1/2$ cup	chopped green onions	125 mL
1	medium-large Granny Smith apple, peeled and shredded	1
$1^1/2$ tbsp	packed light brown sugar	22 mL
$1/4$ cup	freshly squeezed lime juice	60 mL
2 tbsp	Asian fish sauce or GF soy sauce	30 mL
2 tbsp	toasted sesame oil	30 mL
2 tsp	Asian chili sauce (such as Sriracha)	10 mL
	Fine sea salt and freshly ground black pepper	
$1/2$ cup	packed fresh mint or cilantro leaves, chopped	125 mL

1. In a large bowl, combine millet, chicken, cabbage, carrots, green onions and apple.

2. In a small bowl, whisk together brown sugar, lime juice, fish sauce, sesame oil and chili sauce. Add to the millet mixture and gently toss to coat. Season to taste with salt and pepper. Cover and refrigerate for at least 30 minutes, until chilled, or for up to 24 hours.

3. Just before serving, add mint, gently tossing to combine.

Waldorf Steel-Cut Oats Salad

You read correctly: steel-cut oats in a salad. But fear not: these are not your weekday morning porridge-style oats, but dry-cooked oats that will remind you of brown rice or bulgur. Bittersweet radicchio, toasted pecans and dried cranberries further enhance this riff on the New York City original.

Tips

You can skip steps 1 and 2 and replace the oats with an equal amount of cooked millet, quinoa, brown rice or sorghum, cooled. Information on cooking these grains can be found on pages 11–17.

If you do not like the bitter taste of radicchio, substitute shredded purple cabbage.

Chopped toasted walnuts or roughly chopped toasted green pumpkin seeds (pepitas) or sunflower seeds can be used in place of the pecans.

1½ cups	certified GF steel-cut oats	375 mL
	Cold water	
4 tbsp	extra virgin olive oil, divided	60 mL
2	large Granny Smith or other tart apples, peeled and diced	2
1½ cups	red seedless grapes, halved	375 mL
1 cup	thinly sliced celery	250 mL
2 tbsp	sherry vinegar or cider vinegar	30 mL
2 tsp	liquid honey	10 mL
	Fine sea salt and freshly cracked black pepper	
1½ cups	torn radicchio	375 mL
½ cup	dried cranberries or dried tart cherries	125 mL
½ cup	chopped toasted pecans (see page 26)	125 mL

1. Soak oats overnight in enough cold water to cover. Reserve ¼ cup (60 mL) soaking water, then drain oats in a fine-mesh sieve, pressing out excess water.

2. In a large nonstick skillet, melt 1 tbsp (15 mL) oil over medium-low heat. Add oats and reserved water; cook, stirring, for 3 to 5 minutes or until water is evaporated and oats are plump and dry. Spread oats out on a rimmed baking sheet and let cool completely.

3. In a large bowl, combine cooled oats, apples, grapes and celery.

4. In a small bowl, whisk together the remaining oil, vinegar and honey. Add to the oat mixture and gently toss to coat. Season to taste with salt and pepper. Cover and refrigerate for at least 30 minutes, until chilled, or for up to 2 hours.

5. Just before serving, add radicchio, cranberries and pecans, gently tossing to combine.

Peach, Radicchio and Quinoa Salad

The bold colors of this orange, purple and green salad are only outmatched by the dazzling combination of sweet, bitter and fresh. It's grand summer fare.

Tips

Cooked amaranth, millet, brown rice or sorghum, cooled, can be used in place of the quinoa. Information on cooking these grains can be found on pages 8–17.

When peaches are not in season, use two 10-oz (284 mL) cans of mandarin oranges, drained and coarsely chopped, in their place.

Chopped toasted pecans or roughly chopped toasted green pumpkin seeds (pepitas) or sunflower seeds can be used in place of the walnuts.

3 tbsp	extra virgin olive oil	45 mL
1½ tbsp	sherry vinegar	22 mL
½ tsp	Dijon mustard	2 mL
	Fine sea salt and freshly cracked black pepper	
2 cups	cooked quinoa (see page 15), cooled	500 mL
2	large firm-ripe peaches, peeled, if desired, and diced	2
1	head radicchio, coarsely chopped	1
1 cup	packed fresh flat-leaf (Italian) parsley leaves	250 mL
¼ cup	chopped toasted walnuts (see page 26)	60 mL

1. In a small bowl, whisk together oil, vinegar and mustard. Season to taste with salt and pepper.

2. In a large bowl, combine quinoa, peaches, radicchio and parsley. Add dressing and gently toss to coat. Sprinkle with walnuts.

Asparagus and Quinoa Salad

This crunchy spring salad is loaded with plenty of fresh flavor. It's also fast and easy to make.

Tip

To hard-cook eggs, place eggs in a saucepan large enough to hold them in a single layer. Add enough cold water to cover eggs by 1 inch (2.5 cm). Heat over high heat until water is just boiling. Remove from heat and cover pan. Let stand for about 12 minutes for large eggs (9 minutes for medium eggs; 15 minutes for extra-large eggs). Drain eggs and cool completely under cold running water or in a bowl of ice water. Refrigerate until ready to eat.

1 lb	asparagus, trimmed and cut diagonally into $\frac{1}{4}$-inch (0.5 cm) pieces, tips left intact	500 g
2 cups	cooked quinoa (see page 15), cooled	500 mL
1 cup	chopped trimmed radishes	250 mL
1 tsp	dried thyme	5 mL
3 tbsp	extra virgin olive oil	45 mL
1½ tbsp	white wine vinegar	22 mL
1 tsp	Dijon mustard	5 mL
	Fine sea salt and freshly cracked black pepper	
2	hard-cooked large eggs (see tip, at left), peeled and chopped	2

1. In a large saucepan of boiling salted water, cook asparagus for 30 seconds. Drain and rinse under cold water until cool.

2. In a large bowl, combine asparagus, quinoa and radishes.

3. In a small bowl, whisk together thyme, oil, vinegar and mustard. Add to the asparagus mixture and gently toss to coat. Season to taste with salt and pepper. Cover and refrigerate for at least 30 minutes, until chilled, or for up to 2 hours.

4. Just before serving, add eggs, gently tossing to combine.

Shredded Beet, Quinoa and Hazelnut Salad

The quinoa in this magenta salad is more than garnish: it has a fullness of flavor that flatters the fresh parsley and shredded beets.

Tip

Use the coarse side of a box grater to shred the beets. Or, to make quick work of the task, use the shredding disk on a food processor.

3 tbsp	extra virgin olive oil	45 mL
1½ tbsp	sherry vinegar	22 mL
2 cups	cooked quinoa (see page 15), cooled	500 mL
3	beets, peeled and coarsely shredded	3
	Fine sea salt and freshly cracked black pepper	
1 cup	packed fresh flat-leaf (Italian) parsley leaves, chopped	250 mL
⅓ cup	chopped toasted hazelnuts (see page 26)	75 mL

1. In a small bowl, whisk together oil and vinegar.

2. In a large bowl, combine quinoa and beets. Add dressing and gently toss to coat. Season to taste with salt and pepper. Cover and refrigerate for at least 30 minutes, until chilled, or for up to 4 hours.

3. Just before serving, add parsley and hazelnuts, gently tossing to combine.

Broccoli, Grape and Quinoa Salad

Fresh grapes and golden raisins add sweetness, while broccoli and hazelnuts add crunch to this simple, yet uniquely delicious quinoa salad.

Tips

Cooked amaranth, millet, brown rice or sorghum, cooled, can be used in place of the quinoa. Information on cooking these grains can be found on pages 8–17.

You can replace the hazelnuts with an equal amount of toasted seeds (such as green pumpkin seeds or sunflower seeds) or another type of chopped toasted nuts (such as pecans or walnuts).

3 cups	broccoli florets	750 mL
	Ice water	
½ cup	plain yogurt	125 mL
2 tbsp	Dijon mustard	30 mL
1 tbsp	liquid honey	15 mL
1½ cups	cooked quinoa (see page 15), cooled	375 mL
1½ cups	red seedless grapes, halved	375 mL
½ cup	golden raisins	125 mL
	Fine sea salt and freshly cracked black pepper	
2 cups	packed tender watercress sprigs	500 mL
½ cup	chopped toasted hazelnuts (see page 26)	125 mL

1. In a medium saucepan of boiling water, blanch broccoli for 1 minute. Using a slotted spoon, immediately transfer broccoli to a large bowl of ice water to cool. Drain and pat dry with paper towels.

2. In a small bowl, whisk together yogurt, mustard and honey.

3. In a large bowl, combine broccoli, quinoa, grapes and raisins. Add dressing and gently toss to coat. Season to taste with salt and pepper. Cover and refrigerate for at least 30 minutes, until chilled, or for up to 4 hours.

4. Just before serving, add watercress and hazelnuts, gently tossing to combine.

Summer Corn and Quinoa Salad

Here, down-to-earth quinoa offers its nuance, nutty flavor and delicate texture as a foil for sweet summer corn and fresh herbs.

Tips

If you don't have fresh tarragon on hand, you can use 1 tsp (5 mL) dried tarragon.

This salad is especially beautiful when made with red, black or multicolored quinoa, but any variety will do.

2 tsp	minced fresh tarragon	10 mL
3 tbsp	extra virgin olive oil	45 mL
1 tbsp	sherry vinegar	15 mL
	Fine sea salt and freshly cracked black pepper	
2 cups	cooked quinoa (see page 15), cooled	500 mL
3 cups	cooked fresh or thawed frozen corn kernels	750 mL
½ cup	packed fresh parsley leaves, chopped	125 mL
½ cup	minced fresh chives	125 mL

1. In a small bowl, whisk together tarragon, oil and vinegar. Season to taste with salt and pepper.

2. In a large bowl, combine quinoa, corn, parsley and chives. Add dressing and gently toss to coat. Adjust seasoning with salt and pepper to taste.

Kale and Quinoa Salad with Maple Vinaigrette

Makes 4 side-dish servings

In this recipe, kale is transformed into a modern mainstay. Tart-sweet apple pieces and the nuanced, nutty flavor of quinoa lend sweetness and textural contrast.

Tip

Cooked amaranth, millet or sorghum, cooled, can be used in place of the quinoa. Information on cooking these grains can be found on pages 8–17.

3 tbsp	extra virgin olive oil	45 mL
2 tbsp	cider vinegar	30 mL
1 tbsp	pure maple syrup	15 mL
1 tsp	Dijon mustard	5 mL
3 cups	cooked quinoa (see page 15), cooled	750 mL
1	large bunch kale, tough stems and center ribs removed, leaves torn into small pieces (about 6 cups/1.5 L)	1
1	large tart-sweet apple (such as Gala, Braeburn or Golden Delicious), diced	1
½ cup	thinly sliced green onions	125 mL
	Fine sea salt and freshly cracked black pepper	

1. In a small bowl, whisk together oil, vinegar, maple syrup and mustard.

2. In a large bowl, combine quinoa, kale, apple and green onions. Add dressing and gently toss to coat. Season to taste with salt and pepper.

Butternut Squash and Quinoa Harvest Salad

This beautiful autumnal salad is a perfect way to showcase butternut squash. Combining it with nutty quinoa, peppery arugula and tart, chewy cherries results in a different combination of flavors with each bite.

Tip

An equal amount of chopped toasted walnuts or hazelnuts, or whole toasted green pumpkin seeds (pepitas) can be used in place of the pecans.

- Preheat oven to 400°F (200°C)
- Large rimmed baking sheet, lined with foil and sprayed with nonstick cooking spray

1	large butternut squash, cut into 1-inch (2.5 cm) cubes	1
2 tsp	minced fresh rosemary	10 mL
4 tbsp	extra virgin olive oil, divided	60 mL
	Fine sea salt and freshly cracked black pepper	
3 cups	cooked quinoa (see page 15), cooled	750 mL
1/2 cup	dried tart cherries, chopped	125 mL
2 tbsp	sherry vinegar	30 mL
6 cups	packed baby arugula leaves	1.5 L
2/3 cup	chopped toasted pecans (see page 26)	150 mL

1. In a large bowl, combine squash, rosemary and 1 tbsp (15 mL) oil. Season with salt and pepper. Spread in a single layer on prepared baking sheet. Roast in preheated oven for 35 to 40 minutes, stirring occasionally, until squash is tender. Let cool completely.

2. In a large bowl, combine roasted squash and quinoa. Add cherries, the remaining oil and vinegar, gently tossing to coat. Season to taste with salt and pepper. Add arugula and pecans, gently tossing to combine.

Quinoa, Blue Cheese and Pecan Salad

The hearty flavor of quinoa in this salad balances the salty-sweet tang of the blue cheese and the nutty crunch of toasted pecans.

Tip

Crumbled feta or goat cheese can be used in place of the blue cheese.

2	cloves garlic, mashed (see tip, page 143)	2
3 tbsp	extra virgin olive oil	45 mL
1 1/2 tbsp	white wine vinegar	22 mL
1 tsp	Dijon mustard	5 mL
	Fine sea salt and freshly cracked black pepper	
3 cups	cooked quinoa (see page 15), cooled	750 mL
1 cup	packed fresh flat-leaf (Italian) parsley leaves	250 mL
3/4 cup	crumbled blue cheese	175 mL
1/2 cup	chopped toasted pecans (see page 26)	125 mL
1/2 cup	dried tart cherries or cranberries, chopped	125 mL

1. In a small bowl, whisk together garlic, oil, vinegar and mustard. Season to taste with salt and pepper.

2. Place quinoa in a large bowl. Add dressing and gently toss to coat. Cover and refrigerate for at least 30 minutes, until chilled, or for up to 4 hours.

3. Just before serving, add parsley, blue cheese, pecans and cherries, gently tossing to combine.

Eggplant, Lentil and Quinoa Salad

Makes 8 side-dish or 4 main-dish servings

This Middle Eastern–inspired quinoa and lentil salad is lighter than many other eggplant recipes, since no heavy sauces or cheeses weigh it down. The creamy eggplant and the wonderful aromas of fresh cilantro and ground coriander really come through.

Tips

Cooked amaranth, millet, brown rice or sorghum, cooled, can be used in place of the quinoa. Information on cooking these grains can be found on pages 8–17.

An equal amount of fresh flat-leaf (Italian) parsley leaves can be used in place of the cilantro. Alternatively, replace the cilantro with ½ cup (125 mL) parsley and ½ cup (125 mL) fresh mint leaves.

1 cup	dried green lentils, rinsed	250 mL
4½ cups	water, divided	1.125 L
	Fine sea salt	
5 tbsp	extra virgin olive oil, divided	75 mL
1	large eggplant, diced	1
¼ cup	tomato paste	60 mL
1 tsp	ground coriander	5 mL
¼ tsp	cayenne pepper	1 mL
2 tbsp	freshly squeezed lime juice	30 mL
3 cups	cooked quinoa (see page 15), cooled	750 mL
1	large cucumber, peeled, seeded and cubed	1
1 cup	packed fresh cilantro leaves, chopped	250 mL

1. In a medium saucepan, combine lentils and 3 cups (750 mL) water. Bring to a boil over medium-high heat. Reduce heat and simmer for 15 minutes. Add ½ tsp (2 mL) salt and simmer for 10 to 15 minutes or until tender. Drain lentils, transfer to a large bowl and let cool completely.

2. Meanwhile, in a large nonstick skillet, heat 2 tbsp (30 mL) oil over medium heat. Add eggplant and cook, stirring, for 2 minutes. Stir in ½ tsp (2 mL) salt, the remaining water and tomato paste; bring to a simmer. Reduce heat and simmer, stirring occasionally, for about 20 minutes or until eggplant is very tender and no liquid remains in the pan.

3. In a small bowl, whisk together coriander, cayenne, the remaining oil and lime juice. Season to taste with salt.

4. To the lentils, add quinoa, eggplant mixture and dressing, gently tossing to coat. Cover and refrigerate for at least 30 minutes, until chilled, or for up to 4 hours.

5. Just before serving, add cucumber and cilantro, gently tossing to combine. Adjust seasoning with salt to taste.

Chimichurri Chickpea, Quinoa and Queso Salad

European-style cheeses are an important part of Argentinian cuisine thanks to early immigrants from Italy, France and Spain. Here, Romano cheese — akin to Argentina's Sardo cheese — pairs with chimichurri, another of the country's iconic foods, in a fresh, flavorful chickpea and quinoa salad.

Variation

Cilantro Chimichurri and Black Bean Salad: Replace the parsley with an equal amount of fresh cilantro and replace the chickpeas with black beans.

* Blender

2	cloves garlic	2
1¼ cups	packed fresh flat-leaf (Italian) parsley leaves	300 mL
¼ tsp	cayenne pepper	1 mL
¼ cup	extra virgin olive oil	60 mL
2 tbsp	red wine vinegar	30 mL
3 cups	cooked quinoa (see page 15), cooled	750 mL
1	red bell pepper, chopped	1
1	can (14 to 19 oz/398 to 540 mL) chickpeas, drained and rinsed	1
¾ cup	freshly grated Romano cheese	175 mL
	Fine sea salt and freshly cracked black pepper	

1. In blender, combine garlic, parsley, cayenne, oil and vinegar; purée until smooth.

2. In a large bowl, combine quinoa, red pepper, chickpeas and cheese. Add dressing and gently toss to coat. Season to taste with salt and pepper. Cover and refrigerate for at least 30 minutes, until chilled, or for up to 2 hours.

Turkey, Pear and Quinoa Salad with Blue Cheese

Looking for a fast weeknight supper salad? This one tastes fancy but is a snap to prepare. Use leftover turkey in the days following Thanksgiving, or pick up a rotisserie chicken or diced smoked turkey from the deli the rest of the year.

Tips

Cooked amaranth, millet, brown rice or sorghum, cooled, can be used in place of the quinoa. Information on cooking these grains can be found on pages 8–17.

Chopped toasted pecans or roughly chopped toasted green pumpkin seeds (pepitas) or sunflower seeds can be used in place of the walnuts.

3 cups	cooked quinoa (see page 15), cooled	750 mL
1½ cups	diced cooked turkey or chicken	375 mL
2	firm-ripe pears, peeled and diced	2
1 cup	thinly sliced celery	250 mL
½ cup	thinly sliced green onions	125 mL
½ cup	dried cranberries, chopped	125 mL
3 tbsp	extra virgin olive oil	45 mL
2 tbsp	white wine vinegar	30 mL
1½ tbsp	Dijon mustard	22 mL
2 tsp	liquid honey	10 mL
	Fine sea salt and freshly cracked black pepper	
½ cup	chopped toasted walnuts (see page 26)	125 mL
½ cup	crumbled blue cheese	125 mL

1. In a large bowl, combine quinoa, turkey, pears, celery, green onions and cranberries.

2. In a small bowl, whisk together oil, vinegar, mustard and honey. Add to the quinoa mixture and gently toss to coat. Season to taste with salt and pepper. Cover and refrigerate for at least 30 minutes, until chilled, or for up to 4 hours.

3. Just before serving, sprinkle with walnuts and blue cheese.

Warm Linguiça, Kale and Quinoa Salad

The robust flavors of Portugal — garlic, Linguiça, golden raisins and greens — make this otherwise everyday kale salad extraordinary.

Tips

Linguiça is a fully cooked smoked pork sausage seasoned with garlic and paprika. If you cannot find it, any other variety of smoked sausage can be used in its place.

Cooked millet, brown rice or sorghum, cooled, can be used in place of the quinoa. Information on cooking these grains can be found on pages 11–17.

1½ tbsp	olive oil	22 mL
8 oz	GF Linguiça or other smoked sausage, diced	250 g
2	cloves garlic, minced	2
1	large bunch kale, tough stems and center ribs removed, leaves very thinly sliced crosswise (about 6 cups/1.5 L)	1
3 cups	cooked quinoa (see page 15), cooled	750 mL
⅓ cup	golden raisins	75 mL
1 tbsp	red wine vinegar	15 mL
	Fine sea salt and freshly cracked black pepper	

1. In a large nonstick skillet, heat oil over medium-high heat. Add sausage and cook, stirring, for 2 to 3 minutes or until starting to brown. Add garlic and kale; cook, stirring, for 2 to 3 minutes or until kale is just starting to wilt. Transfer to a large bowl and let cool slightly.

2. Add quinoa, raisins and vinegar, gently tossing to coat. Season to taste with salt and pepper.

Coconut, Pineapple and Basmati Rice Salad

Makes 6 side-dish servings

Good-quality jerk seasoning can steer a dish in a Caribbean direction in seconds. Here, it works magic in a pineapple and brown rice salad.

Tip

To toast coconut, preheat oven to 300°F (150°C). Spread coconut in a thin, even layer on an ungreased baking sheet. Bake for 15 to 20 minutes, stirring every 5 minutes, until golden brown and fragrant. Transfer to a plate and let cool completely.

3 cups	cooked brown basmati rice (see page 16), cooled	750 mL
1½ cups	diced fresh or thawed frozen pineapple	375 mL
1 cup	chopped green onions	250 mL
½ cup	unsweetened flaked coconut, toasted (see tip, at left)	125 mL
2 tbsp	melted virgin coconut oil	30 mL
1 tbsp	salt-free dry Jamaican jerk seasoning	15 mL
2 tsp	packed light brown sugar	10 mL
1 tsp	finely grated lime zest	5 mL
2 tbsp	freshly squeezed lime juice	30 mL
	Fine sea salt and hot pepper sauce	
⅔ cup	lightly salted macadamia nuts or roasted cashews, chopped	150 mL

1. In a large bowl, combine rice, pineapple, green onions, coconut and coconut oil.

2. In a small bowl, whisk together jerk seasoning, brown sugar, lime zest and lime juice. Add to the rice mixture and gently toss to coat. Season to taste with salt and hot pepper sauce. Cover and refrigerate for at least 30 minutes, until chilled, or for up to 2 hours.

3. Just before serving, sprinkle with macadamia nuts.

Edamame and Basmati Rice Salad

Here, edamame's pale jade hue and tender texture work in harmony with the delicate fragrance of basmati rice and the nuanced flavor of ground coriander.

Tip

One 12-oz (375 g) bag of frozen shelled edamame yields about 2 cups (500 mL).

2 cups	frozen shelled edamame	500 mL
1 tsp	ground coriander	5 mL
3 tbsp	extra virgin olive oil	45 mL
1 tbsp	finely grated lime zest	15 mL
2 tbsp	freshly squeezed lime juice	30 mL
	Fine sea salt and cracked black pepper	
3 cups	cooked brown basmati rice (see page 16), cooled	750 mL
1 cup	thinly sliced green onions	250 mL
½ cup	chopped lightly salted roasted pistachios	125 mL

1. In a medium saucepan of boiling water, cook edamame over medium-high heat for 4 to 6 minutes or until bright green and tender. Drain and rinse under cold water until cool.

2. In a small bowl, whisk together coriander, oil, lime zest and lime juice. Season to taste with salt and pepper.

3. In a large bowl, combine edamame, rice and green onions. Add dressing and gently toss to coat. Cover and refrigerate for at least 1 hour, until chilled, or for up to 4 hours.

4. Just before serving, sprinkle with pistachios.

California Sushi Salad with Tahini Miso Dressing

Sushi deconstructed: this fabulous salad has many of the distinctive flavors of California rolls with minimal effort and a tahini-miso twist.

Tips

Cooked millet or quinoa, cooled, can be used in place of the brown rice. Information on cooking these grains can be found on pages 11–15.

Use a very sharp knife or kitchen shears to cut the nori into strips (its dryness can make it somewhat tough to cut).

2 tbsp	minced gingerroot	30 mL
1/4 cup	well-stirred tahini	60 mL
3 tbsp	hot water	45 mL
2 tbsp	GF miso paste	30 mL
2 tbsp	unseasoned rice vinegar	30 mL
1 1/2 tbsp	liquid honey or agave nectar	22 mL
4 cups	cooked long-grain brown rice (see page 16), cooled	1 L
1 1/2 cups	diced seeded peeled cucumber	375 mL
3/4 cup	coarsely shredded carrots	175 mL
3/4 cup	thinly sliced green onions	175 mL
1	firm-ripe Hass avocado	1
1	6-inch (15 cm) square toasted nori, cut into very thin strips	1

1. In a small bowl, combine ginger, tahini, hot water, miso, vinegar and honey until blended.

2. In a large bowl, combine rice, cucumber, carrots and green onions. Add dressing and gently toss to coat. Cover and refrigerate for at least 1 hour, until chilled, or for up to 2 hours.

3. Just before serving, dice avocado and sprinkle over salad, along with nori strips.

Lemony Sorghum Salad with Kale Pesto

Makes 6 side-dish servings

In this easy and hugely satisfying salad, kale is used two ways: as a green and as the basis of a creamy emerald pesto. Dried cranberries and toasted walnuts lend sweetness and textural contrast.

Tips

Cooked millet, quinoa or brown rice, cooled, can be used in place of the sorghum. Information on cooking these grains can be found on pages 11–16.

Chopped toasted pecans or roughly chopped toasted green pumpkin seeds (pepitas) or sunflower seeds can be used in place of the walnuts.

- Food processor

1	large bunch kale, tough stems and center ribs removed, leaves very thinly sliced crosswise (about 6 cups/1.5 L), divided	1
1	clove garlic	1
1 tbsp	finely grated lemon zest	15 mL
1 tbsp	freshly squeezed lemon juice	15 mL
1/3 cup	extra virgin olive oil	75 mL
3 cups	cooked sorghum (see page 17), cooled	750 mL
1/2 cup	dried cranberries, chopped	125 mL
	Fine sea salt and freshly cracked black pepper	
1/4 cup	chopped toasted walnuts (see page 26)	60 mL

1. In food processor, finely chop half the kale with the garlic. Add lemon zest and lemon juice. With the motor running, through the feed tube, slowly drizzle in oil, processing until smooth.

2. In a large bowl, combine the remaining kale, sorghum and cranberries. Add kale pesto and gently toss to coat. Season to taste with salt and pepper. Sprinkle with walnuts.

Snap Pea, Sorghum and Tarragon Salad

The components of this understated salad go together brilliantly.

Tips

If you don't have fresh tarragon on hand, you can use 1 tsp (5 mL) dried tarragon.

Replace the snap peas with an equal amount of snow peas, halved on the diagonal.

12 oz	sugar snap peas, strings removed	375 g
2 cups	cooked sorghum (see page 17), cooled	500 mL
2	cloves garlic, mashed (see tip, page 143)	2
2 tsp	minced fresh tarragon	10 mL
½ tsp	fine crystal cane sugar	2 mL
3 tbsp	extra virgin olive oil	45 mL
2 tbsp	freshly squeezed lemon juice	30 mL
	Fine sea salt and freshly cracked black pepper	
3 cups	packed tender watercress sprigs	750 mL

1. In a large saucepan of boiling salted water, cook peas for 1 minute. Drain and rinse under cold water until cool.

2. In a large bowl, combine peas and sorghum.

3. In a small bowl, whisk together garlic, tarragon, sugar, oil and lemon juice. Add to the sorghum mixture and gently toss to coat. Season to taste with salt and pepper. Cover and refrigerate for at least 30 minutes, until chilled, or for up to 2 hours.

4. Just before serving, gently toss in watercress.

Provençal Sorghum Salad

Olives, fennel and roasted red bell peppers, common ingredients in the south of France, give this rustic yet still sophisticated salad Provençal flair.

Tips

To make this dish vegetarian, simply omit the tuna or replace it with 1 cup (250 mL) rinsed drained canned chickpeas or white beans.

Cooked millet, quinoa or brown rice, cooled, can be used in place of the sorghum. Information on cooking these grains can be found on pages 11–16.

1	can (6 oz/170 g) tuna packed in olive oil, with oil	1
2 tsp	finely grated lemon zest	10 mL
3 tbsp	freshly squeezed lemon juice	45 mL
3 cups	cooked sorghum (see page 17), cooled	750 mL
1 cup	chopped fennel bulb	250 mL
½ cup	chopped drained roasted red bell peppers	125 mL
⅓ cup	pitted kalamata or other brine-cured black olives, chopped	75 mL
	Fine sea salt and freshly cracked black pepper	
1 cup	packed fresh flat-leaf (Italian) parsley leaves, chopped	250 mL
2	hard-cooked large eggs (see tip, page 151), sliced into wedges	2

1. Drain tuna, reserving 2 tbsp (30 mL) oil. In a small bowl, whisk together the reserved oil, lemon zest and lemon juice.

2. In a large bowl, combine tuna, sorghum, fennel, roasted peppers and olives. Add dressing and gently toss to coat. Season to taste with salt and pepper. Cover and refrigerate for at least 1 hour, until chilled, or for up to 6 hours.

3. Just before serving, add parsley, gently tossing to combine. Top with egg wedges.

Green Bean and Teff Salad with Tahini Dressing

This teff salad is a fast and beautiful way to showcase summer green beans with style. For the best presentation, consider serving the salad on a platter rather than a bowl.

Tip

If you don't have fresh dill on hand, you can use 1 tbsp (15 mL) dried dillweed.

- Steamer basket

1 lb	green beans, trimmed and halved crosswise	500 g
	Ice water	
1	clove garlic, mashed (see tip, page 143)	1
3 tbsp	tahini	45 mL
1½ tbsp	freshly squeezed lemon juice	22 mL
1 tbsp	extra virgin olive oil	15 mL
1 tsp	liquid honey	5 mL
	Fine sea salt and freshly cracked black pepper	
1¼ cups	dry-cooked teff (see page 18)	300 mL
2 tbsp	chopped fresh dill	30 mL
¼ cup	chopped toasted walnuts (see page 26)	60 mL

1. Place green beans in a steamer basket set over a large pot of boiling water. Cover and steam for 4 to 6 minutes or until tender. Transfer to a large bowl of ice water to stop the cooking. Drain and pat dry with paper towels.

2. In a small bowl, whisk together garlic, tahini, lemon juice, oil and honey. Thin with water, if needed. Season to taste with salt and pepper.

3. In a large bowl, combine green beans, teff and dill. Add dressing and gently toss to coat. Cover and refrigerate for at least 1 hour, until chilled, or for up to 6 hours.

4. Just before serving, sprinkle with walnuts.

Arugula, Teff and Pomegranate Salad

Arugula, pomegranate and teff may sound worlds apart — bitter, sweet and earthy — but like so many odd arrangements, they go together beautifully.

½	small red onion, diced	½
2 tsp	fine crystal cane sugar	10 mL
½ tsp	ground cumin	2 mL
1 tbsp	white wine vinegar	15 mL
	Fine sea salt and freshly cracked black pepper	
3 tbsp	extra virgin olive oil	45 mL
6 cups	packed baby arugula (about 4 oz/125 g)	1.5 L
¾ cup	dry-cooked teff (see page 18)	175 mL
⅓ cup	pomegranate seeds	75 mL

1. In a large bowl, combine onion, sugar, cumin and vinegar. Season to taste with salt and pepper. Let stand for 30 minutes.

2. Add oil to the onion mixture. Add arugula, tossing to combine. Adjust seasoning with salt and pepper to taste. Add teff, gently tossing to combine. Sprinkle with pomegranate seeds.

Coconut Millet

This millet dish proves that simple is often best.

Tips

An equal amount of quinoa, rinsed, or amaranth seeds can be used in place of the millet. Reduce the cooking time to 12 to 15 minutes.

The coconut milk will caramelize slightly as it cooks, producing some brown flecks throughout the millet once it is fluffed.

1½ cups	millet	375 mL
1 tbsp	fine crystal cane sugar	15 mL
⅛ tsp	fine sea salt	0.5 mL
1	can (14 oz/400 mL) coconut milk (full-fat), well stirred	1
1⅓ cups	water	325 mL

1. In a medium saucepan, combine millet, sugar, salt, coconut milk and water. Bring to a boil over medium-high heat. Reduce heat to low, cover and simmer for 15 minutes or until liquid is absorbed. Remove from heat and let stand for 5 minutes. Fluff with a fork.

Lemon Parsley Millet

Here, millet returns to its early Roman roots in a striking side dish flavored with classic Italian ingredients.

Tips

The easiest way to peel a piece of fresh gingerroot is with the tip of a metal spoon. Simply rub the edge of the spoon firmly over the surface of the ginger to remove the skin.

An equal amount of quinoa, rinsed, can be used in place of the millet. Reduce the cooking time to 12 to 15 minutes.

Variation

Cilantro Jalapeño Millet: Replace the parsley with cilantro, use lime zest and juice in place of the lemon zest and juice, and add 1 tbsp (15 mL) minced seeded jalapeño pepper to the blender in step 2. To make the dish spicier, add some or all of the jalapeño seeds.

- Blender

1 cup	millet	250 mL
2 cups	water	500 mL
	Fine sea salt	
1	clove garlic, minced	1
1¼ cups	packed fresh parsley leaves	300 mL
1 tsp	finely grated lemon zest	5 mL
2 tbsp	freshly squeezed lemon juice	30 mL
2 tbsp	extra virgin olive oil	30 mL

1. In a medium saucepan, combine millet, water and ½ tsp (2 mL) salt. Bring to a boil over medium-high heat. Reduce heat to low, cover and simmer for 15 minutes. Remove from heat and let stand for 5 minutes. Fluff with a fork. Transfer to a medium bowl.

2. Meanwhile, in blender, combine garlic, parsley, lemon zest, lemon juice and oil; pulse until smooth. Add to millet, tossing with a fork to combine. Season to taste with salt.

Moroccan Millet and Black-Eyed Pea Pilaf

This intensely flavored, North African–inspired pilaf takes straightforward quinoa to an exotic place.

Tip

Chickpeas, white beans (such as cannellini or Great Northern beans) or butter beans can be used in place of the black-eyed peas.

2 tbsp	olive oil	30 mL
1	red bell pepper, chopped	1
1¼ cups	millet	300 mL
2 tsp	ground cumin	10 mL
1 tsp	ground cinnamon	5 mL
½ tsp	fine sea salt	2 mL
¼ tsp	cayenne pepper	1 mL
2 cups	water	500 mL
¼ cup	chopped pitted brine-cured black olives (such as kalamata)	60 mL
2 tbsp	dried currants	30 mL
1	can (14 to 19 oz/398 to 540 mL) black-eyed peas, drained and rinsed	1
½ cup	packed fresh mint leaves, chopped	125 mL
1 tbsp	freshly squeezed lemon juice	15 mL

1. In a large skillet, heat oil over medium-high heat. Add red pepper and cook, stirring, for 2 to 3 minutes or until pepper is slightly softened. Add millet, cumin, cinnamon, salt and cayenne; cook, stirring, for 1 minute or until fragrant.

2. Stir in water and bring to a boil. Reduce heat to low, cover and simmer for 15 minutes. Remove from heat and add olives, currants and black-eyed peas (do not stir). Cover and let stand for 10 minutes. Fluff millet with a fork, stirring in mint and lemon juice.

Butternut Squash and Toasted Pecan Quinoa

Introducing your new favorite cold-weather side dish. It's ideal for Thanksgiving, but you will love it so much you won't want to limit it to once-a-year status.

Tips

To save time, look for packages of ready-to-use cubed peeled butternut squash in the produce section of the supermarket.

Hot cooked millet, brown rice or sorghum can be used in place of the quinoa. Information on cooking these grains can be found on pages 11–17.

An equal amount of roughly chopped toasted green pumpkin seeds (pepitas) can be used in place of the pecans.

- Preheat oven to 450°F (230°C)
- Large rimmed baking sheet, lined with foil and sprayed with nonstick cooking spray

4 cups	cubed peeled butternut squash (1-inch/2.5 cm cubes)	1 L
2 tsp	dried thyme	10 mL
2 tbsp	olive oil	30 mL
	Fine sea salt and freshly cracked black pepper	
3 cups	hot cooked tricolor quinoa (see page 15)	750 mL
1 cup	chopped toasted pecans (see page 26)	250 mL
1/4 cup	minced fresh chives	60 mL
1 tbsp	cider vinegar	15 mL

1. In a large bowl, combine squash, thyme and oil. Spread in a single layer on prepared baking sheet and season with salt and pepper. Roast in preheated oven for 18 to 23 minutes, stirring once or twice, until squash is golden brown and tender.

2. In a large bowl, combine roasted squash, quinoa, pecans, chives and vinegar, tossing to combine. Season to taste with salt and pepper.

Sorghum with Broccoli Rabe and Sun-Dried Tomatoes

Packed with flavor, rich with chewy sorghum grains and kicked up with hot pepper flakes, the satisfaction value of this impressive dish belies its short list of ingredients.

Tips

An equal amount of brown rice (long-, medium- or short-grain) may be used in place of the sorghum.

Make sure to use fine sea salt in the water you use to cook the sorghum and broccoli rabe. Conventional table salt contains chemicals and additives, whereas sea salt contains an abundance of naturally occurring trace minerals.

1 cup	sorghum	250 mL
1 lb	broccoli rabe, trimmed and roughly chopped	500 g
½ cup	drained oil-packed sun-dried tomatoes, chopped	125 mL
¼ tsp	hot pepper flakes	1 mL
2 tsp	finely grated lemon zest	10 mL
2 tbsp	freshly squeezed lemon juice	30 mL
½ cup	chopped toasted walnuts (see page 26)	125 mL
½ cup	freshly grated Parmesan cheese	125 mL

1. In a medium pot of boiling salted water (see tip, at left), cook sorghum for 50 to 60 minutes or until tender. Add broccoli rabe and cook, stirring occasionally, for 3 to 4 minutes or until tender-crisp. Drain, reserving ¼ cup (60 mL) cooking water, and return sorghum and broccoli rabe to pot.

2. To the sorghum mixture, add tomatoes, hot pepper flakes, lemon zest and lemon juice, gently tossing to combine. If necessary, stir in enough of the reserved water to moisten. Serve sprinkled with walnuts and cheese.

Teff Polenta

Tiny teff grains make an incredibly creamy polenta that is hearty without being heavy. Here is a basic template that you can vary in countless ways and serve as a side with an endless variety of dishes.

Tips

If you do not have broth on hand, use an equal amount of water plus $\frac{1}{2}$ tsp (2 mL) fine sea salt in its place.

To make the polenta dairy-free, either omit the Parmesan cheese or replace it with $\frac{1}{4}$ cup (60 mL) nutritional yeast flakes, and use an equal amount of olive oil in place of the butter.

4 cups	ready-to-use GF chicken or vegetable broth	1 L
1 cup	teff	250 mL
$\frac{1}{3}$ cup	freshly grated Parmesan cheese	75 mL
1 tbsp	unsalted butter	15 mL
	Fine sea salt and freshly ground black pepper	

1. In a medium saucepan, bring broth to a boil over medium-high heat. Slowly whisk in teff. Reduce heat to low, cover and simmer, whisking occasionally, for 15 to 20 minutes or until liquid is absorbed and teff is thickened and creamy. Remove from heat and whisk in cheese and butter. Season to taste with salt and pepper.

Variations

Pan-Fried Teff Polenta Squares: Prepare teff polenta and immediately spread into an oiled 8- or 9-inch (20 or 23 cm) square baking pan. Let cool to room temperature. Loosely cover and refrigerate for at least 2 hours, until firm, or for up to 1 day. When ready to serve, invert onto a cutting board and cut into 9 squares. In a large skillet, heat 1 tbsp (15 mL) olive oil over medium-high heat. Add 4 or 5 squares and cook, turning once, for 3 to 4 minutes per side or until darker brown. Repeat with an equal amount of olive oil and the remaining squares. Serve with your favorite sauce or a side dish.

Teff Polenta "Fries": Prepare teff polenta and immediately spread into an oiled 8- or 9-inch (20 or 23 cm) square baking pan. Let cool to room temperature. Loosely cover and refrigerate for at least 2 hours, until firm, or for up to 1 day. When ready to serve, invert onto a cutting board and cut into sixteen 4- by 1-inch (10 by 2.5 cm) sticks. Position broiler rack 4 inches (10 cm) from the heat source and preheat broiler. Line a baking sheet with foil and brush liberally with olive oil. Space polenta sticks evenly on sheet and brush with olive oil. Broil for 15 to 20 minutes, turning once, until deep brown. Serve immediately.

Broccoli, Cauliflower and Cheddar Gratin

With a teff and golden cheese topping that yields to a cozy combination of cauliflower and broccoli, this gratin is a sensational side dish.

Tip
Make sure to use fine sea salt in the water you use to cook the broccoli and cauliflower. Conventional table salt contains chemicals and additives, whereas sea salt contains an abundance of naturally occurring trace minerals.

- Preheat oven to 400°F (200°C)
- 12-cup (3 L) baking dish, sprayed with nonstick cooking spray

4 cups	broccoli florets	1 L
4 cups	cauliflower florets	1 L
3 tbsp	olive oil, divided	45 mL
2	cloves garlic, minced	2
1/4 tsp	hot pepper flakes	1 mL
2 cups	shredded sharp (old) Cheddar cheese	500 mL
1 1/4 cups	dry-cooked teff (see page 18)	300 mL
	Fine sea salt and freshly ground black pepper	

1. In a large pot of boiling salted water (see tip, at left), cook broccoli and cauliflower for 3 minutes. Drain.

2. In a large skillet, heat 2 tbsp (30 mL) oil over medium heat. Add garlic and hot pepper flakes; cook, stirring, for 1 minute. Remove from heat and add broccoli and cauliflower, tossing to coat. Stir in half the cheese. Transfer to prepared baking dish and sprinkle with the remaining cheese.

3. In a small bowl, toss teff with the remaining oil. Season to taste with salt and pepper. Sprinkle teff over cheese.

4. Bake in preheated oven for 10 to 13 minutes or until cheese is bubbling. Serve hot.

Gruyère, Grains and Zucchini Gratin

Makes 6 servings

Nutty Gruyère, garden zucchini and a generous helping of ancient grains are delectable bedfellows in this easily assembled gratin.

Tips

Other summer squash, such as crookneck or pattypan, may be used in place of the zucchini. You'll need about 3 cups (750 mL) shredded.

Information on cooking the whole grains named in this recipe can be found on pages 8–15.

Feel free to use a combination of cooled cooked grains to equal the 3 cups (750 mL) needed for this recipe.

- Preheat oven to 375°F (190°C)
- 8-cup (2 L) baking dish, sprayed with nonstick cooking spray

2 tbsp	unsalted butter	30 mL
1½ cups	chopped onions	375 mL
4	cloves garlic, minced	4
3	medium-large zucchini, shredded (about 3 cups/750 mL)	3
½ tsp	ground nutmeg	2 mL
	Fine sea salt and freshly cracked black pepper	
4	large eggs	4
3 cups	cooked amaranth, millet or quinoa, cooled	750 mL
1 cup	shredded Gruyère or Swiss cheese	250 mL
½ cup	freshly grated Parmesan cheese	125 mL

1. In a large skillet, melt butter over medium-high heat. Add onions and cook, stirring, for 5 to 6 minutes or until softened. Add garlic, zucchini and nutmeg; cook, stirring, for 1 to 2 minutes or until zucchini is slightly softened. Let cool slightly. Season to taste with salt and pepper.

2. In a large bowl, whisk eggs. Stir in zucchini mixture, amaranth and Gruyère. Spread evenly in prepared baking dish. Sprinkle with Parmesan.

3. Bake in preheated oven for 25 to 30 minutes or until browned on top and just set. Let cool on a wire rack for at least 10 minutes before cutting. Serve warm or let cool completely.

Ancient Grains, Brussels Sprouts and Pecan Dressing

Makes 8 servings

This streamlined dressing covers all the Thanksgiving bases, from the sage to the pecans to the cranberries. You can stick with one variety of ancient grains, or use a combination to heighten the beauty, flavor and texture of the dish.

Tips

Information on cooking the whole grains named in this recipe can be found on pages 8–17.

The dressing can be prepared through step 2 up to 1 day ahead. Cover and refrigerate. Warm, covered, in a 350°F (180°C) oven for 20 minutes before adding the pecans and parsley.

To use as a stuffing in meat or poultry, let cool completely before using.

2 tbsp	olive oil	30 mL
1½ cups	chopped onions	375 mL
12 oz	Brussels sprouts, trimmed (see tip, page 142) and chopped	375 g
4 cups	cooked quinoa, amaranth, millet or sorghum	1 L
1 cup	dried cranberries, coarsely chopped	250 mL
2 tsp	dried rubbed sage	10 mL
½ cup	ready-to-use GF chicken or vegetable broth	125 mL
	Fine sea salt and freshly cracked black pepper	
1 cup	chopped toasted pecans (see page 26)	250 mL
1 cup	packed fresh flat-leaf (Italian) parsley leaves, chopped	250 mL

1. In a large nonstick skillet, heat oil over medium-high heat. Add onions and Brussels sprouts; cook, stirring, for 8 to 10 minutes or until softened.

2. Stir in quinoa, cranberries, sage and broth; cook, stirring, for 3 minutes. Remove from heat, cover and let stand for about 5 minutes or until broth is absorbed. Season to taste with salt and pepper.

3. Stir in pecans and parsley.

Fennel, Italian Sausage and Sorghum Dressing

This is a swoon-worthy dressing that will have your Thanksgiving guests reaching for seconds — or thirds. A large part of the appeal is the simplicity of the flavors, a pleasing contrast to the more complex flavors on the table. Best yet? It is a breeze to prepare.

Tips

Cooked millet or quinoa, cooled, can be used in place of the sorghum. Information on cooking these grains can be found on pages 11–15.

The dressing can be prepared through step 2 up to 1 day ahead. Cover and refrigerate. Warm, covered, in a 350°F (180°C) oven for 20 minutes before adding the chopped fennel fronds and walnuts.

To use as a stuffing in meat or poultry, let cool completely before using.

1 lb	GF sweet Italian sausage (bulk or casings removed)	500 g
2½ cups	chopped fennel bulb (about 2 medium bulbs), fronds reserved	625 mL
2 cups	chopped onions	500 mL
2 tsp	fennel seeds	10 mL
4 cups	cooked sorghum (see page 17)	1 L
¾ cup	dried tart cherries or cranberries, chopped	175 mL
¼ cup	Marsala or cooking sherry	60 mL
	Fine sea salt and freshly cracked black pepper	
¾ cup	chopped toasted walnuts (see page 26)	175 mL

1. In a large nonstick skillet, cook sausage over medium-high heat, breaking it up with a spoon, for 10 to 12 minutes or until no longer pink. Using a slotted spoon, transfer sausage to a plate lined with paper towels.

2. To the fat in the skillet, add chopped fennel and onions; cook, stirring, for 10 to 12 minutes or until golden and softened. Add fennel seeds and cook, stirring, for 1 minute.

3. Return sausage to the pan, along with sorghum, cherries and Marsala. Cook, stirring, for 3 to 4 minutes or until heated through and liquid has evaporated. Season to taste with salt and pepper.

4. Chop the reserved fennel fronds. Add fennel fronds and walnuts to the dressing, stirring to combine. Transfer dressing to a serving bowl or dish. Serve warm.

Meatless Main Dishes

continued...

Lemony Lentil, Quinoa and Zucchini Skillet

Summery and satisfying, this lentil and quinoa dish shines green. The zucchini is shredded and added at the end, simply to warm it through, so that it retains its delicate, fresh flavor.

Tip

Hot cooked amaranth, millet, brown rice or sorghum can be used in place of the quinoa. Information on cooking these grains can be found on pages 8–17.

1 cup	dried brown lentils, rinsed	250 mL
2 cups	water	500 mL
2 tbsp	olive oil	30 mL
3	cloves garlic, minced	3
3 cups	hot cooked quinoa (see page 15)	750 mL
3	zucchini, shredded	3
1 cup	packed fresh parsley leaves, chopped	250 mL
1/2 cup	packed fresh mint leaves, chopped	125 mL
2 tsp	finely grated lemon zest	10 mL
2 tbsp	freshly squeezed lemon juice	30 mL
	Fine sea salt and freshly cracked black pepper	
1 cup	crumbled feta cheese	250 mL

1. In a large saucepan, combine lentils and water. Bring to a boil over medium-high heat. Reduce heat and simmer, stirring occasionally, for 40 to 45 minutes or until very tender. Drain off any excess liquid.

2. In a large skillet, heat oil over medium-high heat. Add garlic and cook, stirring, for 30 to 60 seconds or until golden brown. Stir in lentils and quinoa; cook, stirring, for 2 to 3 minutes to blend the flavors. Add zucchini and cook, stirring, for 1 minute.

3. Remove from heat and stir in parsley, mint, lemon zest and lemon juice. Season to taste with salt and pepper. Serve sprinkled with cheese.

Persian-Spiced Lentils and Millet

This gorgeous, fragrant supper is based on *adas polou*, a Persian dish comprising rice, lentils and a bevy of spices. Here, millet stands in for the rice, for a more delicate variation.

Tips

Hot cooked amaranth, quinoa or sorghum can be used in place of the millet. Information on cooking these grains can be found on pages 8–17.

You can quickly toast sliced almonds on the stovetop. Spread them in a dry medium skillet set over medium heat. Stir until the almonds are golden brown and fragrant. Immediately transfer to a plate to cool.

2 tsp	olive oil	10 mL
3	cloves garlic, minced	3
3 cups	chopped onions	750 mL
1 tsp	ground cumin	5 mL
1 tsp	ground cinnamon	5 mL
1/2 tsp	ground coriander	2 mL
1/4 tsp	ground cardamom	1 mL
3/4 cup	chopped pitted dates	175 mL
2 tsp	finely grated lime zest	10 mL
1 cup	dried yellow or red lentils, rinsed	250 mL
3 cups	water	750 mL
3 cups	hot cooked millet (see page 11)	750 mL
2 tbsp	freshly squeezed lime juice	30 mL
	Fine sea salt and freshly cracked black pepper	
1/2 cup	sliced almonds, toasted (see tip, at left)	125 mL

1. In a large skillet, heat oil over medium-high heat. Add garlic, onions, cumin, cinnamon, coriander and cardamom; reduce heat to medium-low, cover and cook, stirring occasionally, for 20 to 25 minutes or until onions are very tender and golden. Remove from heat and stir in dates and lime zest.

2. Meanwhile, in a medium saucepan, combine lentils and water. Bring to a boil over medium-high heat. Reduce heat and simmer for about 22 minutes or until lentils are very tender but not mushy. Drain and add to onion mixture.

3. Add millet and lime juice to lentil mixture, tossing to combine. Season to taste with salt and pepper. Serve sprinkled with almonds.

Lowcountry Okra, Tomatoes and Black-Eyed Peas with Creamy Millet

Makes 6 servings

Crisp okra and hearty black-eyed peas are staple ingredients in the coastal Carolina regions of the United States (part of the "Lowcountry"). Creamy millet stands in, with delicious success, for the more usual corn grits.

Tip

White beans, such as cannellini, Great Northern or white navy, can be used in place of the black-eyed peas.

4 tsp	olive oil, divided	20 mL
1 lb	fresh or thawed frozen okra, trimmed and cut into 1/2-inch (1 cm) slices	500 g
1/2 tsp	fine sea salt, divided	2 mL
1	large red bell pepper, finely chopped	1
1 1/4 cups	chopped onions	300 mL
3	cloves garlic, minced	3
2	bay leaves	2
1/4 tsp	cayenne pepper	1 mL
1 cup	packed fresh flat-leaf (Italian) parsley leaves, chopped, divided	250 mL
1	can (14 to 15 oz/398 to 425 mL) diced tomatoes, with juice	1
1	can (14 to 19 oz/398 to 540 mL) black-eyed peas, drained and rinsed	1
1/2 cup	ready-to-use GF vegetable broth or water	125 mL
4 cups	hot creamy millet (see page 12)	1 L

1. In a large saucepan, heat half the oil over medium-high heat. Add okra and half the salt; cook, stirring, for 12 to 15 minutes or until okra is browned. Transfer okra to a plate.

2. In the same pan, heat the remaining oil over medium-high heat. Add red pepper and onions; cook, stirring, for 6 to 8 minutes or until softened. Add garlic, bay leaves, cayenne and the remaining salt; cook, stirring, for 30 seconds.

3. Stir in half the parsley, tomatoes, black-eyed peas and broth; bring to a boil. Reduce heat to medium-low, cover, leaving lid ajar, and simmer, stirring once or twice, for 10 minutes. Return okra to the pan and simmer for 3 minutes to heat through and blend the flavors. Discard bay leaves.

4. Serve over millet, sprinkled with the remaining parsley.

Sorghum with Zucchini Chickpea Ragù

Fragrant with smoky paprika and sweet cinnamon, this otherwise humble assemblage of ingredients — zucchini, tomatoes and chickpeas — becomes an exotic ragù, made all the better by a bed of plump sorghum grains.

Tip

Other varieties of summer squash, such as crookneck or pattypan, can be used in place of the zucchini.

Variation

Sorghum with Zucchini, Basil and White Bean Ragù: Omit the paprika and cinnamon and add 3 cloves garlic, minced, with the zucchini. Replace the chickpeas with white beans (such as Great Northern or cannellini), and replace the cilantro with 1 cup (250 mL) packed fresh basil leaves, chopped. Garnish with ½ cup (125 mL) freshly grated Parmesan cheese in place of the yogurt.

1 tbsp	olive oil	15 mL
1 cup	chopped onions	250 mL
3	zucchini, diced	3
1½ tsp	hot smoked paprika	7 mL
¾ tsp	ground cinnamon	3 mL
1	can (14 to 15 oz/398 to 425 mL) diced tomatoes, with juice	1
1	can (14 to 19 oz/398 to 540 mL) chickpeas, drained and rinsed	1
¾ cup	ready-to-use GF vegetable broth	175 mL
¼ cup	packed fresh cilantro leaves, chopped	60 mL
2 tbsp	freshly squeezed lemon juice	30 mL
	Fine sea salt and freshly cracked black pepper	
3 cups	hot cooked sorghum (see page 17)	750 mL
½ cup	plain yogurt	125 mL

1. In a large saucepan, heat oil over medium-high heat. Add onions and cook, stirring, for 5 minutes or until starting to soften. Add zucchini, paprika and cinnamon; cook, stirring, for 2 to 4 minutes or until softened.

2. Stir in tomatoes, chickpeas and broth; bring to a boil. Reduce heat, cover and simmer, stirring occasionally, for 10 minutes. Stir in cilantro and lemon juice; simmer, uncovered, stirring occasionally, for 5 minutes to heat through and blend the flavors. Season to taste with salt and pepper.

3. Serve ragù over sorghum, with dollops of yogurt.

Sorghum with Fire-Roasted Tomatoes and Crispy Chickpeas

Chickpeas add meatiness to a speedy tomato topping for sorghum grains. Fresh lemon and smoky paprika round out the flavors.

Tips

If you can't find fire-roasted tomatoes, use regular diced tomatoes instead.

An equal amount of fresh flat-leaf (Italian) parsley can be used in place of the cilantro.

1 tbsp	olive oil	15 mL
1	can (14 to 19 oz/398 to 540 mL) chickpeas, drained and rinsed	1
1 tsp	hot or sweet smoked paprika	5 mL
3 cups	hot cooked sorghum (see page 17)	750 mL
1	can (14 to 15 oz/398 to 425 mL) diced fire-roasted tomatoes, with juice	1
½ cup	packed fresh cilantro leaves, chopped	125 mL
1 tsp	finely grated lemon zest	5 mL
1 tbsp	freshly squeezed lemon juice	15 mL
¾ cup	crumbled feta cheese	175 mL

1. In a large skillet, heat oil over medium-high heat. Add chickpeas and paprika; cook, stirring, for 5 minutes or until chickpeas are crispy.

2. Stir in sorghum and tomatoes; cook, tossing to coat, for 1 minute. Gently stir in cilantro, lemon zest and lemon juice. Serve sprinkled with cheese.

Greek Quinoa Skillet

Here's a mélange of oh-so-satisfying textures and flavors.

Tips

One 14- to 15-oz (398 to 425 mL) can of diced tomatoes, with juice, can be used in place of the cherry tomatoes. Bring to a boil in the skillet before adding the garlic and chickpeas.

If you don't have fresh dill on hand, you can add 1 tbsp (15 mL) dried dillweed with the garlic in step 1.

1½ tbsp	olive oil	22 mL
2½ cups	cherry or grape tomatoes	625 mL
2	cloves garlic, minced	2
1	can (14 to 19 oz/398 to 540 mL) chickpeas, drained and rinsed	1
3 cups	hot cooked quinoa (see page 15)	750 mL
1 cup	packed fresh flat-leaf (Italian) parsley leaves, chopped	250 mL
½ cup	thinly sliced green onions	125 mL
¼ cup	chopped fresh dill	60 mL
½ cup	crumbled feta cheese	125 mL

1. In a large skillet, heat oil over medium-high heat. Add tomatoes and cook, stirring, for 5 minutes or until slightly browned and beginning to burst. Add garlic and chickpeas; cook, stirring, for 4 to 5 minutes or until chickpeas are warmed through.

2. Stir in quinoa, parsley, green onions and dill, tossing to combine. Serve sprinkled with cheese.

Chili Pot Pie
with Millet Polenta Topping

This hearty pie is everything you need to be cozy and satisfied on a cold winter evening. Beans and fire-roasted tomatoes bake underneath an easy, cheesy-creamy millet topping to create a scrumptious entrée that can be served warm or at room temperature.

Tip

If you can only find larger 19-oz (540 mL) cans of beans, you will need about 2¼ cans (4½ cups/1.125 L drained).

- Preheat oven to 400°F (200°C)
- 12-cup (3 L) baking dish, greased

Millet Polenta Topping

1 cup	millet	250 mL
4 cups	ready-to-use GF vegetable broth	1 L
1 cup	freshly grated Romano or Parmesan cheese, divided	250 mL
	Fine sea salt and freshly ground black pepper	
1 cup	shredded sharp (old) Cheddar cheese	250 mL

Chili Pot Pie

2 tbsp	olive oil	30 mL
1	large green bell pepper, chopped	1
1½ cups	chopped onions	375 mL
3	cloves garlic, chopped	3
3 tbsp	chili powder	45 mL
2 tbsp	ground cumin	30 mL
2 tbsp	unsweetened natural cocoa powder	30 mL
3	cans (each 14 to 15 oz/398 to 425 mL) red kidney beans, drained and rinsed	3
2	cans (each 14 to 15 oz/398 to 425 mL) diced fire-roasted tomatoes, with juice	2
	Fine sea salt and freshly ground black pepper	

1. *Topping:* In a medium saucepan, combine millet and broth. Bring to a boil over medium-high heat. Reduce heat to low, cover and simmer, stirring every 5 to 6 minutes to prevent sticking, for 25 to 30 minutes or until mixture appears very creamy.

Tips

Black beans or pinto beans can be used in place of the kidney beans.

If fire-roasted tomatoes are unavailable, use regular diced tomatoes.

2. *Pot Pie:* Meanwhile, in a large saucepan, heat oil over medium-high heat. Add green pepper and onions; cook, stirring, for 6 to 7 minutes or until onions are starting to soften. Add garlic, chili powder, cumin and cocoa powder; cook, stirring, for 30 seconds. Stir in beans and tomatoes; bring to a boil. Reduce heat to low, cover and simmer, stirring occasionally, for 15 minutes. Season to taste with salt and pepper. Spoon into prepared baking dish.

3. Remove topping from heat and stir in half the Romano cheese. Season to taste with salt and pepper. Spread over bean mixture and sprinkle with Cheddar and the remaining Romano cheese.

4. Bake in preheated oven for 20 to 25 minutes or until heated through and cheese is melted and golden brown. Let stand for 5 minutes before serving.

Moroccan Chickpea and Basmati Skillet

Rich in texture and full of healthy goodness, this North African–inspired dish is proof that a well-stocked pantry is all it takes to make an amazing dinner.

Tip

White beans (such as cannellini or Great Northern) or butter beans can be used in place of the chickpeas.

2 tbsp	olive oil	30 mL
1	red bell pepper, chopped	1
1¼ cups	brown basmati rice	300 mL
2 tsp	ground cumin	10 mL
1 tsp	ground cinnamon	5 mL
½ tsp	fine sea salt	2 mL
¼ tsp	cayenne pepper	1 mL
3⅓ cups	water	825 mL
1	can (14 to 19 oz/398 to 540 mL) chickpeas, drained and rinsed	1
¼ cup	chopped pitted brine-cured black olives (such as kalamata)	60 mL
2 tbsp	dried currants	30 mL
½ cup	packed fresh mint leaves, chopped	125 mL
1 tbsp	freshly squeezed lemon juice	15 mL

1. In a large skillet, heat oil over medium-high heat. Add red pepper and cook, stirring, for 2 to 3 minutes or until slightly softened. Add rice, cumin, cinnamon, salt and cayenne; cook, stirring, for 1 minute or until fragrant.

2. Stir in water and bring to a boil. Reduce heat to low, cover and cook for 45 to 55 minutes or until rice is tender and water is absorbed.

3. Remove from heat and add chickpeas, olives and currants (do not stir). Let stand, covered, for 5 minutes. Fluff rice with a fork, stirring in mint and lemon juice.

Central American Black Beans and Amaranth

Black beans, amaranth and cumin make the perfect trio for a quick dinner dish: delicious, easy and healthy. Gussy it up with assorted accompaniments to your heart's and palate's content.

Tip

An equal amount of quinoa, rinsed, can be used in place of the amaranth.

1 tbsp	olive oil	15 mL
1	red bell pepper, chopped	1
1½ cups	chopped onions	375 mL
1 cup	amaranth	250 mL
2 tsp	ground cumin	10 mL
1 tsp	chipotle chile powder	5 mL
2 cups	ready-to-use GF vegetable broth	500 mL
1	can (14 to 19 oz/398 to 540 mL) black beans, drained and rinsed	1

Suggested Accompaniments

Millet, Sorghum and Chia Tortillas (page 260)
Tomato or tomatillo salsa
Fresh cilantro leaves
Chopped radishes
Plain Greek yogurt
Crumbled queso fresco or feta cheese

1. In a medium saucepan, heat oil over medium-high heat. Add red pepper and onions; cook, stirring, for 5 to 6 minutes or until slightly softened.

2. Stir in amaranth, cumin, chile powder and broth; bring to a boil. Reduce heat to medium-low, cover and simmer for 12 to 15 minutes or until amaranth is barely tender.

3. Remove from heat and stir in beans; let stand for 5 minutes, then fluff with fork. Serve with any of the suggested accompaniments, as desired.

Ancient Grain, Avocado and Mango Tacos

Simple and fast, these ancient grain tacos are great for busy weeknights. Fresh avocado, mango and lime make them taste like a tropical luxury.

Tips

Information on cooking the whole grains named in this recipe can be found on pages 8–15.

If you can only find a larger 19-oz (540 mL) can of beans, you will need about ¾ can (1½ cups/375 mL drained).

Store-bought 6-inch (15 cm) GF tortillas can be used in place of the Quinoa or Oat Tortillas.

1 tbsp	olive oil	15 mL
2	cloves garlic, minced	2
1 tbsp	minced seeded jalapeño pepper	15 mL
1 cup	hot cooked amaranth, quinoa, buckwheat or millet	250 mL
1	can (14 to 15 oz/398 to 425 mL) white beans (such as cannellini or Great Northern), drained and rinsed	1
1 tsp	finely grated lime zest	5 mL
1 tbsp	freshly squeezed lime juice	15 mL
8	Quinoa Tortillas (page 258) or Oat Tortillas (page 259)	8
2	small firm-ripe Hass avocados, sliced	2
1 cup	chopped fresh or thawed frozen mango	250 mL
½ cup	packed fresh cilantro leaves	125 mL
	Lime wedges	

1. In a large skillet, heat oil over medium-high heat. Add garlic and jalapeño; cook, stirring, for 30 seconds or until fragrant. Add amaranth and beans; reduce heat to medium and cook, stirring, for 3 to 4 minutes or until heated through. Remove from heat and stir in lime zest and lime juice.

2. Fill tortillas with amaranth mixture, avocados, mango and cilantro. Serve with lime wedges.

Smoky Chipotle Quinoa Burgers

Carnivores and vegetarians will be equally delighted with these "meaty" quinoa burgers. They get their smokiness from chipotle chile powder and smoked Gouda, but you could increase it with some barbecue sauce spread on the buns.

Tip

Cooked amaranth or sorghum, cooled, can be used in place of the quinoa. Information on cooking these grains can be found on pages 8–17.

- Food processor

½ cup	lightly salted roasted sunflower seeds	125 mL
2 cups	cooked red or white quinoa (see page 15), cooled	500 mL
1 cup	shredded smoked Gouda or smoked Cheddar cheese	250 mL
1 cup	rinsed drained canned red kidney beans	250 mL
1½ tsp	chipotle chile powder	7 mL
¼ tsp	fine sea salt	1 mL
1	large egg, lightly beaten	1
2 tsp	olive oil	10 mL
4	GF hamburger buns, split and toasted	4
4	large tomato slices	4
2 cups	packed baby spinach or arugula	500 mL

1. In food processor, process sunflower seeds until finely chopped. Add quinoa, cheese, beans, chipotle chile powder, salt and egg; pulse until blended but still chunky. Form into four ¾-inch (2 cm) thick patties.

2. In a large skillet, heat oil over medium heat. Add patties and cook for 4 minutes. Turn patties over and cook for 3 to 5 minutes or until crispy on the outside and hot in the center.

3. Transfer patties to bottom halves of toasted buns and top with tomato, spinach and top halves of buns.

Asian-Style Amaranth Burgers

Pungent aromatics —
fresh ginger, garlic,
sesame oil and hot
sauce — give this easily
assembled burger a major
punch of flavor. A quick
and crunchy slaw adds
bright, crisp contrast.

Tips

If you can only find larger
19-oz (540 mL) cans of
beans, you will need about
1½ cans (3 cups/750 mL
drained).

For vegan burgers, use
3 tbsp (45 mL) vegan
mayonnaise alternative in
place of the egg.

- Food processor

Coleslaw

1 tsp	packed light brown sugar	5 mL
1 tbsp	GF soy sauce	15 mL
2 tsp	unseasoned rice vinegar or cider vinegar	10 mL
1 tsp	Asian chili sauce (such as Sriracha)	5 mL
1 tsp	toasted sesame oil	5 mL
2 cups	shredded coleslaw mix (with cabbage and carrots)	500 mL
½ cup	chopped green onions	125 mL

Burgers

1 cup	cooked amaranth (see page 8), cooled	250 mL
3	cloves garlic, minced	3
1 tbsp	minced fresh gingerroot	15 mL
2	cans (each 14 to 15 oz/398 to 425 mL) white beans (such as cannellini or Great Northern), drained and rinsed, divided	2
1	large egg	1
1 tbsp	Asian chili sauce (such as Sriracha)	15 mL
2 tsp	toasted sesame oil	10 mL
1 tbsp	olive oil	15 mL
4	GF hamburger buns, split and toasted	4

1. *Coleslaw:* In a medium bowl, whisk together brown sugar, soy sauce, vinegar, chili sauce and sesame oil. Add coleslaw mix and green onions, tossing to coat. Set aside.

2. *Burgers:* In food processor, combine amaranth, garlic, ginger, half the beans, egg, chili sauce and sesame oil; pulse until a chunky purée forms.

3. Transfer purée to another medium bowl and stir in the remaining beans. Form into four ¾-inch (2 cm) thick patties.

4. In a large skillet, heat olive oil over medium heat. Add patties and cook for 4 minutes. Turn patties over and cook for 3 to 4 minutes or until crispy on the outside and hot in the center.

5. Transfer patties to bottom halves of toasted buns. Top with coleslaw and top halves of buns.

Crispy Amaranth Cakes with
Mint Raita (page 207)

Quinoa Risotto with
Bacon and Peas (page 211)

Five-Spice Salmon with
Chia-Sesame Sprinkle (page 229)

Hoisin Chicken and Chard
with Chili Garlic Quinoa (page 239)

Cumin Pork and Millet Bowls
with Avocado and Mango (page 246)

Sesame Ginger Pork with Millet Slaw (page 247)

Thai Grilled Steak and Quinoa Bowls (page 248)

Multi-Seed Bread (page 257)

Amaranth and Tofu Stir-Fry

....

Background notes of coconut and ginger enhance delicate amaranth grains and fresh vegetables, making this simple dish taste deep and complex.

Tips

It is important that the amaranth be chilled (not simply cooled) so that the grains do not clump together.

Cooked millet, quinoa, brown rice or sorghum, chilled, can be used in place of the amaranth. Information on cooking these grains can be found on pages 11–17.

2 tbsp	warmed virgin coconut oil, divided	30 mL
8 oz	extra-firm tofu, drained, cut into 1-inch (2.5 cm) cubes and patted dry	250 g
3	cloves garlic, minced	3
1	red bell pepper, cut into strips	1
8 oz	sliced mushrooms	250 g
1 tbsp	minced gingerroot	15 mL
3 cups	cooked amaranth (see page 8), chilled	750 mL
1 cup	sliced green onions	250 mL
2 tsp	fine crystal cane sugar	10 mL
3 tbsp	GF soy sauce	45 mL
1 tbsp	unseasoned rice vinegar or cider vinegar	15 mL
1 tbsp	toasted sesame seeds (optional)	15 mL

1. In a large skillet, melt half the coconut oil over low heat. Add tofu and increase heat to medium-high; cook, stirring, for 3 to 4 minutes or until golden. Using a slotted spoon, transfer tofu to a plate.

2. In the same skillet, melt the remaining coconut oil over low heat. Add garlic, red pepper, mushrooms and ginger; increase heat to medium-high and cook, stirring, for 4 minutes or until vegetables are tender.

3. Return tofu to the pan and add amaranth, green onions, sugar, soy sauce and vinegar; cook, stirring, for 2 to 3 minutes or until well coated and warmed through. Serve sprinkled with sesame seeds, if desired.

Stir-Fried Buckwheat and Bok Choy

Makes 4 servings

The secret to this dish is coating and cooking the buckwheat in egg. It's an old-fashioned method, used to keep the grains separate, that works perfectly in this newfangled stir-fry.

Tip

If you do not have hoisin sauce on hand, combine the following ingredients to create a substitute: 2 tsp (10 mL) packed dark brown sugar, 1/4 tsp (1 mL) Chinese five-spice powder or ground ginger, 2 tbsp (30 mL) GF barbecue sauce, 1 tbsp (15 mL) GF soy sauce and 1 tsp (5 mL) toasted sesame oil. You will end up with about 1/4 cup (60 mL) sauce.

• Large rimmed baking sheet

1	large egg	1
1 cup	buckwheat groats	250 mL
2 cups	water	500 mL
1 tbsp	toasted sesame oil	15 mL
4	cloves garlic, thinly sliced	4
1 tbsp	minced gingerroot	15 mL
1 lb	bok choy, trimmed and cut crosswise into 1/2-inch (1 cm) slices	500 g
1/4 cup	ready-to-use GF vegetable broth	60 mL
1/4 cup	hoisin sauce	60 mL
2 tsp	Asian chili sauce (such as Sriracha)	10 mL

1. In a large bowl, whisk egg. Add buckwheat, stirring to coat.

2. In a large nonstick skillet, cook buckwheat mixture over medium heat for 2 to 3 minutes, stirring to separate the grains, until the egg coating appears completely dry and the grains are separated. Add water, increase heat to high and bring to a boil. Reduce heat to low, cover and simmer for 13 to 15 minutes or until liquid is absorbed.

3. Immediately spread buckwheat on baking sheet, separating the grains. Let cool completely, about 15 minutes. Wipe out the skillet.

4. In the skillet, heat oil over medium-high heat. Add garlic and ginger; cook, stirring, for 30 seconds. Stir in bok choy and broth; cover and cook for 1 to 2 minutes or until bok choy is wilted. Add buckwheat, hoisin sauce and chili sauce; cook, stirring, for 1 minute.

Thai Stir-Fried Oats

Makes 4 servings

I originally created this as an entry into Bob's Red Mill's Spar for the Spurtle contest back in 2012. My sister was visiting while I was working on the recipe, and I knew I had a great dish when I saw her take her first bite. Soaking the oats overnight yields plump, tender grains that are perfect for a quick stir-fry. The result is exponentially more delicious than fried rice — and simpler and more nutritious, too!

Tips

Lightly salted roasted cashews can be used in place of the peanuts.

You can replace the oats with 2½ cups (625 mL) cooked amaranth, millet or quinoa, cooled. Information on cooking these grains can be found on pages 8–15.

1½ cups	certified GF steel-cut oats Cold water	375 mL
2 tbsp	warmed virgin coconut oil	30 mL
3	green onions, thinly sliced, green and white parts separated	3
1	red bell pepper, chopped	1
8 oz	button or cremini mushrooms, sliced	250 g
2 tsp	packed light brown sugar	10 mL
3 tbsp	GF soy sauce	45 mL
1½ tbsp	Thai green curry paste	22 mL
2	large eggs, beaten	2
1 cup	diced fresh pineapple	250 mL
½ cup	lightly salted roasted peanuts, coarsely chopped	125 mL
¼ cup	unsweetened flaked coconut	60 mL
½ cup	packed fresh basil or mint leaves, chopped	125 mL
2 tsp	finely grated lime zest	10 mL
1 tbsp	freshly squeezed lime juice	15 mL

1. Soak oats overnight in enough cold water to cover. Drain in a fine-mesh sieve, pressing out excess water. Set aside.

2. In a large nonstick skillet, melt coconut oil over medium-low heat. Add white part of green onions, red pepper and mushrooms; increase heat to medium-high and stir-fry for 1 minute. Add oats, sugar, soy sauce and curry paste; stir-fry for 3 minutes.

3. Push oat mixture to side of pan and add eggs to cleared space; cook, stirring, until eggs are just set, then mix in with oat mixture.

4. Add pineapple, peanuts and coconut; stir-fry for 30 seconds. Remove from heat and stir in green part of green onions, basil, lime zest and lime juice.

Edamame and Ginger Stir-Fried Quinoa

Ditch the delivery fried rice in favor of this DIY quinoa version that combines a bounty of vegetables with nutty sesame oil and peppery fresh ginger.

Tips

It is important that the quinoa be chilled (not simply cooled) so that the grains do not clump together.

Cooked amaranth, millet, brown rice or sorghum, chilled, can be used in place of the quinoa. Information on cooking these grains can be found on pages 8–17.

2 tbsp	toasted sesame oil, divided	30 mL
2	large eggs, beaten	2
4	cloves garlic, minced	4
1	red bell pepper, chopped	1
4 cups	broccoli florets	1 L
2 cups	sliced button or cremini mushrooms	500 mL
3 tbsp	minced gingerroot	45 mL
3 cups	cooked quinoa (see page 15), chilled	750 mL
2 cups	frozen shelled edamame, thawed	500 mL
¼ cup	GF soy sauce	60 mL
2	green onions, thinly sliced	2

1. In a large skillet, heat 1 tsp (5 mL) oil over medium-high heat. Add eggs and cook, stirring, for 30 seconds or until cooked through. Transfer eggs to a plate.

2. In the same skillet, heat 1 tbsp (15 mL) oil over medium-high heat. Add garlic, red pepper, broccoli, mushrooms and ginger; cook, stirring, for 4 to 5 minutes or until softened.

3. Push vegetables to side of pan and add the remaining oil to cleared space. Add quinoa and cook, stirring, for 1 to 2 minutes or until lightly browned. Add edamame and soy sauce; cook, stirring all ingredients together, for 1 minute. Stir in eggs and green onions.

Creamy Millet with Eggs, Green Onions and Dukkah

Makes 4 servings

Dukkah is a Middle Eastern spice blend made up of ground nuts, seeds and spices and used as a topping or general seasoning in a wealth of recipes. Here, it stars atop a creamy millet polenta with sautéed green onions and hard-cooked eggs.

Tip

To hard-cook eggs, place eggs in a saucepan large enough to hold them in a single layer. Add enough cold water to cover eggs by 1 inch (2.5 cm). Heat over high heat until water is just boiling. Remove from heat and cover pan. Let stand for about 12 minutes for large eggs (9 minutes for medium eggs; 15 minutes for extra-large eggs). Drain eggs and cool completely under cold running water or in a bowl of ice water. Refrigerate until ready to eat.

- Food processor
- Steamer basket

1/4 cup	toasted almonds (see page 26)	60 mL
2 tbsp	toasted sesame seeds (see page 27)	30 mL
1 tsp	ground coriander	5 mL
1/2 tsp	ground cumin	2 mL
	Fine sea salt	
1	large bunch green onions, trimmed	1
1 tbsp	olive oil	15 mL
1 tbsp	freshly squeezed lemon juice	15 mL
	Freshly ground black pepper	
3 cups	hot creamy millet (see page 12)	750 mL
3	hard-cooked large eggs (see tip, at left), peeled and chopped	3

1. In food processor, combine almonds, sesame seeds, coriander, cumin and $1/8$ tsp (0.5 mL) salt; process until finely chopped (be careful not to overprocess).

2. Cut green part of green onions into 1-inch (2.5 cm) lengths. Thinly slice white part of green onions. In a large skillet, heat oil over medium-high heat. Add green and white parts of green onions and cook, stirring, for 1 to 2 minutes or until wilted. Remove from heat and stir in lemon juice. Season to taste with salt and pepper.

3. Divide millet among four shallow bowls or dinner plates. Top with green onions and eggs. Sprinkle with almond mixture.

Ancient Grain Huevos Rancheros

Homemade huevos rancheros are well worth the effort, and making them is the perfect task to share with family and friends for a relaxed weekend breakfast or brunch.

Tips

If you can only find a larger 19-oz (540 mL) can of beans, you will need about ¾ can (1½ cups/375 mL drained).

Store-bought 6-inch (15 cm) GF tortillas can be used in place of the Oat or Quinoa Tortillas.

Cooked millet, quinoa, brown rice, sorghum or teff can be used in place of the amaranth. Information on cooking these grains can be found on pages 11–18.

- Preheat oven to 400°F (200°C)
- Large rimmed baking sheet

1	can (14 to 15 oz/398 to 425 mL) pinto beans, drained and rinsed	1
1 tsp	finely grated lime zest	5 mL
2 tbsp	freshly squeezed lime juice	30 mL
4	Oat Tortillas (page 259) or Quinoa Tortillas (page 258)	4
1 cup	cooked amaranth (see page 8)	250 mL
1½ cups	shredded Monterey Jack cheese	375 mL
1 cup	salsa	250 mL
2 tbsp	olive oil	30 mL
4	large eggs	4
	Fine sea salt and freshly ground black pepper	

Suggested Accompaniments

Hot pepper sauce
Diced avocado
Chopped fresh cilantro
Thinly sliced green onions
Plain Greek yogurt

1. In a small bowl, coarsely mash beans with a fork. Stir in lime zest and lime juice.

2. Place tortillas on baking sheet. Spread beans over tortillas, dividing evenly. Spread amaranth over beans. Top with cheese and salsa. Bake in preheated oven for 5 to 8 minutes or until cheese begins to melt.

3. Meanwhile, in a large nonstick skillet, heat oil over medium heat. Break eggs into skillet and season with salt and pepper. Cook for 5 to 7 minutes or until whites are just set and yolks are just beginning to set.

4. Remove tortillas from oven. Top each with 1 egg, being careful to not break yolks. Return to oven and bake for 3 to 5 minutes or until warmed through and yolks are set. Serve warm, with any of the suggested accompaniments, as desired.

French Chickpeas and Quinoa with Poached Eggs

This chickpea dish gets richness and verve from an easy tomato-tarragon sauce. Gently poached eggs add to the dish's succulence, while quinoa makes a perfect foundation for soaking up every drop of flavor.

Tip

Hot cooked amaranth or millet can be used in place of the quinoa. Information on cooking these grains can be found on pages 8–11.

2 cups	thick and chunky GF marinara sauce	500 mL
1 tsp	dried tarragon	5 mL
1	can (14 to 19 oz/398 to 540 mL) chickpeas, drained and rinsed	1
4	large eggs	4
	Freshly cracked black pepper	
½ cup	packed fresh flat-leaf (Italian) parsley leaves, chopped	125 mL
3 cups	hot cooked quinoa (see page 15)	750 mL
	Fine sea salt	

1. In a large skillet, heat marinara sauce and tarragon over medium heat. Add chickpeas and cook, stirring, for 4 to 5 minutes or until warmed through.

2. Make four holes for the eggs in the tomato mixture. Crack an egg into each hole and season with pepper. Cover and cook for 2 to 5 minutes or until eggs are set as desired.

3. Stir parsley into quinoa and season to taste with salt and pepper. Divide quinoa among four shallow bowls. Top each with tomato mixture and an egg.

Spinach and Teff Omelet

Makes 4 servings

Here, dry-cooked teff, fresh spinach and Romano cheese jazz up a simple omelet with ease and flair.

Tip

Cooked amaranth, millet or quinoa can be used in place of the dry-cooked teff. Information on cooking these grains can be found on pages 8–15.

6	large eggs	6
1/2 tsp	fine sea salt	2 mL
1/4 tsp	freshly cracked black pepper	1 mL
2 tbsp	unsalted butter	30 mL
1 cup	chopped onions	250 mL
2	cloves garlic, minced	2
4 cups	packed baby spinach, roughly torn	1 L
1 cup	dry-cooked teff (see page 18)	250 mL
1/2 cup	freshly grated Romano or Parmesan cheese	125 mL

1. In a large bowl, whisk together eggs, salt and pepper. Set aside.

2. In a large skillet, melt butter over medium-high heat. Add onions and cook, stirring, for 7 to 10 minutes or until browned and tender. Reduce heat to medium and add garlic and spinach; cook, stirring, for 1 to 2 minutes or until spinach is wilted. Stir in teff.

3. Pour egg mixture over teff mixture. Cook, lifting edges to allow uncooked eggs to run underneath and shaking skillet occasionally to loosen omelet, for 4 to 5 minutes or until almost set. Slide out onto a large plate. Invert skillet over omelet and, using pot holders, firmly hold plate and skillet together. Invert omelet back into skillet and cook for 1 to 2 minutes to set eggs. Slide out onto plate and sprinkle with cheese.

Garden Vegetable Quinoa Quiche for a Crowd

Makes 10 servings

This take on a 1970s mainstay pairs hearty quinoa with a wagonload of fresh, colorful vegetables. Because there is no crust, the preparation is a breeze.

Tips

An equal amount of quinoa flour or sorghum flour can be used in place of the millet flour.

Cooked amaranth or millet, cooled, or dry-cooked teff can be used in place of the quinoa. Information on cooking these grains can be found on pages 8–18.

- Preheat oven to 400°F (200°C)
- 12-cup (3 L) shallow casserole dish, greased

8	large eggs	8
1/3 cup	millet flour	75 mL
1 tsp	GF baking powder	5 mL
3/4 tsp	fine sea salt	3 mL
1/2 cup	milk	125 mL
2 cups	cottage cheese	500 mL
3 cups	shredded Swiss cheese, divided	750 mL
1 tbsp	olive oil	15 mL
1	red bell pepper, chopped	1
4 cups	diced zucchini (about 3 medium)	1 L
2 cups	sliced button or cremini mushrooms	500 mL
1/2 cup	chopped green onions	125 mL
2 1/2 cups	cooked quinoa (see page 15)	625 mL
2	medium-large tomatoes, thinly sliced	2

1. In a large bowl, whisk eggs until blended. Whisk in flour, baking powder, salt and milk. Stir in cottage cheese and half the Swiss cheese. Set aside.

2. In a large nonstick skillet, heat oil over medium-high heat. Add red pepper, zucchini, mushrooms and green onions; cook, stirring, for 6 to 8 minutes or until vegetables are tender.

3. Stir quinoa and vegetables into the egg mixture. Pour into prepared casserole dish and sprinkle with the remaining Swiss cheese. Arrange tomatoes over cheese.

4. Bake in preheated oven for 15 minutes. Reduce oven temperature to 350°F (180°C) and bake for 30 to 35 minutes or until golden brown and set.

Mushroom Quiche with Teff Crust

This sumptuous mushroom quiche, which is equally delicious warm, at room temperature or chilled, has one of the easiest crusts ever: teff flour, oil and water, mixed together then pressed into the pan. This low-tech method yields a tender, nutty crust, thanks to the absence of gluten in the teff flour. Try serving the quiche with a big green salad to balance the richness.

Tips

Other semi-hard cheeses, such as Cheddar, Monterrey Jack or Swiss, can be used in place of the smoked Gouda.

To make the quiche dairy-free, use an equal amount of olive oil in place of the butter, non-dairy milk (such as almond, cashew or hemp milk) in place of the milk, and non-dairy cheese in place of the Gouda.

- Preheat oven to 350°F (180°C)
- 9-inch (23 cm) glass pie plate, greased

1/3 cup	olive oil	75 mL
1/3 cup	water	75 mL
1 1/4 cups	teff flour	300 mL
3/4 tsp	fine sea salt, divided	3 mL
2 tbsp	unsalted butter	30 mL
3/4 cup	finely chopped onions	175 mL
1 lb	button or cremini mushrooms, sliced	500 g
4	large eggs	4
1/2 tsp	freshly ground black pepper	2 mL
1/2 tsp	ground nutmeg	2 mL
1 cup	whole milk	250 mL
1 1/2 cups	shredded smoked Gouda cheese, divided	375 mL

1. In a medium bowl, whisk oil and water. Add flour and 1/4 tsp (1 mL) salt, stirring until blended. Press dough into the bottom and sides of prepared pie plate. Set aside.

2. In a large nonstick skillet, melt butter over medium-high heat. Add onions and cook, stirring, for 2 minutes. Add mushrooms and cook, stirring, for 7 to 8 minutes or until tender. Remove from heat and let cool slightly.

3. In a large bowl, whisk eggs until blended. Whisk in the remaining salt, pepper, nutmeg and milk until blended. Stir in mushroom mixture and 1 cup (250 mL) cheese. Pour filling into crust and sprinkle with the remaining cheese.

4. Bake in preheated oven for 45 to 50 minutes or until golden brown and just set in the center. Let cool on a wire rack for at least 30 minutes before serving or let cool completely. Cut into wedges to serve.

Amaranth and Gruyère Soufflé

Makes 6 servings

Don't be afraid of soufflés — they are really quite simple to prepare. They are also a great way to highlight the flavor of ancient grains, such as the amaranth used in this rendition.

Tips

Cooked millet, quinoa or sorghum, cooled, can be used in place of the amaranth. Information on cooking these grains can be found on pages 11–17.

You can store the leftover egg yolks in an airtight container in the refrigerator for up to 3 days or in the freezer for up to 3 months. If you freeze them, it is important to whisk in $1/8$ tsp (0.5 mL) salt for each $1/4$ cup (60 mL) of yolks (about 4 yolks); without the added salt, the yolks will become overly gelatinous after thawing and will not work properly in recipes. Be sure to label the container with the number of yolks, the date and the amount of salt added. Use the yolks in a variety of yolk-rich dishes, such as lemon curd, custards and custard sauces, puddings and hollandaise sauce.

- Preheat oven to 400°F (200°C)
- 8-cup (2 L) soufflé dish

	Unsalted butter	
6 tbsp	freshly grated Parmesan cheese, divided	90 mL
1 cup	whole milk	250 mL
2 tbsp	amaranth flour	30 mL
4	large egg yolks	4
1 cup	cooked amaranth (see page 8), cooled	250 mL
$1\frac{1}{4}$ cups	shredded Gruyère cheese, divided	300 mL
$\frac{1}{2}$ tsp	fine sea salt	2 mL
$\frac{1}{4}$ tsp	ground nutmeg	1 mL
$\frac{1}{8}$ tsp	cayenne pepper	0.5 mL
1 tbsp	Dijon mustard	15 mL
6	large egg whites	6

1. Generously butter soufflé dish and sprinkle with 2 tbsp (30 mL) Parmesan, rotating dish to coat evenly.

2. In a small saucepan, bring milk to a simmer over medium-high heat.

3. Meanwhile, in a heavy-bottomed medium saucepan, melt 2 tbsp (30 mL) butter over medium-high heat. Whisk in flour and cook, whisking, for about 30 seconds (do not let it brown). Whisk in hot milk and cook, whisking, for 1 to 2 minutes or until blended and thickened.

4. Reduce heat to low and whisk in egg yolks, one at a time, until blended. Remove from heat and whisk in amaranth, the remaining Parmesan, 1 cup (250 mL) Gruyère, salt, nutmeg, cayenne and mustard.

5. In a medium bowl, using an electric mixer, beat egg whites until stiff peaks form (be careful not to overbeat). Stir one-quarter of the whites into amaranth mixture. Fold in the remaining whites. Pour into prepared soufflé dish and sprinkle with the remaining Gruyère.

6. Reduce oven temperature to 375°F (190°C). Bake for 30 to 35 minutes or until lightly browned on top and firm around the edges, but center still jiggles slightly. Serve immediately.

Cheesy Spinach, Artichoke and Amaranth Casserole

Makes 6 servings

A riff on a much-favored hot dip, this casserole is pure comfort on a chilly night. I predict you'll have the recipe committed to memory in no time.

Tip

Cooked millet or quinoa, or dry-cooked teff, can be used in place of the amaranth. Information on cooking these grains can be found on pages 11–18.

- Preheat oven to 375°F (190°C)
- 8-cup (2 L) baking dish, greased

1	package (16 oz/500 g) frozen chopped spinach, thawed	1
3	cloves garlic, minced	3
2	large eggs, beaten	2
1½ cups	ricotta cheese	375 mL
1½ cups	shredded mozzarella cheese, divided	375 mL
3 cups	cooked amaranth (see page 8)	750 mL
1 cup	drained marinated artichoke hearts, chopped	250 mL
	Fine sea salt and freshly cracked black pepper	
½ cup	freshly grated Parmesan cheese	125 mL

1. Place spinach in a clean, lint-free tea towel and squeeze out as much excess liquid as possible.

2. In a large bowl, combine garlic, eggs, ricotta and half the mozzarella. Stir in spinach, amaranth and artichoke hearts. Season with salt and pepper. Transfer to prepared baking dish and sprinkle with Parmesan and the remaining mozzarella.

3. Bake in preheated oven for 30 to 35 minutes or until cheese is browned and bubbly.

Spaghetti Squash, Quinoa and Ricotta Casserole

Makes 6 servings

Ricotta is great in cheesecakes and a host of other desserts, but its buttery flavor and creamy texture also shine in simple savory dishes, such as this squash casserole.

Tips

The spaghetti squash can also be prepared in the oven. Preheat oven to 325°F (160°C), and oil or lightly spray a small rimmed baking sheet with nonstick cooking spray. Cut squash in half lengthwise and remove the seeds. Place squash, cut side down, on prepared baking sheet and bake for 35 to 40 minutes or until a knife is easily inserted. Let cool for 5 to 10 minutes, then scoop out pulp and proceed with the remainder of step 1.

Cooked amaranth, millet or sorghum, cooled, can be used in place of the quinoa. Information on cooking these grains can be found on pages 8–17.

- 8-cup (2 L) baking dish, greased

1	spaghetti squash (about 2 lbs/1 kg)	1
1 tbsp	olive oil	15 mL
	Fine sea salt and freshly cracked black pepper	
3	cloves garlic, minced	3
2	large eggs, beaten	2
2 cups	ricotta cheese	500 mL
$\frac{1}{4}$ tsp	ground nutmeg	1 mL
$1\frac{1}{2}$ cups	cooked quinoa (see page 15), cooled	375 mL
$1\frac{1}{2}$ cups	shredded mozzarella cheese	375 mL

1. Pierce squash all over with a fork. Place on a paper towel in the microwave. Microwave on Medium-High (70%) for 13 to 15 minutes or until tender. Let cool for 5 to 10 minutes. Cut squash in half, remove seeds and scoop out pulp. Transfer pulp to a bowl and, using a fork, rake into strands. Add oil, tossing to coat. Season to taste with salt and pepper.

2. Preheat oven to 400°F (200°C).

3. In a large bowl, combine garlic, eggs, ricotta, 1 tsp (5 mL) salt, $\frac{1}{4}$ tsp (1 mL) pepper and nutmeg. Stir in squash and quinoa until blended. Transfer to prepared baking dish and sprinkle with mozzarella.

4. Bake in preheated oven for 18 to 22 minutes or until browned and bubbling.

Millet and Ricotta Crocchette

Forget about deep-frying: these crispy millet cakes are tender on the inside, crisp on the outside and require only a few tablespoons of oil.

Tips

To make dry GF bread crumbs, toast 1 to 2 slices of GF bread, let cool completely, tear into pieces, then place the pieces in a food processor and process to even crumbs.

You can make the patties half the size and serve them as an appetizer.

• Rimmed baking sheet

3 cups	cooked millet (see page 11), cooled	750 mL
2	cloves garlic, minced	2
1 cup	freshly grated Parmesan cheese	250 mL
½ cup	ricotta cheese	125 mL
	Fine sea salt and freshly cracked black pepper	
1	large egg, lightly beaten	1
1 cup	dry GF bread crumbs (see tip, at left)	250 mL
3 tbsp	olive oil, divided	45 mL
1½ cups	GF marinara sauce, warmed	375 mL

1. In a large bowl, combine millet, garlic, Parmesan and ricotta until well blended. Season generously with salt and pepper. Form into twelve 1-inch (2.5 cm) thick patties.

2. Place egg and bread crumbs in separate shallow dishes. Carefully dip each patty in egg, then in bread crumbs, turning to coat. Place on baking sheet. Cover and place in freezer for 15 minutes. Discard any excess egg and crumbs.

3. In a large nonstick skillet, heat 1 tbsp (15 mL) oil over medium heat. Add 4 patties and cook, turning once, for 2 to 3 minutes per side or until golden brown on both sides and hot in the center. Transfer to a plate and loosely cover with foil to keep warm. Repeat with the remaining oil and patties, adjusting heat as necessary between batches. Serve with warm marinara sauce.

Crispy Amaranth Cakes with Mint Raita

A minted, tart yogurt raita gives sprightliness to crisp, spiced amaranth cakes in a quick supper that manages to be both substantial and refreshing.

Tips

Freshly squeezed lemon juice can be used in place of the lime juice.

To make dry GF bread crumbs, toast 1 to 2 slices of GF bread, let cool completely, tear into pieces, then place the pieces in a food processor and process to even crumbs.

An equal amount of curry powder (any heat level) or Thai curry paste can be used in place of the garam masala.

Mint Raita

1	clove garlic, minced	1
1/4 cup	packed fresh mint leaves, chopped	60 mL
2 tsp	minced gingerroot	10 mL
Pinch	fine sea salt	Pinch
3/4 cup	plain yogurt	175 mL
1 tsp	freshly squeezed lime juice	5 mL

Amaranth Cakes

2 cups	cooked amaranth (see page 8), cooled	500 mL
1/3 cup	finely chopped green onions	75 mL
1 cup	dry GF bread crumbs (see tip, at left)	250 mL
1 tsp	garam masala	5 mL
1/2 tsp	fine sea salt	2 mL
2	large eggs, beaten	2
4 tsp	olive oil, divided	20 mL

1. *Raita:* In a small bowl, whisk together garlic, mint, ginger, salt, yogurt and lime juice. Cover and refrigerate while you prepare the cakes.

2. *Amaranth Cakes:* In a large bowl, combine amaranth, green onions, bread crumbs, garam masala, salt and eggs. Let stand for 5 minutes. Form into eight 1/2-inch (1 cm) thick patties.

3. In a large skillet, heat half the oil over medium-high heat. Add 4 patties and cook, turning once, for 2 to 3 minutes per side or until golden brown on both sides and hot in the center. Transfer to a plate and loosely tent with foil to keep warm. Repeat with the remaining oil and patties, adjusting heat as necessary between batches. Serve with mint raita.

Millet Polenta with Cherry Tomato Sauté

Celebrate the final days of summer with this easy, elegant polenta topped with a perfect cherry tomato sauce that is ready in under 5 minutes.

Tip

Consider this recipe a template, much as you would a basic recipe for corn polenta. The cheese, herbs and topping can be varied in a multitude of ways to suit your taste.

1 cup	millet	250 mL
4 cups	ready-to-use GF vegetable broth	1 L
1 cup	freshly grated Romano or Parmesan cheese, divided	250 mL
3 tbsp	minced fresh chives, divided	45 mL
	Fine sea salt and freshly ground black pepper	
1 tbsp	olive oil	15 mL
4 cups	cherry tomatoes	1 L

1. In a medium saucepan, toast millet over medium heat, stirring constantly, for 2 to 3 minutes or until grains smell toasty and begin to make a popping sound.

2. Stir in broth and bring to a boil. Reduce heat to low, cover and simmer, stirring every 5 to 6 minutes to prevent sticking, for 25 to 30 minutes or until mixture appears very creamy. Remove from heat and stir in half the cheese and 2 tbsp (30 mL) chives. Season to taste with salt and pepper.

3. Meanwhile, in a large skillet, heat oil over medium-high heat. Add tomatoes and cook, stirring, for 3 to 4 minutes or until just starting to pop. Stir in the remaining chives. Season to taste with salt and pepper.

4. Spoon polenta into shallow bowls and top with tomato mixture. Sprinkle with the remaining cheese.

Grilled Portobellos with Pesto Quinoa

Meaty mushrooms with a pesto-enriched quinoa and tomato stuffing make for a surprisingly filling meal with minimal effort. Add a big green salad and dinner is done.

Tip

To make the mushrooms indoors, preheat the oven to 500°F (260°C). Place the mushrooms, hollow side down, on a large rimmed baking sheet sprayed with nonstick cooking spray. Bake in preheated oven for 5 minutes. Turn mushrooms over and stuff with quinoa mixture, dividing equally. Sprinkle with cheese. Bake for 3 to 5 minutes or until cheese is melted.

• Preheat barbecue grill to medium-high

1½ cups	hot cooked quinoa (see page 15)	375 mL
¾ cup	diced tomatoes	175 mL
3 tbsp	basil pesto	45 mL
8	large portobello mushrooms, stems trimmed and gills removed	8
	Olive oil	
	Fine sea salt	
1 cup	shredded mozzarella cheese	250 mL

1. In a medium bowl, combine quinoa, tomatoes and pesto.

2. Brush mushrooms with oil and sprinkle with salt. Place on preheated barbecue and grill, turning once, for 4 to 5 minutes per side or until tender and deep golden brown on both sides.

3. Stuff mushroom caps with quinoa mixture, dividing equally, and sprinkle with cheese. Return to barbecue, cover and grill for 3 minutes or until cheese is melted.

Red Pepper Pesto, Asparagus and Quinoa Bowls

This Italian-inspired red, white and green bowl of goodness has just the right proportion of sauce to quinoa.

Tip

Almonds or walnuts may be used in place of the pine nuts.

- Blender or food processor

Red Pepper Pesto

1	jar (8 oz/227 mL) roasted red bell peppers, drained	1
1	clove garlic, minced	1
1/2 cup	packed fresh basil leaves	125 mL
1 tbsp	pine nuts	15 mL
1/4 tsp	fine sea salt	1 mL
2 tbsp	olive oil	30 mL

Quinoa

1 tbsp	olive oil	15 mL
12 oz	asparagus, trimmed and cut crosswise into 1/4-inch (0.5 cm) pieces	375 g
3 tbsp	water	45 mL
4 cups	hot cooked quinoa (see page 15)	1 L
	Fine sea salt and freshly cracked black pepper	
1/3 cup	freshly grated Romano or Parmesan cheese	75 mL
1/4 cup	packed fresh basil leaves, thinly sliced	60 mL

1. *Pesto:* In blender, combine roasted peppers, garlic, basil, pine nuts, salt and oil; purée until smooth.

2. *Quinoa:* In a large nonstick skillet, heat oil over medium-high heat. Add asparagus and cook, stirring, for 1 minute. Add water, cover and cook for 2 to 3 minutes or until asparagus is tender-crisp. Stir in quinoa and cook, uncovered, for 1 minute. Season to taste with salt and pepper.

3. Divide quinoa among bowls and top with pesto, cheese and thinly sliced basil.

Quinoa Risotto with Bacon and Peas

Makes 4 servings

Risotto is a breeze to prepare, and a fast weeknight meal, when made with quinoa in place of rice. Verdant peas and parsley, plus crisp bacon, make it an irresistible choice.

Variation

Butternut Squash Quinoa Risotto: Replace the peas with 2 cups (500 mL) cooked cubed butternut squash.

3	slices thick-cut bacon, chopped	3
1¼ cups	quinoa, rinsed	300 mL
1 tsp	dried thyme	5 mL
½ cup	dry white wine	125 mL
2 cups	ready-to-use GF vegetable broth	500 mL
1 cup	frozen petite peas, thawed	250 mL
1 cup	freshly grated Parmesan cheese, divided	250 mL
¼ cup	packed fresh flat-leaf (Italian) parsley leaves, chopped	60 mL
1 tbsp	freshly squeezed lemon juice	15 mL
	Fine sea salt and freshly cracked black pepper	

1. In a large saucepan, cook bacon over medium-high heat until crisp. Using a slotted spoon, transfer bacon to a plate lined with paper towels. Drain off all but 1 tbsp (15 mL) fat.

2. Add quinoa to the pan and cook, stirring, for 1 minute. Add thyme and wine; cook, stirring, for 3 to 5 minutes or until liquid is evaporated.

3. Stir in broth and bring to a boil, stirring often. Reduce heat and simmer, stirring occasionally, for 12 minutes.

4. Stir in peas, half the cheese, parsley and lemon juice; simmer for 1 minute or until heated through. Season to taste with salt and pepper. Serve sprinkled with bacon and the remaining cheese.

Sorghum with Parmesan and Broccoli Rabe

The bittersweet undertones of broccoli rabe and the brightness of fresh lemon juice play up the earthy qualities of sorghum, and a topping of toasted walnuts lends a pleasant crunch.

Tips

You can skip step 1 and substitute 3 cups (750 mL) hot cooked buckwheat, millet, quinoa or brown rice for the sorghum. Information on cooking these grains can be found on pages 9–16.

Make sure to use fine sea salt in the water you use to cook the sorghum and broccoli rabe. Conventional table salt contains chemicals and additives, whereas sea salt contains an abundance of naturally occurring trace minerals.

1½ cups	sorghum	375 mL
5 cups	water	1.25 L
1 lb	broccoli rabe, trimmed and roughly chopped	500 g
¾ cup	freshly grated Parmesan cheese, divided	175 mL
¼ tsp	hot pepper flakes	1 mL
1 tbsp	finely grated lemon zest	15 mL
2 tbsp	freshly squeezed lemon juice	30 mL
½ cup	chopped toasted walnuts (see page 26)	125 mL

1. In a large saucepan, combine sorghum and 5 cups (1.25 L) water. Bring to a boil over medium-high heat. Reduce heat and simmer, stirring occasionally, for 50 to 60 minutes or until very tender. Drain off excess water.

2. Meanwhile, in a medium pot of boiling salted water (see tip, at left), cook broccoli rabe for 3 to 4 minutes, stirring occasionally, until tender-crisp. Drain and add to sorghum.

3. Add half the cheese, hot pepper flakes, lemon zest and lemon juice, gently tossing to combine. Serve sprinkled with walnuts and the remaining cheese.

Broccoli, Cheddar and Quinoa–Stuffed Sweet Potatoes

These gorgeous sweet potatoes, stuffed with emerald broccoli and tiny pearls of quinoa before being crowned with golden Cheddar, are guaranteed to be a hit.

Tip

Hot cooked amaranth, buckwheat, brown rice or sorghum can be used in place of the quinoa. Information on cooking these grains can be found on pages 8–17.

- Preheat oven to 425°F (220°C)
- Rimmed baking sheet

4	sweet potatoes (each about 12 oz/375 g)	4
1½ tbsp	olive oil	22 mL
3	cloves garlic, minced	3
3 cups	coarsely chopped broccoli florets	750 mL
⅓ cup	dry white wine or water	75 mL
1½ cups	hot cooked quinoa (see page 15)	375 mL
1 cup	shredded sharp (old) Cheddar cheese	250 mL

1. Pierce sweet potatoes all over with a fork. Place on baking sheet. Bake in preheated oven for about 1 hour or until tender.

2. Meanwhile, in a large nonstick skillet, heat oil over medium-high heat. Add garlic and cook, stirring, for 30 seconds. Add broccoli and wine; cover and cook for 4 to 5 minutes or until broccoli is tender-crisp. Stir in quinoa and cook, uncovered, for 1 minute.

3. Transfer sweet potatoes to dinner plates and let cool for 5 minutes. Slit each lengthwise, press to open, then spoon quinoa mixture into the center. Sprinkle with cheese.

Sorghum Skillet Casserole with Smoky Sweet Potato Topping

Everyone needs at least one single-skillet supper dish in their repertoire, and this one — hearty with sorghum, flavorful with smoky paprika and Spanish sherry, and capped with a cheesy sweet potato topping — is a great place to start.

Tips

Hot Cooked amaranth, millet, quinoa or brown rice can be used in place of the sorghum. Information on cooking these grains can be found on pages 8–16.

Other semi-firm cheeses, such as Cheddar, fontina or Monterey Jack, can be used in place of the Gouda.

- Preheat oven to 400°F (200°C)
- Large cast-iron or other ovenproof skillet

1½ lbs	sweet potatoes (about 2 medium), peeled and cut into chunks	750 g
2 tbsp	olive oil, divided	30 mL
1	red bell pepper, chopped	1
1 cup	chopped onion	250 mL
3	cloves garlic, minced	3
1 lb	cremini or button mushrooms, halved (or quartered if large)	500 g
1 tbsp	potato starch or tapioca starch	15 mL
½ cup	dry sherry	125 mL
¾ cup	ready-to-use GF vegetable broth	175 mL
3 cups	hot cooked sorghum (see page 17)	750 mL
	Fine sea salt and freshly cracked black pepper	
1½ tsp	hot smoked paprika	7 mL
1 cup	shredded smoked Gouda cheese, divided	250 mL

1. Place sweet potatoes in a large pot of cold water. Bring to a boil over high heat. Reduce heat to medium-high and boil for 15 to 20 minutes or until very tender.

2. Meanwhile, in the cast-iron skillet, heat half the oil over medium-high heat. Add red pepper and onion; cook, stirring, for 6 to 7 minutes or until starting to soften. Add garlic and mushrooms; cook, stirring, for 5 minutes or until mushrooms release their liquid.

3. In a small cup, combine potato starch and sherry until completely dissolved. Stir into mushroom mixture, along with broth; bring to a boil. Reduce heat to low, cover and simmer, stirring occasionally, for 5 minutes. Remove from heat and stir in sorghum. Season to taste with salt and pepper. Spread evenly in skillet.

Tip

The casserole can be prepared ahead through step 4. At the end of step 3, transfer the sorghum mixture to an 8-cup (2 L) baking dish and complete step 4 as directed. Let cool completely, then cover and refrigerate for up to 2 days. Increase the baking time to 25 to 30 minutes, tenting with foil during the last 10 minutes to prevent overbrowning.

4. Drain sweet potatoes, reserving $\frac{1}{4}$ cup (60 mL) cooking water. Return sweet potatoes and reserved water to the pot, along with paprika and the remaining oil; mash until smooth. Stir in half the cheese. Season to taste with salt and pepper. Spread over sorghum mixture and sprinkle with the remaining cheese.

5. Bake in preheated oven for 15 to 20 minutes or until heated through and cheese is melted and golden brown.

Miso Squash, Kale and Buckwheat Burritos

A panoply of flavors — malt-like buckwheat, bittersweet kale and umami roasted butternut squash — combine to make one very special burrito.

Tips

Hot cooked amaranth, quinoa, brown rice or sorghum can be used in place of the buckwheat. Information on cooking these grains can be found on pages 8–17.

Store-bought 8-inch (20 cm) GF tortillas can be used in place of the Millet, Sorghum and Chia Tortillas.

- Preheat oven to 425°F (220°C)
- Large rimmed baking sheet, lined with parchment paper

3 cups	finely diced butternut squash	750 mL
1½ tbsp	olive oil, divided	22 mL
1½ tbsp	GF miso paste	22 mL
1	large bunch kale, tough stems and center ribs removed, leaves very thinly sliced crosswise (about 6 cups/1.5 L)	1
1½ cups	hot cooked buckwheat (see page 9)	375 mL
2 tbsp	water	30 mL
2 tsp	unseasoned rice vinegar or cider vinegar	10 mL
	Fine sea salt and Asian chili sauce (such as Sriracha)	
4	Millet, Sorghum and Chia Tortillas (page 260), warmed	4

1. In a large bowl, combine squash, 1 tbsp (15 mL) oil and miso, coating squash thoroughly. Spread evenly on prepared baking sheet. Roast in preheated oven for 20 to 25 minutes, stirring once, until tender and browned.

2. Meanwhile, in a large pot, heat the remaining oil over medium-high heat. Add kale and cook, stirring, for 5 minutes. Reduce heat to medium-low and cook, stirring, for 12 to 15 minutes or until kale is very tender.

3. Stir in roasted squash, buckwheat and water; cook, stirring, for 2 minutes or until heated through. Stir in vinegar. Season to taste with salt and hot sauce.

4. Spoon buckwheat mixture down the center of each warmed tortilla, leaving a 2-inch (5 cm) border. Roll up like burritos, enclosing filling, or like a cigar (ends open).

White Cheddar and Millet Enchiladas

Ready-to-use chipotle salsa adds mellow, smoky heat and tangy balance to the rich, cheesy filling of these cauliflower enchiladas.

Tips

Hot cooked amaranth, quinoa, brown rice or sorghum can be used in place of the millet. Information on cooking these grains can be found on pages 8–17.

Store-bought 8-inch (20 cm) GF tortillas can be used in place of the Millet, Sorghum and Chia Tortillas.

- Preheat oven to 350°F (180°C)
- 9-inch (23 cm) square glass baking dish or metal baking pan, sprayed with nonstick cooking spray

1 tbsp	olive oil	15 mL
1 cup	chopped onions	250 mL
2½ cups	finely chopped cauliflower florets	625 mL
1 tsp	ground cumin	5 mL
1½ cups	chipotle salsa, divided	375 mL
1½ cups	cooked millet (see page 11)	375 mL
2 cups	shredded sharp (old) white Cheddar cheese, divided	500 mL
1 cup	ricotta cheese	250 mL
8	Millet, Sorghum and Chia Tortillas (page 260), warmed	8

1. In a large skillet, heat oil over medium heat. Add onions and cook, stirring, for 6 to 8 minutes or until softened. Add cauliflower, cumin and ⅓ cup (75 mL) salsa; cook, stirring, for 1 minute. Remove from heat and stir in millet, half the Cheddar and ricotta.

2. Spoon about ⅓ cup (75 mL) of the millet mixture down the center of each warmed tortilla. Roll up like a cigar and place, seam side down, in prepared baking dish. Spoon the remaining salsa over top.

3. Cover and bake in preheated oven for 20 to 25 minutes or until heated through. Sprinkle with the remaining Cheddar. Bake, uncovered, for 5 minutes or until cheese is bubbling.

Roasted Fennel, Mushroom and Tomato Sorghum

Makes 4 servings

Fennel and garlic caramelize when roasted at high heat, releasing their sweet essence. Blending the two with nutty sorghum yields an irresistible, easy weeknight supper.

Tip

Hot cooked amaranth, millet, quinoa or brown rice can be used in place of the sorghum. Information on cooking these grains can be found on pages 8–16.

- Preheat oven to 450°F (230°C)
- Large roasting pan, lined with foil and sprayed with nonstick cooking spray

4	cloves garlic, roughly chopped	4
1	large fennel bulb, cut into 1-inch (2.5 cm) pieces, fronds reserved	1
1 lb	cremini mushrooms, trimmed and thickly sliced	500 g
¾ tsp	fine sea salt	3 mL
½ tsp	freshly cracked black pepper	2 mL
2 tbsp	olive oil	30 mL
2 cups	cherry or grape tomatoes	500 mL
½ cup	dry white wine	125 mL
3 cups	hot cooked sorghum (see page 17)	750 mL

1. In a large bowl, combine garlic, fennel, mushrooms, salt, pepper and oil. Spread in a single layer in prepared roasting pan. Roast in preheated oven for 18 to 21 minutes, stirring occasionally, until fennel and mushrooms begin to brown. Add tomatoes and roast for 7 to 10 minutes or until tomatoes begin to burst and shrivel. Return vegetables to large bowl.

2. Add wine to the roasting pan, scraping up any browned bits from bottom of pan. Place pan over medium heat and simmer for 2 to 3 minutes (or return pan to oven for 5 minutes if pan is not stovetop-safe), until wine has evaporated by half.

3. Return roasted vegetables to the pan, along with sorghum. Reduce heat to medium-low and cook, tossing, for 1 minute or until heated through (or return to oven for 1 to 2 minutes or until heated through).

4. Chop enough of the reserved fennel fronds to measure ¼ cup (60 mL). Stir into sorghum mixture.

Roasted Eggplant and Cherry Tomatoes with Sorghum

Makes 4 servings

It takes a little while for the eggplant and cherry tomatoes to roast, but it's hands-free time that you can spend doing something else (like kicking up your heels). The sorghum cooks in just about the same time, too. The end result couldn't be more satisfying!

Tip

Hot cooked amaranth, millet, quinoa or brown rice can be used in place of the sorghum. Information on cooking these grains can be found on pages 8–16.

- Preheat oven to 400°F (200°C)
- Large rimmed baking sheet, sprayed with nonstick cooking spray

1½ lbs	eggplant, trimmed and cubed	750 g
2 cups	cherry or grape tomatoes	500 mL
4	cloves garlic, roughly chopped	4
1½ tsp	dried thyme	7 mL
	Fine sea salt and freshly cracked black pepper	
¼ cup	olive oil	60 mL
3 cups	hot cooked sorghum (see page 17)	750 mL
	Freshly grated Parmesan cheese (optional)	

1. In a large bowl, combine eggplant, tomatoes, garlic, thyme, ¾ tsp (3 mL) salt, ½ tsp (2 mL) pepper and oil. Spread in a single layer on prepared baking sheet. Roast in preheated oven for 30 minutes. Stir. Roast for 20 to 30 minutes or until eggplant is very tender.

2. Season sorghum to taste with salt and pepper. Divide sorghum among four shallow bowls and top with eggplant mixture. Sprinkle with cheese, if desired.

Green Curry with Eggplant and Sorghum

Makes 4 servings

Asian eggplant retains its shape and a slight chewiness in this boldly spiced curry. Fresh lime juice and basil brighten everything, while cashews add nutty crunch.

Tips

Asian eggplants work best in this dish because they are denser and have smaller seeds. For 3 lbs (1.5 kg), you'll need about 6 medium Asian eggplants. Alternatively, you can use 2 medium-large regular eggplants.

Hot cooked amaranth, millet, quinoa or brown rice can be used in place of the sorghum. Information on cooking these grains can be found on pages 8–16.

1 tbsp	warmed virgin coconut oil	15 mL
1¼ cups	chopped onions	300 mL
3 lbs	Asian eggplants, trimmed and cut into 1-inch (2.5 cm) cubes	1.5 kg
1 tbsp	packed light brown sugar	15 mL
1 tsp	ground ginger	5 mL
¾ cup	ready-to-use GF vegetable broth	175 mL
2 tbsp	Thai green curry paste	30 mL
2 cups	hot cooked sorghum (see page 17)	500 mL
1 cup	packed fresh basil leaves, roughly chopped, divided	250 mL
1 cup	well-stirred coconut milk (full-fat)	250 mL
2 tbsp	freshly squeezed lime juice	30 mL
½ cup	lightly salted roasted cashews, coarsely chopped	125 mL

1. In a large saucepan, melt coconut oil over low heat. Add onions, increase heat to medium-high and cook, stirring, for 5 minutes or until starting to soften. Add eggplants and cook, stirring, for 6 to 7 minutes or until starting to brown.

2. Stir in brown sugar, ginger, broth and curry paste; bring to a boil. Stir in sorghum, reduce heat to medium-low, cover and simmer, stirring occasionally, for 5 minutes.

3. Stir in half the basil, coconut milk and lime juice; simmer, uncovered, stirring occasionally, for 5 minutes to heat through and blend the flavors. Serve sprinkled with cashews and the remaining basil.

Seafood, Poultry and Meat Main Dishes

Oven-Baked Amaranth Fish Sticks

Makes 4 servings

Amaranth looks like the world's smallest popcorn once popped — just the incentive any kid (of any age) needs to dig in to these crispy-on-the-outside, moist-on-the-inside fish sticks.

Tip

Sea bass, halibut or any other firm white fish fillets may be used in place of the tilapia.

Storage Tip

The fish sticks can be prepared through step 2 and frozen. Wrap the fish sticks in plastic wrap, then foil, completely enclosing them, and freeze for up to 3 months. When ready to bake, unwrap the frozen fish sticks (do not thaw), place on rack on prepared baking sheet and bake at 450°F (230°C) for 18 to 22 minutes, turning once halfway through, until coating is golden brown and fish is opaque and flakes easily when tested with a fork.

- Preheat oven to 375°F (190°C)
- Large rimmed baking sheet, lined with foil, wire rack set on top

1¼ lbs	skinless tilapia fillets, cut into 3-inch (7.5 cm) strips	625 g
	Fine sea salt and freshly ground black pepper	
2 cups	popped amaranth (see page 9)	500 mL
¼ cup	melted virgin coconut oil or unsalted butter, melted	60 mL

1. Season all sides of fish with salt and pepper. Place amaranth in a shallow dish. Place coconut oil in another shallow dish.

2. Dip fish in coconut oil, shaking off excess, then in amaranth, turning to coat and pressing to adhere. Place on rack on prepared baking sheet. Drizzle fish with any remaining coconut oil. Discard any excess amaranth.

3. Bake in preheated oven for 10 to 14 minutes or until coating is golden brown and fish is opaque and flakes easily when tested with a fork.

Fish Tacos with Quinoa Tortillas

Quick pickled red onions, combined with mango, avocado and quinoa, make a vibrant counterpoint to flaky cod in these scrumptious tacos.

Tips

Other mild, lean white fish, such as orange roughy, snapper, tilapia or striped bass, may be used in place of the cod.

Cooked amaranth, millet or sorghum, cooled, can be used in place of the quinoa. Information on cooking these grains can be found on pages 8–17.

Store-bought 6-inch (15 cm) GF tortillas can be used in place of the Quinoa Tortillas.

- Preheat broiler, with rack set 4 to 6 inches (10 to 15 cm) from the heat source
- Broiler pan, greased

1 cup	thinly sliced red onion	250 mL
2 tsp	fine crystal cane sugar	10 mL
½ tsp	fine sea salt, divided	2 mL
2 tbsp	freshly squeezed lime juice	30 mL
4	skinless fresh or thawed frozen cod fillets (each about 6 oz/175 g)	4
1 tbsp	melted virgin coconut oil or olive oil	15 mL
1 tsp	chipotle chile powder, divided	5 mL
½ tsp	ground cumin	2 mL
1 cup	cooked quinoa (see page 15), cooled	250 mL
1 cup	fresh or thawed frozen chopped mango	250 mL
1	large firm-ripe Hass avocado, diced	1
8	6-inch (15 cm) Quinoa Tortillas (page 258), warmed	8
½ cup	packed fresh cilantro leaves	125 mL
4	lime wedges	4

1. In a medium bowl, combine red onion, sugar, half the salt and lime juice. Let stand for 5 minutes.

2. Meanwhile, place fish on prepared pan. Brush both sides of fish with oil, then sprinkle with ¾ tsp (3 mL) chipotle chile powder, cumin and the remaining salt. Broil for 4 to 6 minutes or until fish is opaque and flakes easily when tested with a fork. Flake fish into small pieces.

3. To the onion mixture, add quinoa, mango, avocado and the remaining chipotle chile powder, gently tossing to combine.

4. Fill warmed tortillas with fish, quinoa mixture and cilantro. Serve with lime wedges.

Cod with Roasted Tomatoes and Lemon Thyme Quinoa

Makes 4 servings

This cod, tomato and quinoa dish is simplicity itself. The lemon thyme quinoa helps to soak up every last drop of the incredibly flavorful roasted cherry tomatoes.

Tips

Sea bass, halibut or any other firm white fish fillets may be used in place of the cod.

Hot cooked amaranth, millet, long-grain brown rice or sorghum can be used in place of the quinoa. Information on cooking these grains can be found on pages 8–17.

- Preheat oven to 400°F (200°C)
- Large rimmed baking sheet

3 cups	cherry or grape tomatoes	750 mL
3 tbsp	olive oil, divided	45 mL
	Fine sea salt and freshly cracked black pepper	
4	skinless Pacific cod fillets (each about 6 oz/175 g)	4
3 cups	hot cooked quinoa (see page 15)	750 mL
1½ tsp	minced fresh thyme	7 mL
1 tsp	finely grated lemon zest	5 mL
1 tbsp	freshly squeezed lemon juice	15 mL

1. Place tomatoes on baking sheet. Toss with 1 tbsp (15 mL) oil and sprinkle with salt and pepper. Roast in preheated oven for 5 minutes or until skins begin to burst.

2. Brush both sides of fish with oil, using another 1 tbsp (15 mL) oil total, then sprinkle with salt and pepper. Place fish on baking sheet with tomatoes. Roast for 7 to 10 minutes or until fish is opaque and flakes easily when tested with a fork.

3. Meanwhile, in a large bowl, toss quinoa with thyme, lemon zest, lemon juice and the remaining oil. Season to taste with salt.

4. Serve quinoa alongside cod. Spoon tomatoes over fish.

Miso Cod with Lemon Amaranth

Delicate, sophisticated flavors come together almost effortlessly in this cod dish, with the help of miso and ginger, two Japanese staples. Lemon amaranth provides the perfect counterpoint.

Tips

Sea bass, halibut or any other firm white fish fillets may be used in place of the cod.

Hot cooked millet, quinoa, long-grain brown rice or sorghum can be used in place of the amaranth. Information on cooking these grains can be found on pages 11–17.

2 tbsp	minced gingerroot	30 mL
3 tbsp	water	45 mL
2 tbsp	GF miso paste	30 mL
4	skinless Pacific cod fillets (each about 5 oz/150 g)	4
3 cups	hot cooked amaranth (see page 8)	750 mL
1/4 cup	minced fresh chives	60 mL
1 tsp	finely grated lemon zest	5 mL
1 tbsp	freshly squeezed lemon juice	15 mL
	Fine sea salt	

1. In a large skillet, combine ginger, water and miso. Add fish and bring to a boil over medium-high heat. Reduce heat to low, cover and simmer for 6 to 9 minutes or until fish is opaque and flakes easily when tested with a fork.

2. Meanwhile, in a large bowl, toss amaranth with chives, lemon zest and lemon juice. Season to taste with salt.

3. Serve amaranth alongside cod. Spoon sauce over fish.

Tuna and Millet Croquettes

Millet and tuna yield fantastic croquettes, especially when they're seasoned with aromatic tarragon and tangy Dijon mustard and cooked to a crisp golden brown.

Tip

Cooked amaranth or quinoa, cooled, may be used in place of the millet. Information on cooking these grains can be found on pages 8–15.

2	large eggs, lightly beaten	2
1 1/2 tbsp	Dijon mustard	22 mL
1 tsp	dried tarragon	5 mL
1 cup	cooked millet (see page 11), cooled	250 mL
3 tbsp	minced fresh chives	45 mL
2	cans (each 6 oz/170 g) water-packed chunk light tuna, drained	2
1 1/2 tbsp	olive oil	22 mL

1. In a medium bowl, whisk together eggs, mustard and tarragon. Gently stir in millet, chives and tuna, flaking tuna into small pieces. Form into four 3/4-inch (2 cm) thick patties.

2. In a large skillet, heat oil over medium-high heat. Add patties and cook for 4 minutes. Turn and cook for 4 to 5 minutes or until browned and hot in the center.

Sorghum with Tuna, Fennel and Green Olives

Makes 4 servings

For this comforting meal, hearty sorghum and licorice fennel are layered with citrus, sweet and sea-salty flavors. The result? Your new favorite fast-food dinner.

Tips

Hot cooked amaranth, millet or quinoa may be used in place of the sorghum. Information on cooking these grains can be found on pages 8–15.

Dark raisins can be used in place of the golden raisins.

1	can (6 oz/170 g) oil-packed tuna	1
1	large bulb fennel, chopped, fronds reserved	1
2	cloves garlic, minced	2
2½ cups	hot cooked sorghum (see page 17)	625 mL
⅓ cup	pitted green olives, coarsely chopped	75 mL
¼ cup	golden raisins, chopped	60 mL
½ tsp	fine sea salt	2 mL
2 tbsp	freshly squeezed lemon juice	30 mL
4 cups	packed arugula or tender watercress sprigs, roughly chopped	1 L

1. Drain tuna, reserving 2 tsp (10 mL) oil. Flake tuna with a fork and set aside.

2. Chop enough of the reserved fennel fronds to measure 3 tbsp (45 mL). Set aside.

3. In a medium saucepan, heat the reserved tuna oil over medium heat. Add fennel bulb and garlic; cook, stirring, for 6 to 8 minutes or until softened.

4. Stir in sorghum and cook, stirring, for 2 minutes. Add tuna, fennel fronds, olives, raisins, salt and lemon juice; cook, stirring, until warmed through. Stir in arugula. Serve immediately.

Salmon Amaranth Cakes

Makes 6 servings

A sprinkle of fresh lemon zest, a handful of chopped green onion and sharp Dijon mustard highlight the flavor of pantry-friendly canned salmon and earthy amaranth.

Tip

Cooked millet or quinoa, cooled, can be used in place of the amaranth. Information on cooking these grains can be found on pages 11–15.

• Food processor

1 cup	chopped green onions (about 1 small bunch)	250 mL
1½ cups	cooked amaranth (see page 8), cooled	375 mL
2 tsp	dried dillweed	10 mL
½ tsp	fine sea salt	2 mL
¼ tsp	freshly ground black pepper	1 mL
1	large egg	1
1 tbsp	Dijon mustard	15 mL
1 tbsp	finely grated lemon zest	15 mL
3	cans (each 7 oz/213 g) wild Alaskan salmon, drained and flaked (skin removed, if necessary)	3
2 tbsp	olive oil, divided	30 mL

1. In food processor, process green onions until finely chopped. Add amaranth, dill, salt, pepper, egg, mustard and lemon zest; process until well blended, scraping down sides as needed. Add salmon and process using on/off pulses until blended and mixture begins to come together. Form into twelve ¾-inch (2 cm) thick patties.

2. In a large skillet, heat half the oil over medium-high heat. Add half the patties and cook, turning once, for 2 to 3 minutes per side or until golden brown on both sides and hot in the center. Transfer to a plate and tent with foil to keep warm. Repeat with the remaining oil and patties, adjusting heat between batches as necessary.

Spicy-Sweet Salmon with Corn and Chive Amaranth

Makes 4 servings

No need to head outside: this salmon achieves its great barbecue flavor from a bit of sauce and a super-hot oven.

Tips

According to the Monterey Bay Aquarium Seafood Watch, some of the best choices for wild salmon are those caught in Alaska, British Columbia, California, Oregon and Washington. Compared with salmon caught in other regions, these options are abundant, well managed and caught in an environmentally friendly way.

Hot cooked millet, quinoa, long-grain brown rice or sorghum can be used in place of the amaranth. Information on cooking these grains can be found on pages 11–17.

- Preheat oven to 500°F (260°C)
- Small rimmed baking sheet, sprayed with nonstick cooking spray

4	skinless wild salmon fillets (each about 6 oz/175 g)	4
¼ cup	GF barbecue sauce	60 mL
⅛ tsp	cayenne pepper	0.5 mL
1 tbsp	olive oil	15 mL
1½ cups	fresh or thawed frozen corn kernels	375 mL
1½ cups	hot cooked amaranth (see page 8)	375 mL
3 tbsp	chopped fresh chives	45 mL
	Fine sea salt and freshly cracked black pepper	

1. Place fish, skinned side down, on prepared baking sheet. In a small cup, combine barbecue sauce and cayenne. Generously brush fish with sauce. Bake in preheated oven for 7 to 11 minutes or until fish is opaque and flakes easily when tested with a fork.

2. Meanwhile, in a large skillet, heat oil over medium-high heat. Add corn and cook, stirring, for 2 minutes. Remove from heat and stir in amaranth and chives. Season to taste with salt and black pepper. Serve alongside fish.

Five-Spice Salmon with Chia-Sesame Sprinkle

A crunchy, sweet-savory chia and sesame seed sprinkle enhances this hot and spicy salmon to delicious effect.

Tips

According to the Monterey Bay Aquarium Seafood Watch, some of the best choices for wild salmon are those caught in Alaska, British Columbia, California, Oregon and Washington. Compared with salmon caught in other regions, these options are abundant, well managed and caught in an environmentally friendly way.

An equal amount of Dijon mustard can be used in place of the hot Chinese mustard. If you like, add a pinch of cayenne pepper to match the heat of the Chinese mustard.

• Preheat barbecue grill to medium-high

2½ tbsp	sesame seeds	37 mL
2 tbsp	liquid honey or agave nectar, divided	30 mL
2½ tbsp	chia seeds	37 mL
	Fine sea salt and freshly cracked black pepper	
1 tsp	Chinese five-spice powder	5 mL
1 tbsp	unseasoned rice vinegar	15 mL
1 tbsp	hot Chinese mustard	15 mL
1 tbsp	toasted sesame oil	15 mL
4	skinless wild salmon fillets (each about 6 oz/175 g)	4

1. In a small dry skillet, toast sesame seeds over medium-low heat, stirring constantly, for 1 to 2 minutes or until fragrant and golden. Add half the honey; cook, tossing often, until glossy clumps form, about 1 minute. Remove from heat and stir in chia seeds. Season to taste with salt and pepper. Spread out on a plate and let cool completely.

2. In a small bowl or cup, whisk together five-spice powder, the remaining honey, vinegar and mustard. Set aside.

3. Brush both sides of fish with oil and sprinkle with salt and pepper. Grill on preheated barbecue, brushing with mustard sauce and turning once, for 3 to 4 minutes per side or until fish is opaque and flakes easily when tested with a fork.

4. Serve fish sprinkled with chia-sesame seed mixture.

Lemony Shrimp, Asparagus and Quinoa Stir-Fry

Plump-sweet shrimp, tender-crisp asparagus and nutty quinoa together make one heck of a trio. Make the quinoa a day ahead and chill it; when dinnertime arrives the next day, this dish will come together in a matter of minutes.

Tips

Chilling the quinoa before stir-frying helps to keep it from clumping and sticking to the pan.

Cooked amaranth, millet, long-grain brown rice or sorghum, chilled, can be used in place of the quinoa. Information on cooking these grains can be found on pages 8–17.

1 tbsp	minced garlic	15 mL
1 tsp	cornstarch	5 mL
1 tbsp	olive oil	15 mL
1 tsp	finely grated lemon zest	5 mL
3 tbsp	freshly squeezed lemon juice	45 mL
12 oz	asparagus, trimmed and cut into 1-inch (2.5 cm) pieces	375 g
12 oz	fresh or thawed frozen medium-large shrimp, peeled and deveined	375 g
1/4 cup	dry white wine	60 mL
2 cups	cooked quinoa (see page 15), chilled	500 mL

1. In a small bowl, whisk together garlic, cornstarch, oil, lemon zest and lemon juice.

2. In a large skillet, heat garlic mixture over medium-high heat until bubbling. Add asparagus and cook, stirring, for 2 minutes or until slightly softened.

3. Add shrimp and wine; cook, stirring, for 2 to 3 minutes or until shrimp are pink, firm and opaque.

4. Add quinoa and cook, stirring, for 2 to 3 minutes to heat through and blend the flavors. Serve immediately.

Greek Sorghum Skillet with Shrimp and Feta

Makes 4 servings

This fresh but filling skillet supper is full of Mediterranean flavor. Equally enticing, the dish comes together in a matter of minutes.

Tip

Hot cooked amaranth, millet, quinoa or brown rice can be used in place of the sorghum. Information on cooking these grains can be found on pages 8–16.

1 tbsp	olive oil	15 mL
12 oz	fresh or thawed frozen medium shrimp, peeled and deveined	375 g
2	cloves garlic, minced	2
1	can (14 to 15 oz/398 to 425 mL) diced tomatoes, with juice	1
3 cups	hot cooked sorghum (see page 17)	750 mL
1/3 cup	pitted brine-cured black olives (such as kalamata), chopped	75 mL
1/2 cup	packed fresh parsley leaves, roughly chopped	125 mL
	Fine sea salt and freshly cracked black pepper	
1/3 cup	crumbled feta cheese	75 mL

1. In a large skillet, heat oil over medium-high heat. Add shrimp and garlic; cook, stirring, for 30 seconds.

2. Stir in tomatoes, reduce heat and simmer, stirring occasionally, for 3 minutes or until thickened.

3. Stir in sorghum and olives; simmer, stirring, for 1 minute or until shrimp are pink, firm and opaque. Stir in parsley. Season to taste with salt and pepper. Serve sprinkled with cheese.

Shrimp Pilau with Pistachios

The distinctive, almost floral fragrance of basmati rice — an Indian staple — finds perfect expression in this quick-to-the-table, South Indian–style dish.

Tip

Other varieties of long-grain brown rice can be substituted for the brown basmati rice.

2 tbsp	virgin coconut oil	30 mL
1 cup	chopped onion	250 mL
1 cup	brown basmati rice	250 mL
1 tsp	ground coriander	5 mL
¾ tsp	ground turmeric	3 mL
2½ cups	ready-to-use GF chicken or vegetable broth	625 mL
12 oz	fresh or thawed frozen medium shrimp, peeled and deveined	375 g
¼ cup	raisins, chopped	60 mL
2 tbsp	freshly squeezed lime juice	30 mL
⅓ cup	chopped lightly salted roasted pistachios or cashews	75 mL

1. In a large skillet, melt coconut oil over low heat. Add onion, increase heat to medium-high and cook, stirring, for 6 to 8 minutes or until softened. Add rice, coriander and turmeric; cook, stirring, for 1 minute.

2. Stir in broth and bring to a boil. Reduce heat to low, cover and simmer for 45 to 50 minutes or until liquid is absorbed.

3. Add shrimp, cover, leaving lid ajar, and cook for 2 to 3 minutes or until shrimp are pink, firm and opaque. Fluff rice with a fork.

4. Stir in raisins and lime juice; cook, stirring, for 1 to 2 minutes or until warmed through. Serve sprinkled with pistachios.

Amaranth Paella

White wine and a pinch of saffron add authentic oomph to this quick and easy version of paella. The clean spark of lemon at the end brightens the dish.

Tip

An equal amount of ready-to-use GF chicken or vegetable broth can be used in place of the wine.

Variation

Vegan Paella: Replace the sausage with a 14- to 19-oz (398 to 540 mL) can of chickpeas or white beans (such as Great Northern, navy or cannellini), drained and rinsed. Omit the shrimp.

1 tbsp	olive oil	15 mL
1	red bell pepper, chopped	1
1 cup	chopped onion	250 mL
2	cloves garlic, minced	2
8 oz	GF smoked chicken or pork sausage, diced	250 g
Pinch	saffron threads	Pinch
1/2 cup	dry white wine	125 mL
12 oz	fresh or thawed frozen medium shrimp, peeled and deveined	375 g
1 cup	frozen petite peas, thawed	250 mL
3 cups	hot cooked amaranth (see page 8)	750 mL
2 tbsp	freshly squeezed lemon juice	30 mL

1. In a large skillet, heat oil over medium-high heat. Add red pepper and onion; cook, stirring, for 6 to 8 minutes or until softened. Add garlic and sausage; cook, stirring, for 2 minutes.

2. Stir in saffron and wine; bring to a boil. Add shrimp and peas; reduce heat to low, cover, leaving lid ajar, and simmer for 2 to 3 minutes or until shrimp are pink, firm and opaque.

3. Remove from heat and stir in amaranth. Cover and let stand for 3 minutes. Fluff amaranth with a fork, stirring in lemon juice.

Jeweled Quinoa with Chicken Sausage

Jeweled rice — rice cooked with spices and studded with dried fruits, nuts and herbs — is a prize dish in Persian cuisine. I've used it as inspiration for a simple quinoa skillet meal.

Tips

An equal amount of millet or amaranth can be used in place of the quinoa.

Look for chicken sausages that are fully cooked. Other varieties of cooked sausage (smoked or unsmoked), such as those made with turkey, pork or a combination, can be used in place of the chicken sausages.

4 tsp	olive oil, divided	20 mL
1½ cups	chopped onions	375 mL
1 cup	quinoa, rinsed	250 mL
¾ tsp	fine sea salt	3 mL
¼ tsp	ground cinnamon	1 mL
Pinch	saffron threads	Pinch
1⅔ cups	water	400 mL
½ cup	chopped dried tart cherries or cranberries	125 mL
12 oz	GF cooked chicken sausages, diced	375 g
½ cup	packed fresh flat-leaf (Italian) parsley leaves, roughly chopped	125 mL
¼ cup	lightly salted roasted pistachios or almonds, chopped	60 mL

1. In a large skillet, heat half the oil over medium-high heat. Add onions and cook, stirring, for 7 to 8 minutes or until lightly browned. Add quinoa and cook, stirring, for 1 minute. Stir in salt, cinnamon, saffron and water; bring to a boil. Reduce heat to low, cover and simmer for 12 minutes. Stir in cherries, cover and simmer for 3 to 6 minutes or until water is absorbed.

2. Meanwhile, in a medium skillet, heat the remaining oil over medium-high heat. Add sausage and cook, stirring, for 2 to 3 minutes or until browned.

3. Add sausage to the quinoa mixture and cook over medium heat, stirring, for 1 to 2 minutes to blend the flavors. Remove from heat and stir in parsley and pistachios.

Amaranth with Roasted Sweet Potatoes, Chicken and Apples

An ode to fall in one dish, this sweet potato, apple and chicken amaranth is quintessential comfort fare.

Tip

Hot cooked buckwheat, millet, quinoa, brown rice or sorghum can be used in place of the amaranth. Information on cooking these grains can be found on pages 9–17.

- Preheat oven to 425°F (220°C)
- Large rimmed baking sheet

2	sweet potatoes (about 1 lb/500 g), peeled and cut into ½-inch (1 cm) pieces	2
1	large Granny Smith apple, peeled and cut into ½-inch (1 cm) pieces	1
2 tbsp	olive oil	30 mL
1½ tsp	dry rubbed sage	7 mL
	Fine sea salt and freshly cracked black pepper	
1	bunch green onions, trimmed and coarsely chopped	1
3 cups	hot cooked amaranth (see page 8)	750 mL
2 cups	diced cooked rotisserie chicken breast, warmed	500 mL
2 tsp	cider vinegar or white wine vinegar	10 mL

1. Place sweet potatoes and apple on prepared baking sheet. Toss with oil and sprinkle with sage, salt and pepper. Spread out in a single layer. Roast in preheated oven for 12 minutes. Add green onions to baking sheet, stirring to coat with oil and combine. Spread out and roast for 10 to 12 minutes or until sweet potatoes are browned and tender. Transfer mixture to a large bowl.

2. Add amaranth, chicken and vinegar, gently tossing to combine. Season to taste with salt and pepper.

Millet with Thyme-Scented Chicken and White Beans

Makes 4 servings

Millet may have its roots in Ancient China and Rome, but it takes beautifully to French flavors — thyme, garlic and white wine — in this flavorful skillet dish.

Tips

Chickpeas can be used in place of the white beans.

Hot cooked amaranth, quinoa, brown rice or sorghum can be used in place of the millet. Information on cooking these grains can be found on pages 8–17.

2 tsp	olive oil	10 mL
1 cup	chopped onion	250 mL
1 lb	boneless skinless chicken breasts, cut into 1-inch (2.5 cm) cubes	500 g
4	cloves garlic, minced	4
1½ tsp	dried thyme	7 mL
½ tsp	fine sea salt	2 mL
½ tsp	freshly cracked black pepper	2 mL
1	can (14 to 19 oz/398 to 540 mL) white beans (such as navy or Great Northern), drained and rinsed	1
1	can (14 to 15 oz/398 to 425 mL) diced tomatoes, with juice	1
⅓ cup	dry white wine	75 mL
3 cups	hot cooked millet (see page 11)	750 mL

1. In a large skillet, heat oil over medium-high heat. Add onion and cook, stirring, for 5 minutes or until slightly softened. Add chicken, garlic, thyme, salt and pepper; cook, stirring, for 4 minutes or until chicken is browned on all sides.

2. Stir in beans, tomatoes and wine. Reduce heat and simmer, stirring occasionally, for 5 to 7 minutes or until sauce is slightly thickened and chicken is no longer pink inside.

3. Divide millet among four shallow bowls and top with chicken mixture.

Jerk Chicken Quinoa

This easy, breezy, down-island dish is great for busy weeknights, but impressive for weekend guests, too.

Tips

A 1-lb (500 g) pork tenderloin, trimmed and cut into 1-inch (2.5 cm) cubes, can be used in place of the chicken.

Hot cooked amaranth, millet, brown rice or sorghum can be used in place of the quinoa. Information on cooking these grains can be found on pages 8–17.

To toast coconut, preheat oven to 300°F (150°C). Spread coconut in a thin, even layer on an ungreased baking sheet. Bake for 15 to 20 minutes, stirring every 5 minutes, until golden brown and fragrant. Transfer to a plate and let cool completely.

12 oz	boneless skinless chicken breasts, cut into 1-inch (2.5 cm) cubes	375 g
1 tbsp	salt-free dry Jamaican jerk seasoning	15 mL
1/2 tsp	fine sea salt	2 mL
1 1/2 tbsp	virgin coconut oil	22 mL
3 cups	hot cooked quinoa (see page 15)	750 mL
2 tsp	finely grated lime zest	10 mL
2 tbsp	freshly squeezed lime juice	30 mL
1/2 cup	raisins, chopped	125 mL
3/4 cup	thinly sliced green onions	175 mL
1/2 cup	unsweetened flaked coconut, toasted (optional)	125 mL
1/2 cup	lightly salted roasted cashews, chopped	125 mL

1. In a large sealable plastic bag, combine chicken, jerk seasoning and salt, shaking to coat chicken.

2. In a large skillet, melt coconut oil over low heat. Add chicken, increase heat to medium-high and cook, stirring, for 6 to 8 minutes or until no longer pink inside.

3. Stir in quinoa, lime zest, lime juice and raisins. Remove from heat, cover and let stand for 5 minutes. Fluff quinoa with a fork. Stir in green onions, coconut (if using) and cashews.

Quinoa Chicken Biryani

Makes 4 servings

Biryani is a traditional rice dish from India and Pakistan featuring rice, meat and spices. This version is easy enough to make any night of the week, and you can adjust the heat level based on the heat of the curry powder you choose.

Tips

An equal amount of millet or amaranth can be used in place of the quinoa.

You can quickly toast sliced almonds on the stovetop. Spread them in a dry medium skillet set over medium heat. Stir until the almonds are golden brown and fragrant. Immediately transfer to a plate to cool.

1 tbsp	olive oil	15 mL
1 cup	chopped onion	250 mL
1½ tbsp	curry powder (any heat level)	22 mL
¾ tsp	ground cardamom	3 mL
½ tsp	ground cinnamon	2 mL
1 lb	boneless skinless chicken breasts, cut into 1-inch (2.5 cm) cubes	500 g
1 cup	quinoa, rinsed	250 mL
⅓ cup	golden or dark raisins	75 mL
1¾ cups	ready-to-use GF chicken broth	425 mL
2 tbsp	freshly squeezed lime juice	30 mL
	Fine sea salt and freshly ground black pepper	
¼ cup	sliced almonds, toasted (see tip, at left)	60 mL
¼ cup	packed fresh cilantro leaves, roughly chopped	60 mL

1. In a large skillet, heat oil over medium-high heat. Add onion and cook, stirring, for 5 to 6 minutes or until softened. Add curry powder, cardamom and cinnamon; cook, stirring, for 30 seconds. Add chicken and cook, stirring, for 3 to 5 minutes or until browned on all sides.

2. Stir in quinoa, raisins and broth; bring to a boil. Reduce heat to low, cover and simmer for 10 to 12 minutes or until most of the liquid is absorbed. Remove from heat and let stand, covered, for 5 minutes. Fluff quinoa with a fork, stirring in lime juice. Season to taste with salt and pepper. Serve sprinkled with almonds and cilantro.

Hoisin Chicken and Chard with Chili Garlic Quinoa

A bed of spicy quinoa and a sprinkling of cashews add body and crunch to this filling entrée. The Swiss chard and ginger contribute hits of freshness and heat, as well as vivid flavor.

Tip

Hot cooked amaranth, millet, brown rice or sorghum can be used in place of the quinoa. Information on cooking these grains can be found on pages 8–17.

1 tbsp	olive oil	15 mL
1	large red bell pepper, thinly sliced	1
1 lb	boneless skinless chicken breasts, cut into thin strips	500 g
3 tbsp	minced gingerroot	45 mL
1	large bunch red Swiss chard, tough stems and center ribs removed, leaves thinly sliced crosswise (about 5 cups/1.25 L), divided	1
¼ cup	hoisin sauce	60 mL
2 tbsp	water	30 mL
1 tbsp	Asian chili-garlic sauce	15 mL
3 cups	hot cooked quinoa (see page 15)	750 mL
⅓ cup	lightly salted roasted cashews, coarsely chopped	75 mL

1. In a large skillet, heat oil over medium-high heat. Add red pepper and cook, stirring, for 5 to 6 minutes or until slightly softened. Add chicken and ginger; cook, stirring, for 2 minutes.

2. Add half the Swiss chard, hoisin sauce and water; cook, stirring, for 2 to 3 minutes or until Swiss chard is wilted. Add the remaining Swiss chard and cook, stirring, for 1 to 2 minutes or until Swiss chard is wilted and chicken is no longer pink inside.

3. Stir chili-garlic sauce into hot quinoa. Divide quinoa mixture among four bowls and top with chicken mixture. Sprinkle with cashews.

Miso Chicken, Edamame and Quinoa Skillet

Miso can do so much more than make soup; it also works as a great multipurpose seasoning for vegetables, meat, fish and chicken. Here, it lends deep umami flavor to chicken breasts.

Tips

Cooked amaranth, millet, brown rice or sorghum, cooled, can be used in place of the quinoa. Information on cooking these grains can be found on pages 8–17.

Make sure to use fine sea salt in the water you use to cook the edamame. Conventional table salt contains chemicals and additives, whereas sea salt contains an abundance of naturally occurring trace minerals.

12 oz	boneless skinless chicken breasts, cut into thin strips	375 g
1 tbsp	GF yellow miso paste	15 mL
2 cups	frozen shelled edamame	500 mL
1½ tbsp	toasted sesame oil	22 mL
1 tbsp	minced gingerroot	15 mL
2 cups	cooked quinoa (see page 15), cooled	500 mL
½ cup	thinly sliced green onions	125 mL
2 tsp	unseasoned rice vinegar	10 mL

1. Place chicken in a shallow dish and rub all over with miso paste. Cover and refrigerate for 15 minutes.

2. Meanwhile, in a large pot of boiling salted water (see tip, at left), cook edamame for 8 minutes. Drain and set aside.

3. In a large skillet, heat oil over medium-high heat. Add chicken and cook, stirring, for 5 to 6 minutes or until no longer pink inside. Add ginger and cook, stirring, for 1 minute. Add edamame, quinoa and green onions; cook, stirring, for 2 to 3 minutes to heat quinoa and blend the flavors. Sprinkle with vinegar, stirring to combine.

Carrot Bread with Coconut and
Cardamom (page 267)

Multigrain Blueberry Muffins (page 273)

British Cream Currant
Scones (page 278)

Ancient Grain Chocolate Chip Cookies (page 290)

Olive Oil Cake with Cherries and
Dark Chocolate Chunks (page 304)

Chocolate, Lime and Coconut Cake (page 305)
with Whipped Coconut Cream (page 326)

Key Lime Pie (page 312)

Berry Crisp with Brown Sugar
Ginger Topping (page 316)

Greek Amaranth and Turkey–Stuffed Swiss Chard Leaves

Makes 6 servings

Consider this a simplified main-dish reinvention of stuffed grape leaves. The mild flavor of the Swiss chard will win over everyone in the family.

Tips

Any variety of Swiss chard leaves may be used in this recipe.

Cooked millet, quinoa, brown rice or sorghum, cooled, can be used in place of the amaranth. Information on cooking these grains can be found on pages 11–17.

12 oz	lean ground turkey	375 g
2 cups	cooked amaranth (see page 8), cooled	500 mL
1 cup	finely chopped onion	250 mL
2 tsp	dried dillweed	10 mL
3/4 tsp	fine sea salt	3 mL
1/2 tsp	freshly cracked black pepper	2 mL
1	large egg, beaten	1
12	large Swiss chard leaves, tough stems removed	12
1 1/2 cups	ready-to-use GF chicken or vegetable broth	375 mL
1	jar (26 oz/700 mL) GF marinara sauce	1
1 cup	crumbled feta cheese	250 mL

1. In a large bowl, gently combine turkey, amaranth, onion, dill, salt, pepper and egg. Form into twelve 3-inch (7.5 cm) oblong portions.

2. Place Swiss chard leaves on a work surface, underside of leaves facing up. Place a portion of turkey mixture in the center of each leaf. Tuck in ends, then tightly roll leaf around filling.

3. Place rolls, seam side down, in a large skillet. Pour in broth, cover and bring to a boil over high heat. Reduce heat and simmer, stirring occasionally, for 8 to 10 minutes or until rolls are no longer pink inside. Discard broth.

4. Meanwhile, in a medium saucepan, warm marinara sauce over medium heat, stirring often.

5. Serve rolls topped with marinara sauce and sprinkled with cheese.

Pizza Quinoa Casserole

A universal favorite (pizza) and a newfangled ingredient (quinoa) unite in this fast, family-friendly casserole.

Tips

If you do not have a 9-inch (23 cm) cast-iron skillet, use a regular skillet for step 1. In step 3, spoon the quinoa mixture into a 9-inch (23 cm) square glass or metal baking dish, spreading evenly. Continue with step 3 as directed.

Hot cooked amaranth, millet, brown rice or sorghum can be used in place of the quinoa. Information on cooking these grains can be found on pages 8–17.

- Preheat oven to 375°F (190°C)
- 9-inch (23 cm) cast-iron skillet (see tip, at left)

8 oz	GF Italian pork or turkey sausage (bulk or casings removed)	250 g
3 cups	hot cooked quinoa (see page 15)	750 mL
	Fine sea salt and freshly cracked black pepper	
1	large egg, beaten	1
2 cups	shredded mozzarella cheese, divided	500 mL
3/4 cup	GF marinara sauce	175 mL
1 1/2 cups	sliced mushrooms	375 mL
2 tbsp	freshly grated Parmesan cheese	30 mL

1. In the cast-iron skillet, cook sausage over medium-high heat, breaking it up with a spoon, for 6 to 8 minutes or until no longer pink. Using a slotted spoon, transfer sausage to a plate lined with paper towels. Drain off all but 1 tsp (5 mL) fat from skillet.

2. In a large bowl, season quinoa to taste with salt and pepper. Stir in egg and half the mozzarella.

3. Spoon quinoa mixture into skillet, spreading evenly. Spoon marinara sauce over quinoa, spreading evenly. Top with the remaining mozzarella, mushrooms, sausage and Parmesan.

4. Bake in preheated oven for 23 to 28 minutes or until cheese is melted and beginning to brown in spots. Let cool on a wire rack for 5 minutes, then cut into wedges and serve.

Millet and Ham Hoppin' John

Hoppin' John is a traditional Southern dish often eaten to bring good luck for the New Year. Here, light and fluffy millet takes the place of the rice, and frozen mustard greens and canned black-eyed peas make the dish weeknight-friendly by shaving off several hours of preparation and cooking time.

Tips

One pound (500 g) of chopped trimmed fresh mustard greens may be used in place of the frozen greens. After adding the greens in step 2, boil, without stirring, for 4 to 5 minutes or until greens are wilted but not yet tender. Continue with step 2.

Hot cooked amaranth, quinoa, long-grain brown rice or sorghum can be used in place of the millet. Information on cooking these grains can be found on pages 8–17.

1 tbsp	olive oil	15 mL
1 cup	chopped onion	250 mL
3	cloves garlic, minced	3
1 tsp	dried thyme	5 mL
1 cup	ready-to-use GF vegetable or chicken broth	250 mL
1	package (10 oz/300 g) frozen chopped mustard greens	1
1	can (14 to 19 oz/398 to 540 mL) black-eyed peas, drained and rinsed	1
1½ cups	diced cooked ham	375 mL
2 cups	hot cooked millet (see page 11)	500 mL
	Fine sea salt and hot pepper sauce	

1. In a large pot, heat oil over medium-high heat. Add onion and cook, stirring, for about 5 minutes or until slightly softened. Add garlic and thyme; cook, stirring, for 30 seconds.

2. Stir in broth and bring to a boil. Add mustard greens and boil, without stirring, for 2 to 3 minutes or until greens are thawed. Stir to combine. Reduce heat to low, cover and simmer, stirring occasionally, for 10 to 15 minutes or until greens are tender.

3. Stir in black-eyed peas and ham; simmer, uncovered, for 5 minutes or until warmed through. Stir in millet. Season to taste with salt and hot pepper sauce.

Rosemary Pork with Quinoa and Sweet Potato Hash

Infusing pork tenderloin with rosemary elevates its flavor in one fell swoop. The sweet potato and quinoa hash alongside is both simple and simply great.

Tips

If you don't have fresh rosemary on hand, you can use ½ tsp (2 mL) dried rosemary, crumbled.

Hot cooked amaranth, millet, brown rice or sorghum can be used in place of the quinoa. Information on cooking these grains can be found on pages 8–17.

- Preheat oven to 400°F (200°C)
- Large ovenproof skillet

1 lb	pork tenderloin, trimmed	500 g
1 tsp	minced fresh rosemary	5 mL
½ tsp	fine sea salt, divided	2 mL
2 tbsp	olive oil, divided	30 mL
1 cup	chopped onion	250 mL
1	large sweet potato (about 12 oz/375 g), peeled and shredded	1
1½ cups	hot cooked quinoa (see page 15)	375 mL
2 tbsp	pure maple syrup	30 mL
⅓ cup	packed fresh flat-leaf (Italian) parsley leaves, chopped	75 mL

1. Sprinkle pork with rosemary and half the salt. In the ovenproof skillet, heat half the oil over medium-high heat. Add pork and cook, turning several times, for 3 to 4 minutes or until browned all over.

2. Transfer skillet to preheated oven and roast for 12 to 14 minutes or until an instant-read thermometer inserted in the thickest part of the tenderloin registers 145°F (63°C) for medium-rare, or until desired doneness. Let rest for at least 5 minutes before slicing.

3. Meanwhile, in another large skillet, heat the remaining oil over medium-high heat. Add onion and cook, stirring, for 2 minutes. Add sweet potato and the remaining salt; cook, stirring, for 8 to 10 minutes or until sweet potato is tender. Add quinoa and maple syrup; cook, stirring, for 1 to 2 minutes to blend the flavors. Stir in parsley. Serve with pork.

Sicilian Pork and Peppers with Millet Polenta

Makes 4 servings

Who says stir-fries are limited to Asian food? This Sicilian-inspired pork and pepper dish proves otherwise. Be sure to start the polenta before cooking the pork, as the latter comes together very quickly.

Tip

You can replace the pork with 1 lb (500 g) boneless skinless chicken breasts, cut into thin strips. Cook until chicken is no longer pink inside.

1 lb	pork tenderloin, trimmed	500 g
1 tbsp	olive oil	15 mL
3	cloves garlic, minced	3
1	red bell pepper, cut into very thin strips	1
1	green bell pepper, cut into very thin strips	1
1 tsp	dried oregano	5 mL
1/3 cup	dry white wine	75 mL
3 tbsp	tomato paste	45 mL
	Millet Polenta (page 208, prepared through step 2) or Teff Polenta (page 174)	

1. Cut pork crosswise into $1/2$-inch (1 cm) thick slices. Place slices cut side down and cut into $1/2$-inch (1 cm) wide strips.

2. In a large skillet, heat oil over medium-high heat. Add pork and garlic; cook, stirring, for 2 minutes. Add red pepper, green pepper and oregano; cook, stirring, for 2 minutes. Stir in wine and tomato paste; reduce heat and simmer, stirring, for 1 minute or until sauce is slightly thickened and just a hint of pink remains inside pork. Serve over Millet Polenta.

Cumin Pork and Millet Bowls with Avocado and Mango

This comforting bowlful marries the simplicity of quickly stir-fried pork with millet and the big, fresh flavors of Central America.

Tip

An equal amount of diced pineapple can be used in place of the mango.

1 lb	pork tenderloin, trimmed and cut into thin strips	500 g
1½ tsp	ground cumin	7 mL
	Fine sea salt and freshly ground black pepper	
1 tbsp	olive oil	15 mL
1 cup	millet	250 mL
2 cups	water	500 mL
2 tbsp	freshly squeezed lime juice	30 mL
1	firm-ripe Hass avocado, diced	1
1½ cups	diced mango	375 mL
½ cup	packed fresh cilantro leaves	125 mL

Suggested Accompaniments

Crumbled queso fresco

Thinly sliced (crosswise) red chile peppers

Chia seeds

Lime wedges

1. Season pork with cumin, salt and pepper. In a large skillet, heat oil over medium-high heat. Add pork and cook, stirring, for 5 to 6 minutes or until just a hint of pink remains inside. Remove pork to a plate.

2. Add millet and water to the skillet; bring to a boil. Reduce heat to low, cover and simmer for 15 minutes. Remove from heat, return pork to the pan, cover and let stand for 10 minutes. Fluff with fork, stirring in lime juice. Season to taste with salt and pepper.

3. Divide millet mixture among four bowls and top with avocado, mango and cilantro. Serve with any of the suggested accompaniments, as desired.

Sesame Ginger Pork with Millet Slaw

The combination of sesame, soy and ginger is a trinity used many times over in multiple Asian cuisines. And for good reason: it makes just about everything, from vegetables to noodles to meats, delectable. Here, it works magic in a pork tenderloin dish that is coupled with a crunchy, colorful millet slaw.

Tips

Choose unseasoned rice vinegar over seasoned rice vinegar; the latter has added sugar and salt.

Cooked amaranth or quinoa, cooled, can be used in place of the millet. Information on cooking these grains can be found on pages 8–15.

Green cabbage can be substituted for the purple cabbage.

Millet Slaw

3 tbsp	unseasoned rice vinegar	45 mL
2 tbsp	GF tamari or soy sauce	30 mL
1 tbsp	Asian chili-garlic sauce	15 mL
2 tsp	sesame oil	10 mL
1½ cups	cooked millet (see page 11), cooled	375 mL
2 cups	shredded purple cabbage	500 mL
½ cup	shredded carrot	125 mL
½ cup	chopped green onions	125 mL

Sesame Ginger Pork

1 tbsp	packed brown sugar	15 mL
2 tsp	ground ginger	10 mL
¼ cup	GF soy sauce	60 mL
¼ cup	unsweetened apple juice	60 mL
2 tbsp	sesame oil	30 mL
1 tbsp	Asian chili-garlic sauce	15 mL
1 lb	pork tenderloin, trimmed and cut crosswise into very thin slices	500 g
2 tbsp	sesame or chia seeds (optional)	30 mL

1. *Slaw:* In a large bowl, whisk together vinegar, soy sauce, chili-garlic sauce and oil. Add millet, cabbage, carrot and green onions, gently tossing to combine. Cover and refrigerate for up to 1 hour.

2. *Pork:* In a medium bowl, whisk together sugar, ginger, soy sauce, apple juice, oil and chili-garlic sauce. Add pork and toss to coat. Cover and refrigerate for 15 minutes.

3. Remove half the pork slices from marinade, shaking off excess. In a large, deep skillet, cook pork over medium-high heat, stirring, for 2 to 4 minutes or until browned on all sides and just a hint of pink remains inside. Transfer to a plate. Repeat with the remaining pork, discarding marinade. Return all pork to skillet and cook, stirring, until heated through.

4. Serve pork with slaw. Garnish with sesame seeds, if desired.

Thai Grilled Steak and Quinoa Bowls

Take a trip to Thailand with these boldly flavored steak and quinoa bowls.

Tips

An equal amount of curry powder (any heat level) can be used in place of the curry paste.

When rubbing the steak with melted coconut oil, be sure to measure out the oil for the dressing first and put it in a separate bowl to avoid any cross-contamination with the raw steak. As well, discard any extra melted oil that you've dipped a brush or your fingers into when rubbing the steak.

- Preheat barbecue grill to medium-high

1 cup	quinoa, rinsed	250 mL
1 tbsp	Thai red or green curry paste	15 mL
1½ cups	water	375 mL
12 oz	boneless beef top loin (strip loin) or top sirloin steak, trimmed	375 g
	Melted virgin coconut oil	
	Fine sea salt and freshly cracked black pepper	
1 tsp	packed light brown sugar	5 mL
2 tbsp	freshly squeezed lime juice	30 mL

Suggested Accompaniments

Fresh mint, cilantro or basil leaves
Very thinly sliced red bell pepper
Toasted unsweetened flaked coconut

1. In a medium saucepan, combine quinoa, curry paste and water. Bring to a boil over medium-high heat, stirring to combine curry paste. Reduce heat to low, cover and simmer for 12 to 15 minutes or until liquid is absorbed. Remove from heat and let stand, covered, for 5 minutes. Fluff with a fork.

2. Meanwhile, pat steak dry with paper towels. Lightly rub with coconut oil (see tip, at left). Sprinkle with salt and generously season with pepper. Grill on preheated barbecue, turning once, for 5 to 6 minutes per side for medium-rare, or to desired doneness. Transfer to a cutting board and let rest for 5 minutes.

3. In a small bowl, whisk together brown sugar, 2 tbsp (30 mL) coconut oil and lime juice. Season to taste with salt and pepper.

4. Divide quinoa mixture among four bowls. Thinly slice steak and arrange on top. Sprinkle with any of the suggested accompaniments, as desired. Drizzle with dressing.

Skillet Quinoa Eggplant Parmesan

One of the great Italian comfort food dishes — eggplant Parmesan — inspired this hearty but streamlined supper. Sautéing the eggplant instead of frying it makes the preparation equal parts healthy, easy and delicious.

2 tsp	olive oil	10 mL
1	large eggplant (about 1 lb/500 g), peeled and cut into ½-inch (1 cm) cubes	1
1¼ cups	chopped onions	300 mL
1 lb	extra-lean ground beef	500 g
2	cloves garlic, minced	2
½ tsp	fine sea salt	2 mL
1	can (28 oz/796 mL) crushed tomatoes	1
1 tsp	dried Italian seasoning	5 mL
2 cups	hot cooked quinoa (see page 15)	500 mL
1 cup	shredded mozzarella cheese	250 mL
½ cup	packed fresh basil leaves, roughly chopped (optional)	125 mL
⅓ cup	freshly grated Parmesan cheese	75 mL

1. In a Dutch oven or a large saucepan, heat oil over medium-high heat. Add eggplant and onions; cook, stirring, for 6 to 8 minutes or until softened. Transfer to a bowl.

2. Add beef, garlic and salt to the pan and cook, breaking beef up with a spoon, for 5 to 6 minutes or until beef is no longer pink. Drain off any fat.

3. Stir in eggplant mixture, tomatoes and Italian seasoning; bring to a boil. Reduce heat and simmer, stirring occasionally, for 20 to 25 minutes or until sauce is thickened and eggplant is very tender. Stir in quinoa. Sprinkle with mozzarella and simmer for 1 to 2 minutes or until cheese is melted. Serve sprinkled with basil (if using) and Parmesan.

Keema with Minted Millet

Makes 4 servings

If you are stumped for a quick and easy ground beef recipe, this spicy Indian minced beef is your solution. Packed with great flavor and protein, it will please one and all.

Tip

Hot cooked amaranth, quinoa, brown rice or sorghum can be used in place of the millet. Information on cooking these grains can be found on pages 8–17.

1 lb	extra-lean ground beef	500 g
2	cans (each 10 oz/284 mL) diced tomatoes with chiles and garlic, with juice	2
1	can (14 to 19 oz/398 to 540 mL) chickpeas, drained and rinsed	1
1½ tsp	garam masala	7 mL
1 tsp	curry powder	5 mL
¾ cup	packed fresh mint leaves, chopped	175 mL
3 cups	hot cooked millet (see page 11)	750 mL
	Fine sea salt and freshly cracked black pepper	

Suggested Accompaniments

Plain yogurt

Raisins or currants

Millet, Sorghum and Chia Tortillas (page 260) or other 8-inch (20 cm) GF tortillas

Lime or lemon wedges

1. In a large skillet, cook beef over medium-high heat, breaking it up with a spoon, for 5 to 6 minutes or until no longer pink. Drain off any fat.

2. Stir in tomatoes, chickpeas, garam masala and curry powder; reduce heat and simmer, stirring occasionally, for 5 minutes.

3. Stir mint into millet and season to taste with salt and pepper. Divide millet among four shallow bowls and top with keema. Serve with any of the suggested accompaniments, as desired.

Millet, Beef and Basil Lettuce Wraps

Here is a great example of layering flavors to create a complex-tasting dish in no time: peppery ginger, spicy-sweet hoisin sauce and fresh basil combine to make your new favorite go-to dinner.

Tip
Lean ground turkey or pork can be used in place of the beef.

1 lb	extra-lean ground beef	500 g
2 tbsp	minced gingerroot	30 mL
2/3 cup	chopped green onions	175 mL
1/4 cup	hoisin sauce	60 mL
12	butter or Bibb lettuce leaves	12
2 cups	hot cooked millet (see page 11)	500 mL
1 cup	shredded carrots	250 mL
1/2 cup	packed fresh basil, mint or cilantro leaves	125 mL
1/4 cup	lightly salted roasted peanuts, chopped	60 mL

1. In a large skillet, cook beef over medium-high heat, breaking it up with a spoon, for 5 to 6 minutes or until no longer pink. Add ginger and cook, stirring, for 30 seconds. Drain off any fat.

2. Stir in green onions and hoisin sauce; reduce heat and cook, stirring, for 1 to 2 minutes or until green onions are slightly softened and sauce is slightly thickened.

3. Place lettuce leaves on a work surface, underside of leaves facing up. Spoon millet down the center of each leaf, then top with beef mixture, carrots, basil and peanuts. Tuck in ends, then tightly roll leaf around filling.

Amaranth Meatloaf with Peppers and Kale

Makes 8 servings

A mix of beef, amaranth and three vegetables ensures a moist, flavorful meatloaf. Barbecue sauce, both in and on top of the loaf, adds balance and faint sweetness.

Tips

Lean ground turkey or pork can be used in place of the beef.

Cooked millet or quinoa, cooled, or dry-cooked teff can be used in place of the amaranth. Information on cooking these grains can be found on pages 11–18.

For a more traditional flavor, replace the barbecue sauce with an equal amount of GF marinara sauce.

- Large rimmed baking sheet, lined with parchment paper

2 tbsp	olive oil	30 mL
2 cups	finely chopped red bell peppers	500 mL
1 cup	finely chopped onion	250 mL
2 cups	finely chopped trimmed kale leaves	500 mL
1 lb	extra-lean ground beef	250 mL
2 cups	cooked amaranth (see page 8), cooled	500 mL
1 tsp	fine sea salt	5 mL
1/4 tsp	freshly cracked black pepper	1 mL
1 cup	GF barbecue sauce, divided	250 mL

1. In a large skillet, heat oil over medium-high heat. Add red peppers and onion; cook, stirring, for 6 to 8 minutes or until softened. Add kale and cook, stirring, for 2 minutes or until wilted. Remove from heat and let cool to room temperature.

2. Preheat oven to 375°F (190°C).

3. In a large bowl, thoroughly combine kale mixture, beef, amaranth, salt, pepper and half the barbecue sauce. Form into two 8- by 4-inch (20 by 10 cm) loaves. Place on prepared baking sheet, at least 3 inches (7.5 cm) apart, and brush with the remaining barbecue sauce.

4. Bake for 43 to 48 minutes or until loaves are browned and a thermometer inserted in the center registers 160°F (71°C). Let stand for at least 15 minutes before slicing (to avoid crumbling).

Ancient Grain and Beef Meatballs

This recipe is a basic template from which you can vary the ground meat, ancient grains and seasonings in countless ways — and that's all before you think about adding a sauce! Marinara is a classic choice, but try a bit of hoisin sauce or barbecue sauce for a quick glaze, or perhaps a few spoonfuls of your favorite pesto. Have fun!

Tips

If using non-dairy milk, try hemp, almond or rice.

Lean ground turkey, chicken or pork can be used in place of the beef.

Cooked amaranth or millet, cooled, or dry-cooked teff can be used in place of the quinoa. Information on cooking these grains can be found on pages 8–18.

- Large rimmed baking sheet, lined with parchment paper

1	large egg	1
2	cloves garlic, finely chopped	2
1 1/2 tsp	fine sea salt	7 mL
1/2 tsp	freshly ground black pepper	2 mL
1/2 cup	milk or plain non-dairy milk	125 mL
1 1/2 lbs	extra-lean ground beef	750 g
1 cup	cooked quinoa (see page 15), cooled	250 mL
1 cup	packed fresh parsley leaves, chopped	250 mL

1. In a large bowl, whisk egg until blended. Whisk in garlic, salt, pepper and milk until combined. Using your hands, mix in beef, quinoa and parsley until combined. Cover and refrigerate for at least 1 hour, until chilled, or for up to 24 hours.

2. Preheat oven to 400°F (200°C).

3. Form beef mixture into 24 meatballs. Arrange on prepared baking sheet.

4. Bake for 10 minutes. Turn and bake for 7 to 10 minutes or until browned, firm to the touch and no longer pink inside.

Variations

Albóndigas (Mexican Meatballs): Replace the black pepper with 1 tsp (5 mL) chipotle chile powder, and add 3/4 tsp (3 mL) ground cumin and 1/2 tsp (2 mL) dried oregano. Replace the parsley with an equal amount of packed fresh cilantro leaves, chopped.

Kefta (Middle Eastern Spiced Meatballs): Add 3/4 tsp (3 mL) ground cumin, 1/2 tsp (2 mL) ground allspice and 1/4 tsp (1 mL) ground cinnamon with the pepper. Replace half the parsley with 1/2 cup (125 mL) packed fresh cilantro leaves, chopped.

Fresh and Juicy Beef and Amaranth Burgers

This ancient grain take on the classic beef burger features delicate amaranth (which keeps the burgers moist and tender), an ample amount of garlic and all of the fixings.

Tips

Cooked millet or quinoa, cooled, can be used in place of the amaranth. Information on cooking these grains can be found on pages 11–15.

Substitute lean ground turkey or extra-lean ground pork for the beef.

- Food processor

1 cup	cooked amaranth (see page 8), cooled	250 mL
4	cloves garlic	4
1 tsp	fine sea salt	5 mL
1 lb	extra-lean ground beef	500 g
1 tbsp	olive oil	15 mL
4	GF hamburger buns, split and toasted	4
4	large tomato slices	4
2 cups	packed trimmed spinach leaves	500 mL

Suggested Accompaniments

Ketchup
Spicy mustard
Sliced or crumbled cheese
Sliced Hass avocado

1. In food processor, combine amaranth, garlic and salt; pulse until blended.

2. Transfer amaranth mixture to a large bowl and add beef. Using your hands, gently combine the mixture, being careful not to compact it. Form into four $3/4$-inch (2 cm) thick patties.

3. In a large skillet, heat oil over medium-high heat. Add patties and cook for 4 minutes. Turn and cook for 4 to 5 minutes or until no longer pink inside.

4. Transfer patties to bottom halves of toasted buns and top with tomato, spinach and any of the suggested accompaniments, as desired. Cover with top halves of buns, pressing down gently.

Breads, Muffins and Snacks

No-Knead Sandwich Bread

Delicious, fast and fuss-free (no kneading and only about 5 minutes assembly time), this is definitely the gluten-free sandwich bread you've been seeking. It makes a perfect sandwich loaf, but is a fine complement to dinners and soups, too.

Tips

Be sure to line the bottom of the pan with parchment paper and generously grease or spray the pan with cooking spray, as this loaf tends to stick.

If using non-dairy milk, try hemp, almond or rice.

You can grind the chia seeds with a mortar and pestle or seal them in a small, heavy-duty plastic bag with a zipper top and pound them with a mallet or rolling pin until crushed.

Storage Tip

Store the cooled bread, wrapped in foil or plastic wrap, in the refrigerator for up to 1 week. Alternatively, wrap it in plastic wrap, then foil, completely enclosing bread, and freeze for up to 3 months. Let thaw at room temperature for 4 to 6 hours before serving.

- Stand mixer, fitted with paddle attachment
- 9- by 5-inch (23 by 12.5 cm) metal loaf pan, lined with parchment paper and generously greased or sprayed with nonstick cooking spray

2 tbsp	fine crystal cane sugar	30 mL
1 tbsp	quick-rising (instant) yeast	15 mL
1 cup	warm milk or plain non-dairy milk	250 mL
1 cup	brown rice flour	250 mL
1 cup	sorghum flour	250 mL
1/4 cup	potato starch	60 mL
1/4 cup	tapioca starch	60 mL
1 1/2 tbsp	chia seeds, ground (see tip, at left)	22 mL
1/2 tsp	fine sea salt	2 mL
2	large eggs, beaten	2
3 tbsp	olive oil	45 mL
1 tsp	cider vinegar	5 mL

1. In a small bowl, combine sugar, yeast and milk. Let stand for 5 minutes or until foamy.

2. In a medium bowl, whisk together brown rice flour, sorghum flour, potato starch, tapioca starch, chia seeds and salt.

3. In stand mixer fitted with paddle attachment, combine the yeast mixture, eggs, oil and vinegar. Gradually beat in the flour mixture. Beat on low speed for 1 minute. Beat on medium speed for 2 minutes. (The dough will appear softer and looser than glutinous bread dough.)

4. Transfer dough to prepared pan, smoothing the top with a wet spatula. Place pan in a warm place and cover loosely with a clean, lint-free tea towel. Let rise for 25 to 35 minutes or until dough reaches the top of the pan.

5. Meanwhile, preheat oven to 375°F (190°F).

6. Bake for 20 minutes. Tent with foil to prevent over-browning. Bake for 10 to 15 minutes or until golden brown and set at the center. Let cool in pan on a wire rack for 10 minutes, then transfer to the rack to cool completely.

Multi-Seed Bread

This incredible loaf launches quick bread-baking into a new stratosphere of ease, simplicity and deliciousness. It can be sliced very thin, making it ideal for open-faced sandwiches, and because it is loaded with protein, it is also a superb breakfast on the run when simply toasted and spread with jam.

Tip

Use a serrated knife to cut the bread.

Storage Tip

Store the cooled bread, wrapped in foil or plastic wrap, in the refrigerator for up to 1 week. Alternatively, wrap it in plastic wrap, then foil, completely enclosing bread, and freeze for up to 3 months. Let thaw at room temperature for 4 to 6 hours before serving.

- Preheat oven to 325°F (160°F)
- 9- by 5-inch (23 by 12.5 cm) metal loaf pan, lined with parchment paper
- Baking sheet

4	large eggs	4
2 tbsp	olive oil	30 mL
1 cup	green pumpkin seeds (pepitas), chopped	250 mL
1 cup	sunflower seeds	250 mL
¾ cup	sesame seeds	175 mL
½ cup	ground flax seeds (flaxseed meal)	125 mL
6 tbsp	psyllium husk	90 mL
4 tbsp	chia seeds, divided	60 mL
2 tbsp	buckwheat flour	30 mL
1½ tsp	fine sea salt	7 mL

1. In a large bowl, whisk together eggs and oil until well blended. Add pumpkin seeds, sunflower seeds, sesame seeds, flax seeds, psyllium, 3 tbsp (45 mL) chia seeds, flour and salt, stirring until well blended. Let stand for 10 minutes to thicken.

2. Spread batter evenly in prepared pan and sprinkle with the remaining chia seeds.

3. Bake in preheated oven for 30 minutes. Using the parchment paper, transfer bread (including paper) to the baking sheet. Bake for 30 to 35 minutes or until firm in the center and light golden. Transfer bread to a wire rack and let cool completely.

Quinoa Tortillas

The popularity of tortillas extends far beyond Tex-Mex cooking. These days, they are part of everyday eating, for wraps and sandwiches, and as quick and easy stand-ins for flatbreads from other regions of the globe, from India to China to Morocco. Despite their availability in supermarkets everywhere, nothing beats homemade tortillas, and these quinoa ones — flavorful, fragrant and toothsome — do not disappoint.

Tips

If you do not have a tortilla press, you can use a rolling pin. Place a 6-inch (15 cm) wide bowl upside down on the sealable plastic bag and trace a circle around it. Cut out the circle into two rounds. Place a round on either side of the dough ball before rolling it out.

The plastic rounds help ensure that the tortillas do not stick and are all the same size.

Storage Tip

Store the cooled tortillas, wrapped in foil or plastic wrap, in the refrigerator for up to 5 days. Alternatively, wrap them in plastic wrap, then foil, completely enclosing them, and freeze for up to 3 months. Let thaw at room temperature for 4 to 6 hours before serving.

- Tortilla press (see tip, at left)
- Cast-iron or other heavy skillet

2 cups	quinoa flour	500 mL
1/3 cup	brown rice flour	75 mL
1/2 tsp	fine sea salt	2 mL
2/3 cup	hot (not boiling) water	150 mL
2 tsp	olive oil or virgin coconut oil	10 mL
	Additional brown rice flour or quinoa flour	

1. Cut two rounds from a large, heavy-duty sealable plastic bag to fit the shape of the tortilla press. Set aside.

2. In a large bowl, whisk together quinoa flour, brown rice flour and salt. Stir in hot water and oil until mixture comes together into a smooth dough.

3. Turn dough out onto a surface lightly dusted with brown rice flour. Knead for about 1 minute. Cut dough into 8 equal pieces and shape each into a ball. Cover loosely with plastic wrap.

4. Place a plastic round on the bottom half of the tortilla press. Place a dough ball in the center. Top with the second plastic round. Close press, flattening dough to about 1/8 inch (3 mm) thick and forming a 6-inch (15 cm) round. If thickness of tortilla is uneven, lift dough round, in plastic, and rotate 180 degrees. Press tortilla lightly to even out. Peel off top sheet of plastic.

5. Heat cast-iron skillet over medium-high heat. Peel tortilla off bottom sheet of plastic and cook, turning once, for about 45 seconds per side or until it looks slightly dry at the edges, starts to release from the surface of the skillet and is lightly browned in spots. Transfer to a plate.

6. Repeat steps 4 and 5 with the remaining dough balls.

Oat Tortillas

Light and flavorful, these easy oat tortillas are an ideal gluten-free option to replace flour tortillas.

Tips

If you do not have a tortilla press, you can use a rolling pin. Place a 6-inch (15 cm) wide bowl upside down on the sealable plastic bag and trace a circle around it. Cut out the circle into two rounds. Place a round on either side of the dough ball before rolling it out.

The plastic rounds help ensure that the tortillas do not stick and are all the same size.

Storage Tip

Store the cooled tortillas, wrapped in foil or plastic wrap, in the refrigerator for up to 5 days. Alternatively, wrap them in plastic wrap, then foil, completely enclosing them, and freeze for up to 3 months. Let thaw at room temperature for 4 to 6 hours before serving.

- Tortilla press (see tip, at left)
- Cast-iron or other heavy skillet

2 cups	certified GF oat flour	500 mL
1/2 tsp	fine sea salt	2 mL
1/2 cup	hot water (approx.)	125 mL
2 tsp	olive oil or melted virgin coconut oil	10 mL
	Additional certified GF oat flour	

1. Cut two rounds from a large, heavy-duty sealable plastic bag to fit the shape of the tortilla press. Set aside.

2. In a large bowl, whisk together oat flour and salt. Stir in water and oil until mixture comes together into a smooth dough. If the dough seems somewhat dry, add 1 to 2 tbsp (15 to 30 mL) more water.

3. Turn dough out onto a surface lightly dusted with oat flour. Knead for about 1 minute. Cut dough into 6 equal pieces and shape each into a ball. Cover loosely with plastic wrap.

4. Place a plastic round on the bottom half of the tortilla press. Place a dough ball in the center. Top with the second plastic round. Close press, flattening dough to about 1/8 inch (3 mm) thick and forming a 6-inch (15 cm) round. If thickness of tortilla is uneven, lift dough round, in plastic, and rotate 180 degrees. Press tortilla lightly to even out. Peel off top sheet of plastic.

5. Heat cast-iron skillet over medium-high heat. Peel tortilla off bottom sheet of plastic and cook, turning once, for about 45 seconds per side or until it looks slightly dry at the edges, starts to release from the surface of the skillet and is lightly browned in spots. Transfer to a plate.

6. Repeat steps 4 and 5 with the remaining dough balls.

Millet, Sorghum and Chia Tortillas

Who needs corn tortillas when you can up the flavor and nutrition with millet, sorghum and chia? Flexible yet sturdy, these will serve you well for all of your favorite wraps, tacos and burritos.

Tips

If you do not have a tortilla press, you can use a rolling pin. Place an 8-inch (20 cm) wide bowl upside down on the sealable plastic bag and trace a circle around it. Cut out the circle into two rounds. Place a round on either side of the dough ball before rolling it out.

The plastic rounds help ensure that the tortillas do not stick and are all the same size.

If using non-dairy milk, try hemp, almond or rice.

- Tortilla press (see tip, at left)
- Cast-iron or other heavy skillet

²⁄₃ cup	tapioca starch	150 mL
¹⁄₂ cup	millet flour	125 mL
¹⁄₂ cup	sorghum flour	125 mL
¹⁄₃ cup	potato starch	75 mL
1¹⁄₂ tbsp	chia seeds, ground (see tip, page 256)	22 mL
1¹⁄₂ tsp	GF baking powder	7 mL
¹⁄₂ tsp	fine sea salt	2 mL
³⁄₄ cup	milk or plain non-dairy milk	175 mL
1¹⁄₂ tbsp	olive oil or melted virgin coconut oil	22 mL
	Additional potato starch	

1. Cut two rounds from a large, heavy-duty sealable plastic bag to fit the shape of the tortilla press. Set aside.

2. In a large bowl, whisk together tapioca starch, millet flour, sorghum flour, potato starch, chia seeds, baking powder and salt.

3. In a small saucepan, heat milk over medium heat until warm but not hot. Stir into flour mixture, along with oil, until mixture comes together into a smooth, sticky dough. Let rest for 20 minutes.

4. Turn dough out onto a surface lightly dusted with potato starch. Knead for about 1 minute. Cut dough into 8 equal pieces and shape each into a ball. Cover loosely with plastic wrap and let rest for 10 minutes.

Storage Tip

Store the cooled tortillas, wrapped in foil or plastic wrap, in the refrigerator for up to 5 days. Alternatively, wrap them in plastic wrap, then foil, completely enclosing them, and freeze for up to 3 months. Let thaw at room temperature for 4 to 6 hours before serving.

5. Place a plastic round on the bottom half of the tortilla press. Place a dough ball in the center. Top with the second plastic round. Close press, flattening dough to about $\frac{1}{8}$ inch (3 mm) thick and forming an 8-inch (20 cm) round. If thickness of tortilla is uneven, lift dough round, in plastic, and rotate 180 degrees. Press tortilla lightly to even out. Peel off top sheet of plastic.

6. Heat cast-iron skillet over medium-high heat. Peel tortilla off bottom sheet of plastic and cook, turning once, for about 45 seconds per side until it looks slightly dry at the edges, starts to release from the surface of the skillet and is lightly browned in spots. Transfer to a plate.

7. Repeat steps 5 and 6 with the remaining dough balls.

Ethiopian Injera (Teff Flatbread)

Injera is a unique, slightly spongy flatbread that is the national dish of Ethiopia. The batter is traditionally made with teff flour and is allowed to ferment for at least a day, resulting in a distinctive sourdough flavor. Once the batter has fermented, the method for making the breads is similar to that for making crêpes, with two exceptions. First, injera is not as thin as traditional crêpes: you use more batter than you would for crêpes, but less than for traditional breakfast pancakes. Second, you cook injera all the way through without flipping — no anxiety about flipping it out onto the floor!

Storage Tip

Refrigerate injera between sheets of waxed paper, tightly covered in plastic wrap, for up to 2 days or freeze, enclosed in a sealable plastic bag, for up to 1 month.

- Several clean, lint-free tea towels

2 cups	teff flour	500 mL
3 cups	warm water	750 mL
$\frac{1}{2}$ tsp	fine sea salt	2 mL
	Olive oil	

1. In a large bowl, whisk together teff flour and warm water. Cover loosely with a clean, lint-free tea towel and let stand in a warm spot for at least 1 day, until mixture is foamy on the surface and has a tangy aroma, or for up to 2 days.

2. Skim off any foam from the surface of the batter. Whisk in salt.

3. Heat a medium skillet over medium-high heat. Remove from heat and lightly coat pan with oil. Whisk the batter slightly. For each injera, pour about $\frac{1}{3}$ cup (75 mL) batter into pan, quickly tilting in all directions to spread batter to about $\frac{1}{8}$ inch (3 mm) thick. Cook for 2 to 3 minutes or until surface of injera is covered in small holes and feels dry to the touch. Using a spatula, transfer injera to a clean, lint-free tea towel to cool completely. Repeat with the remaining batter, oiling the skillet and adjusting heat as necessary between injera. Place each hot injera on a towel to cool, without overlapping or stacking. Once injera are cooled, stack them between sheets of waxed paper to prevent sticking.

Corn-Free Millet Cornbread

Makes 9 slices

The flavor of this no-corn cornbread is so spot-on, few will guess that it is made with millet instead. The secret is the addition of coarsely crushed whole millet, which delivers a stone-ground cornmeal flavor and texture. The only giveaway is the bread's pale color, but a bit of turmeric corrects that, lending a just-right golden hue.

Tips

If you don't have a cast-iron skillet, use a 9-inch (23 cm) metal baking pan instead. Do not preheat the pan; simply spray it with nonstick cooking spray or rub it with oil. The bread will not be as crusty as when baked in the skillet.

If using non-dairy milk, try hemp, almond or rice.

Storage Tip

Store the cooled bread, wrapped in foil or plastic wrap, in the refrigerator for up to 3 days. Alternatively, wrap it in plastic wrap, then foil, completely enclosing bread, and freeze for up to 3 months. Let thaw at room temperature for 4 to 6 hours before serving.

- Preheat oven to 375°F (190°C)
- 9-inch (23 cm) cast-iron skillet, oiled

1 cup	millet	250 mL
1½ tbsp	chia seeds	22 mL
⅓ cup	millet flour	75 mL
⅓ cup	sorghum flour	75 mL
⅓ cup	potato starch	75 mL
4 tsp	GF baking powder	20 mL
¾ tsp	ground turmeric (optional)	3 mL
¾ tsp	fine sea salt	3 mL
2	large eggs	2
1 cup	milk or plain non-dairy milk	250 mL
¼ cup	olive oil	60 mL
1 tbsp	liquid honey	15 mL

1. Place prepared skillet in preheated oven for 10 minutes while you prepare the batter.

2. Place millet and chia seeds in a large sealable plastic bag. Press out air and seal. Using a mallet or rolling pin, pound until millet resembles stone-ground cornmeal or grits.

3. Transfer ground millet mixture to a large bowl and whisk in millet flour, sorghum flour, potato starch, baking powder, turmeric (if using) and salt.

4. In a medium bowl, whisk together eggs, milk, oil and honey until well blended.

5. Add the egg mixture to the flour mixture and stir until just blended.

6. Carefully spread batter evenly in hot skillet.

7. Bake for 22 to 25 minutes or until golden and a tester inserted in the center comes out clean. Let cool in skillet on a wire rack for 10 minutes, then transfer to the rack. Serve warm or let cool completely.

Quinoa Banana Bread

Meet one of the best ways to use up the browned bananas on your counter. In fact, the browner and mushier they get, the sweeter and easier they are to mash. This quinoa-flour-enriched bread is simplicity itself, but you can gussy it up (chocolate chips, anyone?) as you like.

Storage Tip

Store the cooled bread, wrapped in foil or plastic wrap, in the refrigerator for up to 5 days. Alternatively, wrap it in plastic wrap, then foil, completely enclosing bread, and freeze for up to 3 months. Let thaw at room temperature for 4 to 6 hours before serving.

Variation

Chocolate Chip Banana Bread: Fold in ³⁄₄ cup (175 mL) GF semisweet chocolate chips with the quinoa.

- Preheat oven to 350°F (180°C)
- 9- by 5-inch (23 by 12.5 cm) metal loaf pan, greased

1 cup	quinoa flour	250 mL
¹⁄₃ cup	ground flax seeds (flaxseed meal)	75 mL
1 tsp	baking soda	5 mL
1 tsp	ground cinnamon	5 mL
¹⁄₂ tsp	fine sea salt	2 mL
2	large eggs	2
³⁄₄ cup	fine crystal cane sugar	175 mL
1¹⁄₃ cups	mashed very ripe bananas	325 mL
¹⁄₃ cup	melted virgin coconut oil	75 mL
2 tsp	GF vanilla extract	10 mL
1 cup	cooked quinoa (see page 15), cooled	250 mL

1. In a large bowl, whisk together quinoa flour, flax seeds, baking soda, cinnamon and salt.

2. In a medium bowl, whisk eggs until blended. Stir in sugar, bananas, coconut oil and vanilla until well blended.

3. Add the egg mixture to the flour mixture and stir until just blended. Gently fold in quinoa.

4. Spread batter evenly in prepared pan.

5. Bake in preheated oven for 55 to 60 minutes or until top is golden brown and a tester inserted in the center comes out clean. Let cool in pan on a wire rack for 10 minutes, then transfer to the rack to cool completely.

Amaranth Apricot Bread

Makes 14 slices

Amaranth is a tiny seed that dates back hundreds of years to the Aztecs in Mexico. It offers a particularly high-quality protein and is high in fiber. What I love best about it, though, is that its toasty, nutty flavor makes it a delicious (and inexpensive) alternative to nuts in a wide range of baking recipes.

Storage Tip

Store the cooled bread, wrapped in foil or plastic wrap, in the refrigerator for up to 5 days. Alternatively, wrap it in plastic wrap, then foil, completely enclosing bread, and freeze for up to 3 months. Let thaw at room temperature for 4 to 6 hours before serving.

Variation

Quinoa Chocolate Chip Bread: Omit the apricots and replace the amaranth with an equal amount of quinoa, rinsed. Gently fold ¾ cup (175 mL) GF semisweet chocolate chips into the batter at the end of step 4.

- 9- by 5-inch (23 by 12.5 cm) metal loaf pan, greased

¾ cup	chopped dried apricots	175 mL
½ cup	amaranth	125 mL
⅓ cup	ground flax seeds (flaxseed meal)	75 mL
1 cup	boiling water	250 mL
1⅔ cups	amaranth flour	400 mL
⅓ cup	potato starch	75 mL
2 tsp	ground ginger	10 mL
2 tsp	GF baking powder	10 mL
½ tsp	fine sea salt	2 mL
2	large eggs	2
½ cup	liquid honey	125 mL
¼ cup	melted virgin coconut oil	60 mL
1 tsp	GF vanilla extract	5 mL

1. In a medium bowl, combine apricots, amaranth, flax seeds and boiling water. Let stand for 20 minutes.

2. Preheat oven to 350°F (180°C).

3. In a large bowl, whisk together amaranth flour, potato starch, ginger, baking powder and salt.

4. In a medium bowl, whisk together eggs, honey, coconut oil and vanilla until well blended.

5. Add the egg mixture to the flour mixture and stir until just blended. Stir in the apricot mixture until just blended.

6. Spread batter evenly in prepared pan.

7. Bake for 50 to 55 minutes or until a tester inserted in the center comes out clean. Let cool in pan on a wire rack for 10 minutes, then transfer to the rack to cool completely.

Teff Date Bread

Teff flour has a unique malty cocoa aroma that matches the caramel flavor of the dates and exotic spices in this easy bread. Be sure to add the psyllium husk — it is essential for the bread's success.

Tip

An equal amount of olive oil or melted butter can be used in place of the coconut oil.

Storage Tip

Store the cooled bread, wrapped in foil or plastic wrap, in the refrigerator for up to 5 days. Alternatively, wrap it in plastic wrap, then foil, completely enclosing bread, and freeze for up to 3 months. Let thaw at room temperature for 4 to 6 hours before serving.

- 9- by 5-inch (23 by 12.5 cm) metal loaf pan, greased

1 cup	chopped pitted dates	250 mL
1 cup	boiling water	250 mL
1½ cups	teff flour	375 mL
2 tbsp	psyllium husk	30 mL
1 tsp	ground cinnamon	5 mL
1 tsp	ground cardamom	5 mL
1 tsp	baking soda	5 mL
½ tsp	fine sea salt	2 mL
⅔ cup	coconut sugar or packed light brown sugar	150 mL
1	large egg, beaten	1
¼ cup	melted virgin coconut oil	60 mL

1. In a medium bowl, combine dates and boiling water. Let stand for 20 minutes.

2. Preheat oven to 350°F (180°C).

3. In a large bowl, whisk together teff flour, psyllium, cinnamon, cardamom, baking soda and salt.

4. Stir coconut sugar, egg and coconut oil into the date mixture until well blended. Add the date mixture to the flour mixture and stir until just blended.

5. Spread batter evenly in prepared pan.

6. Bake for 45 to 55 minutes or until a tester inserted in the center comes out clean. Let cool in pan on a wire rack for 10 minutes, then transfer to the rack to cool completely.

Carrot Bread with Coconut and Cardamom

Makes 12 slices

The exotic scents of coconut and cardamom instantly elevate this quick and easy bread into a very special treat. It is also loaded with good-for-you ingredients, which means you can savor it for breakfast and snacks.

Tip
An equal amount of olive oil or melted unsalted butter can be used in place of the coconut oil.

Storage Tip
Store the cooled bread, wrapped in foil or plastic wrap, in the refrigerator for up to 3 days. Alternatively, wrap it in plastic wrap, then foil, completely enclosing bread, and freeze for up to 3 months. Let thaw at room temperature for 4 to 6 hours before serving.

- Preheat oven to 350°F (180°C)
- 9- by 5-inch (23 by 12.5 cm) metal loaf pan, greased

⅔ cup	sorghum flour	150 mL
⅔ cup	millet flour	150 mL
⅔ cup	potato starch	150 mL
2 tsp	GF baking powder	10 mL
1 tsp	ground cardamom	5 mL
½ tsp	baking soda	2 mL
½ tsp	fine sea salt	2 mL
1 cup	packed light brown sugar	250 mL
2	large eggs	2
½ cup	melted virgin coconut oil	125 mL
2 cups	shredded carrots	500 mL
1¼ cups	unsweetened flaked coconut	300 mL

1. In a large bowl, whisk together sorghum flour, millet flour, potato starch, baking powder, cardamom, baking soda and salt.

2. In a medium bowl, whisk together brown sugar, eggs and coconut oil until well blended.

3. Add the egg mixture to the flour mixture and stir until just blended. Gently fold in carrots and coconut.

4. Spread batter evenly in prepared pan and loosely tent pan with foil.

5. Bake in preheated oven for 80 to 90 minutes or until top is golden and a tester inserted in the center comes out clean. Let cool in pan on a wire rack for 20 minutes, then transfer to the rack to cool completely.

Pumpkin Pecan Bread

A loaf of this homey snack bread is always welcome, no matter what the season. A thick slice — rich with ancient grain, pumpkin and flax seed — is a great portable breakfast, guaranteed to get the day off to a great start.

Storage Tip

Store the cooled bread, wrapped in foil or plastic wrap, in the refrigerator for up to 3 days. Alternatively, wrap it in plastic wrap, then foil, completely enclosing bread, and freeze for up to 3 months. Let thaw at room temperature for 4 to 6 hours before serving.

- Preheat oven to 350°F (180°C)
- 9- by 5-inch (23 by 12.5 cm) metal loaf pan, greased

1¼ cups	amaranth flour	300 mL
⅓ cup	ground flax seeds (flaxseed meal)	75 mL
1 tbsp	pumpkin pie spice	15 mL
2 tsp	GF baking powder	10 mL
¼ tsp	baking soda	1 mL
¼ tsp	fine sea salt	1 mL
1 cup	fine crystal cane sugar or packed light brown sugar	250 mL
2	large eggs	2
1⅓ cups	pumpkin purée (not pie filling)	325 mL
½ cup	unsalted butter, melted, or olive oil	125 mL
2 tsp	GF vanilla extract	10 mL
1 cup	chopped toasted pecans (see page 26)	250 mL

1. In a large bowl, whisk together amaranth flour, flax seeds, pumpkin pie spice, baking powder, baking soda and salt.

2. In a medium bowl, whisk together sugar, eggs, pumpkin, butter and vanilla until well blended.

3. Add the egg mixture to the flour mixture and stir until just blended. Gently fold in pecans.

4. Spread batter evenly in prepared pan.

5. Bake in preheated oven for about 1 hour or until golden and a tester inserted in the center comes out clean. Let cool in pan on a wire rack for 10 minutes, then transfer to the rack to cool completely.

Zucchini Bread

Makes 12 slices

Quick breads are perfect for breakfast, snacks and lunch on the go. This one, with nourishing zucchini, olive oil and whole-grain sorghum flour, is delicious and satisfying.

Tip

If your dates are hard, soak them in warm (not hot) water for 10 to 15 minutes or until soft. Drain and proceed with the recipe.

Storage Tip

Store the cooled bread, wrapped in foil or plastic wrap, in the refrigerator for up to 5 days. Alternatively, wrap it in plastic wrap, then foil, completely enclosing bread, and freeze for up to 3 months. Let thaw at room temperature for 4 to 6 hours before serving.

- Preheat oven to 350°F (180°C)
- Food processor
- 9- by 5-inch (23 by 12.5 cm) metal loaf pan, greased

¾ cup	sorghum flour	175 mL
¾ cup	almond or hazelnut flour	175 mL
2½ tsp	GF baking powder	12 mL
½ tsp	ground cinnamon	2 mL
½ tsp	ground nutmeg	2 mL
½ tsp	fine sea salt	2 mL
1 cup	packed pitted soft dates	250 mL
¾ cup	walnut pieces	175 mL
2	large eggs	2
¼ cup	olive oil	60 mL
¼ cup	liquid honey or pure maple syrup	60 mL
1½ cups	shredded zucchini	375 mL

1. In a large bowl, whisk together sorghum flour, almond flour, baking powder, cinnamon, nutmeg and salt.

2. In food processor, chop dates and walnuts until a paste forms. Add eggs, oil and honey; process until blended and smooth.

3. Add the date mixture to the flour mixture and stir until just blended. Gently fold in zucchini.

4. Spread batter evenly in prepared pan.

5. Bake in preheated oven for 55 to 65 minutes or until top is golden brown and a tester inserted in the center comes out clean. Let cool in pan on a wire rack for 10 minutes, then transfer to the rack to cool completely.

Boston Brown Bread Muffins

Here, I've reconfigured New England's most famous bread — dark, moist, raisin-flecked Boston brown bread — with the help of two of my favorite ancient grain flours, teff and millet.

Tips

An equal amount of quinoa flour, amaranth flour or brown rice flour can be used in place of the teff flour.

You can substitute an equal amount of olive oil or melted virgin coconut oil for the butter.

Non-dairy buttermilk (see page 29) can be used in place of the buttermilk.

Storage Tip

Store the cooled muffins in an airtight container at room temperature for up to 2 days or in the freezer for up to 3 months. Let thaw at room temperature for 1 to 2 hours before serving.

- Preheat oven to 375°F (190°C)
- 12-cup muffin pan, greased

¾ cup	teff flour	175 mL
¾ cup	millet flour	175 mL
½ cup	potato starch	125 mL
2 tsp	GF baking powder	10 mL
1 tsp	baking soda	5 mL
½ tsp	fine sea salt	2 mL
2	large eggs	2
½ cup	dark (cooking) molasses	125 mL
⅓ cup	unsalted butter, melted	75 mL
1 cup	buttermilk	250 mL
½ cup	raisins	125 mL

1. In a large bowl, whisk together teff flour, millet flour, potato starch, baking powder, baking soda and salt.

2. In a medium bowl, whisk together eggs, molasses and butter until well blended. Whisk in buttermilk until blended.

3. Add the egg mixture to the flour mixture and stir until just blended. Gently stir in raisins.

4. Divide batter equally among prepared muffin cups.

5. Bake in preheated oven for 25 to 30 minutes or until a tester inserted in the center comes out clean. Let cool in pan on a wire rack for 5 minutes, then transfer to the rack to cool completely.

All-Oats Muffins

Consider these muffins a bowl of cereal to go. Their faint sweetness makes them perfect for all palates, and you can change them up any which way with different spices and add-ins.

Tips

If using non-dairy milk, try hemp, almond or rice.

For the dried fruit, try raisins, cranberries or cherries.

Storage Tip

Store the cooled muffins in an airtight container in the refrigerator for up to 3 days or in the freezer for up to 3 months. Let thaw at room temperature for 1 to 2 hours before serving.

- Preheat oven to 375°F (190°C)
- Food processor
- 12-cup muffin pan, greased

2½ cups	certified GF quick-cooking or large-flake (old-fashioned) rolled oats	625 mL
1 tbsp	GF baking powder	15 mL
½ tsp	fine sea salt	2 mL
½ tsp	ground cinnamon	2 mL
1	large egg	1
1 cup	milk or plain non-dairy milk	250 mL
¼ cup	liquid honey, pure maple syrup or brown rice syrup	60 mL
2 tbsp	unsalted butter, melted, or melted virgin coconut oil	30 mL
¾ cup	dried fruit (chopped, if necessary)	175 mL

1. In food processor, process oats to the consistency of flour. Add baking powder, salt and cinnamon; pulse to combine.

2. In a large bowl, whisk egg until blended. Whisk in milk, honey and butter until well blended.

3. Add the flour mixture to the egg mixture and stir until just combined. Gently fold in dried fruit.

4. Divide batter equally among prepared muffin cups.

5. Bake in preheated oven for 18 to 23 minutes or until tops are golden and a tester inserted in the center comes out clean. Let cool in pan on a wire rack for 3 minutes, then transfer to the rack to cool completely.

Maple Flax Muffins

These muffins balance the bold flavor of buckwheat flour with the mellow sweetness of maple syrup. A generous portion of ground flax seeds ensures both a stable structure and a moist, tender texture.

Tip

An equal amount of olive oil or melted unsalted butter can be used in place of the coconut oil.

Storage Tip

Store the cooled muffins in an airtight container at room temperature for up to 2 days or in the freezer for up to 3 months. Let thaw at room temperature for 1 to 2 hours before serving.

Variations

Cinnamon Raisin Flax Muffins: Add 1 tsp (5 mL) ground cinnamon to the flour mixture. Gently fold ½ cup (125 mL) raisins into the batter at the end of step 3.

Berry Almond Flax Muffins: Add ½ tsp (2 mL) GF almond extract to the egg mixture. Gently fold ½ cup (125 mL) dried blueberries or cranberries into the batter at the end of step 3.

Spiced Flax Muffins: Add 1 tsp (5 mL) ground cinnamon, 1 tsp (5 mL) ground ginger, ¼ tsp (1 mL) ground nutmeg and ⅛ tsp (0.5 mL) ground cloves to the flour mixture.

- Preheat oven to 375°F (190°C)
- 12-cup muffin pan, greased

¾ cup	buckwheat flour	175 mL
½ cup	sorghum flour	125 mL
½ cup	ground flax seeds (flaxseed meal)	125 mL
¼ cup	potato starch	60 mL
1 tsp	baking soda	5 mL
¼ tsp	fine sea salt	1 mL
2	large eggs	2
1 cup	buttermilk	250 mL
½ cup	unsweetened applesauce	125 mL
⅓ cup	pure maple syrup or liquid honey	75 mL
¼ cup	melted virgin coconut oil	60 mL

1. In a large bowl, whisk together buckwheat flour, sorghum flour, flax seeds, potato starch, baking soda and salt.

2. In a medium bowl, whisk together eggs, buttermilk, applesauce, maple syrup and coconut oil until well blended.

3. Add the egg mixture to the flour mixture and stir until just blended.

4. Divide batter equally among prepared muffin cups.

5. Bake in preheated oven for 25 to 30 minutes or until tops are golden and a tester inserted in the center comes out clean. Let cool in pan on a wire rack for 5 minutes, then transfer to the rack to cool completely.

Multigrain Blueberry Muffins

This hearty, multigrain rendition of blueberry muffins is at once home-style and modern.

Tip

Non-dairy buttermilk (see page 29) can be used in place of the buttermilk.

Storage Tip

Store the cooled muffins in an airtight container in the refrigerator for up to 3 days. Or wrap them in plastic wrap, then foil, completely enclosing them, and freeze for up to 6 months. Let thaw at room temperature for 2 hours before serving.

Variation

Multigrain Cranberry Orange Muffins: Replace the vanilla with 2 tsp (10 mL) finely grated orange zest, and replace the blueberries with an equal amount of fresh or thawed frozen cranberries, chopped.

- Preheat oven to 400°F (200°C)
- Food processor
- 12-cup muffin pan, greased

¾ cup	certified GF quick-cooking rolled oats	175 mL
1 cup	amaranth flour or quinoa flour	250 mL
½ cup	millet flour	125 mL
¼ cup	ground flax seeds (flaxseed meal)	60 mL
1 tbsp	GF baking powder	15 mL
½ tsp	fine sea salt	2 mL
½ cup	fine crystal cane sugar	125 mL
2	large eggs	2
⅓ cup	olive oil	75 mL
1 tsp	GF vanilla extract	5 mL
¾ cup	buttermilk	175 mL
1½ cups	blueberries	375 mL

1. In food processor, pulse oats five or six times or until oats resemble coarse meal.

2. In a large bowl, whisk together oats, amaranth flour, millet flour, flax seeds, baking powder and salt.

3. In a medium bowl, whisk together sugar, eggs, oil and vanilla until well blended. Whisk in buttermilk until blended.

4. Add the egg mixture to the oat mixture and stir until just blended. Gently fold in blueberries.

5. Divide batter equally among prepared muffin cups.

6. Bake in preheated oven for 18 to 23 minutes or until tops are golden and a tester inserted in the center comes out clean. Let cool in pan on a wire rack for 5 minutes, then transfer to the rack to cool completely.

Cranberry Orange Buckwheat Muffins

The bold flavor of buckwheat flour works harmoniously with tart cranberries and fragrant orange zest in these not-too-sweet muffins.

Tips

An equal amount of melted virgin coconut oil or melted unsalted butter can be used in place of the olive oil.

You can substitute an equal amount of pure maple syrup or brown rice syrup for the honey.

Storage Tip

Store the cooled muffins in an airtight container at room temperature for up to 2 days or in the freezer for up to 3 months. Let thaw at room temperature for 1 to 2 hours before serving.

Variation

Blueberry Buttermilk Buckwheat Muffins: Replace the orange zest with 1 tsp (5 mL) GF vanilla extract, the yogurt with an equal amount of buttermilk, and the cranberries with an equal amount of blueberries (do not chop).

- Preheat oven to 375°F (190°C)
- 12-cup muffin pan, greased

1¼ cups	buckwheat flour	300 mL
½ cup	sorghum flour	125 mL
¼ cup	potato starch	60 mL
2 tsp	GF baking powder	10 mL
1 tsp	baking soda	5 mL
½ tsp	fine sea salt	2 mL
2	large eggs	2
½ cup	liquid honey	125 mL
⅓ cup	olive oil	75 mL
2 tsp	finely grated orange zest	10 mL
1½ cups	plain yogurt	375 mL
1 cup	fresh or thawed frozen cranberries, chopped	250 mL

1. In a large bowl, whisk together buckwheat flour, sorghum flour, potato starch, baking powder, baking soda and salt.

2. In a medium bowl, whisk together eggs, honey, oil and orange zest until well blended. Whisk in yogurt until blended.

3. Add the egg mixture to the flour mixture and stir until just blended. Gently fold in cranberries.

4. Divide batter equally among prepared muffin cups.

5. Bake in preheated oven for 25 to 30 minutes or until tops are pale golden and a tester inserted in the center comes out clean. Let cool in pan on a wire rack for 5 minutes, then transfer to the rack to cool completely.

Banana Quinoa Muffins

Quinoa flour adds natural richness and depth of flavor to humble muffins. It also contributes ample protein, making these faintly sweet muffins a great power breakfast or snack any time of day.

Tip
If using non-dairy milk, try hemp, almond or rice.

Storage Tip
Store the cooled muffins in an airtight container in the refrigerator for up to 3 days. Or wrap them in plastic wrap, then foil, completely enclosing them, and freeze for up to 6 months. Let thaw at room temperature for 2 hours before serving.

- Preheat oven to 400°F (200°C)
- 12-cup muffin pan, greased

1½ cups	quinoa flour	375 mL
⅓ cup	ground flax seeds (flaxseed meal)	75 mL
1 tbsp	GF baking powder	15 mL
½ tsp	fine sea salt	2 mL
¼ cup	coconut sugar or packed light brown sugar	60 mL
2	large eggs	2
1 cup	mashed very ripe bananas	250 mL
½ cup	milk or plain non-dairy milk	125 mL
¼ cup	melted virgin coconut oil or olive oil	60 mL
1 tsp	GF vanilla extract	5 mL

1. In a large bowl, whisk together quinoa flour, flax seeds, baking powder and salt.

2. In a medium bowl, whisk together sugar, eggs, bananas, milk, coconut oil and vanilla until well blended.

3. Add the egg mixture to the flour mixture and stir until just blended.

4. Divide batter equally among prepared muffin cups.

5. Bake in preheated oven for 18 to 23 minutes or until tops are golden brown and a tester inserted in the center comes out clean. Let cool in pan on a wire rack for 3 minutes, then transfer to the rack to cool completely.

Variations

Cinnamon Applesauce Quinoa Muffins: Add 1 tsp (5 mL) ground cinnamon with the salt, and replace the banana with an equal amount of unsweetened applesauce.

Spiced Banana, Chia and Quinoa Muffins: Add ⅓ cup (75 mL) chia seeds, 1 tsp (5 mL) ground cinnamon, ½ tsp (2 mL) ground cardamom or nutmeg and ½ tsp (2 mL) ground allspice to the flour mixture.

Dried Fruit and Banana Quinoa Muffins: Replace the vanilla with ½ tsp (2 mL) GF almond extract. Gently fold ½ cup (125 mL) dried fruit (such as raisins, cranberries, chopped apricots or blueberries) into the batter at the end of step 3.

Toasted Nut or Seed Quinoa Muffins: Gently fold 1 cup (250 mL) chopped toasted nuts (such as pecans, walnuts or almonds) or seeds (such as green pumpkin seeds, sunflower seeds or hemp hearts) into the batter at the end of step 3.

Apple Cinnamon Muffins

Makes 12 muffins

These moist, subtly spiced muffins keep beautifully for a couple of days in the refrigerator or for several months in the freezer — perfect for an anytime snack or light meal to go.

Tips

An equal amount of olive oil or melted unsalted butter can be used in place of the coconut oil.

Non-dairy buttermilk (see page 29) can be used in place of the buttermilk.

Gala, Braeburn or Golden Delicious are my apples of choice for these muffins.

Storage Tip

Store the cooled muffins in an airtight container at room temperature for up to 2 days or in the freezer for up to 3 months. Let thaw at room temperature for 1 to 2 hours before serving.

- Preheat oven to 400°F (200°C)
- 12-cup muffin pan, greased

⅔ cup	sorghum flour	150 mL
⅔ cup	millet flour	150 mL
⅔ cup	potato starch	150 mL
2 tbsp	ground flax seeds (flaxseed meal)	30 mL
2 tsp	GF baking powder	10 mL
1½ tsp	ground cinnamon	7 mL
½ tsp	fine sea salt	2 mL
⅓ cup	packed light brown sugar	75 mL
3	large eggs	3
¼ cup	melted virgin coconut oil	60 mL
1⅓ cups	buttermilk	325 mL
1 cup	chopped peeled tart-sweet apple (see tip, at left)	250 mL
½ cup	raisins	125 mL

1. In a large bowl, whisk together sorghum flour, millet flour, potato starch, flax seeds, baking powder, cinnamon and salt.

2. In a medium bowl, whisk together brown sugar, eggs and coconut oil until well blended. Whisk in buttermilk until blended.

3. Add the egg mixture to the flour mixture and stir until just blended. Gently fold in apple and raisins.

4. Divide batter equally among prepared muffin cups.

5. Bake in preheated oven for 23 to 28 minutes or until tops are pale golden and a tester inserted in the center comes out clean. Let cool in pan on a wire rack for 5 minutes, then transfer to the rack to cool completely.

Cheesy Supper Muffins

A generous dose of Dijon mustard in the batter brings out the cheesy goodness of Gruyère in these muffins.

Tip
Non-dairy buttermilk (see page 29) can be used in place of the buttermilk.

Storage Tip
Store the cooled muffins in an airtight container at room temperature for up to 2 days or in the freezer for up to 3 months. Let thaw at room temperature for 1 to 2 hours before serving.

- Preheat oven to 375°F (190°C)
- 12-cup muffin pan, greased

2	large eggs	2
1/3 cup	olive oil	75 mL
2 tbsp	Dijon mustard	30 mL
2 tbsp	ground flax seeds (flaxseed meal)	30 mL
1 1/4 cups	buttermilk	300 mL
2/3 cup	millet flour	150 mL
2/3 cup	sorghum flour	150 mL
2/3 cup	potato starch	150 mL
2 tsp	GF baking powder	10 mL
1 tsp	baking soda	5 mL
1/2 tsp	fine sea salt	2 mL
1 1/2 cups	shredded Gruyère or Swiss cheese, divided	375 mL

1. In a medium bowl, whisk together eggs, oil and mustard until well blended. Whisk in flax seeds and buttermilk until blended. Let stand for 5 minutes to let thicken slightly.

2. In a large bowl, whisk together millet flour, sorghum flour, potato starch, baking powder, baking soda and salt.

3. Add the egg mixture to the flour mixture and stir until just blended. Gently fold in 1 cup (250 mL) cheese.

4. Divide batter equally among prepared muffin cups. Sprinkle with the remaining cheese.

5. Bake in preheated oven for 25 to 30 minutes or until tops are golden and a tester inserted in the center comes out clean. Let cool in pan on a wire rack for 5 minutes, then transfer to the rack. Serve warm or let cool completely.

British Cream Currant Scones

These barely sweet scones will impress one and all with their tender texture and buttery flavor.

Tip

You can grind the chia seeds with a mortar and pestle or seal them in a small, heavy-duty plastic bag with a zipper top and pound them with a mallet or rolling pin until crushed.

Storage Tip

Store the cooled scones in an airtight container at room temperature for up to 2 days or in the freezer for up to 3 months. Let thaw at room temperature for 1 to 2 hours before serving.

Variations

Ginger Scones: Add 2 tsp (10 mL) ground ginger with the salt, and replace the currants with ¾ cup (175 mL) chopped crystallized ginger.

Cinnamon Chocolate Chunk Scones: Add 1½ tsp (7 mL) ground cinnamon with the salt, and replace the currants with 6 oz (175 g) chopped GF semisweet chocolate or 1 cup (250 mL) GF semisweet chocolate chips.

- Preheat oven to 400°F (200°C)
- Large baking sheet, lined with parchment paper

1 cup	millet flour	250 mL
1 cup	potato starch	250 mL
¾ cup	tapioca starch	175 mL
1 tbsp	GF baking powder	15 mL
1 tbsp	chia seeds, ground (see tip, at left)	15 mL
½ tsp	fine sea salt	2 mL
½ cup	cold unsalted butter, cut into small pieces	125 mL
3 tbsp	fine crystal cane sugar	45 mL
2	large eggs	2
½ cup	light (5%) cream	125 mL
1 cup	dried currants	250 mL
	Additional millet flour or sorghum flour	

1. In a large bowl, whisk together millet flour, potato starch, tapioca starch, baking powder, chia seeds and salt. Using a pastry blender or two knives, cut in butter until mixture resembles coarse bread crumbs.

2. In a small bowl, whisk together sugar, eggs and cream until well blended.

3. Add the egg mixture to the flour mixture and stir until just blended. Gently fold in currants.

4. Turn dough out onto a surface lightly dusted with millet flour. Gently pat into a 9-inch (23 cm) square, about 1 inch (2.5 cm) thick. Cut into 9 squares and place 2 inches (5 cm) apart on prepared baking sheet.

5. Bake in preheated oven for 12 to 17 minutes or until golden brown and firm to the touch. Transfer scones to a wire rack and let cool for 5 minutes. Serve warm or let cool completely.

Maple Pecan Scones

Makes 8 scones

Real butter is the catalyst that makes the dual flavors of maple and pecans jump out of the tender interiors of these lovely oat scones.

Tips

You can grind your own oat flour in a food processor or blender. Process 1⅔ cups (400 mL) certified GF rolled oats (large-flake or quick-cooking) to the consistency of flour. This will yield a little more than 1⅓ cups (325 mL), enough for the recipe and for dusting.

You can grind the chia seeds with a mortar and pestle or seal them in a small, heavy-duty plastic bag with a zipper top and pound them with a mallet or rolling pin until crushed.

Storage Tip

Store the cooled scones in an airtight container at room temperature for up to 2 days or in the freezer for up to 3 months. Let thaw at room temperature for 1 to 2 hours before serving.

- Large baking sheet, lined with parchment paper

1⅓ cups	certified GF oat flour	325 mL
⅔ cup	brown rice flour	150 mL
⅓ cup	sorghum flour	75 mL
⅓ cup	tapioca starch	75 mL
1 tbsp	GF baking powder	15 mL
1 tbsp	chia seeds, ground (see tip, at left)	15 mL
¾ tsp	ground cinnamon	3 mL
½ tsp	fine sea salt	2 mL
½ cup	cold unsalted butter, cut into small pieces	125 mL
⅓ cup	packed light brown sugar	75 mL
1	large egg	1
1	large egg yolk	1
⅓ cup	heavy or whipping (35%) cream	75 mL
3 tbsp	pure maple syrup	45 mL
¾ tsp	maple extract (optional)	3 mL
¾ cup	chopped toasted pecans (see page 26)	175 mL
	Additional certified GF oat flour	

1. In a large bowl, whisk together oat flour, rice flour, sorghum flour, tapioca starch, baking powder, chia seeds, cinnamon and salt. Using a pastry blender or two knives, cut in butter until mixture resembles coarse bread crumbs.

2. In a small bowl, whisk together brown sugar, egg, egg yolk, cream, maple syrup and maple extract (if using).

3. Add the egg mixture to the flour mixture and stir until just blended. Gently fold in pecans.

4. Turn dough out onto a surface lightly dusted with oat flour. Gently pat into an 8-inch (20 cm) circle, about 1 inch (2.5 cm) thick. Cut into 8 wedges and place 2 inches (5 cm) apart on prepared baking sheet. Refrigerate for 30 minutes.

5. Meanwhile, preheat oven to 400°F (200°C).

6. Bake for 17 to 20 minutes or until golden brown and firm to the touch. Transfer scones to a wire rack and let cool for 5 minutes. Serve warm or let cool completely.

Cardamom Pear Oat Scones

Fresh pears give these scones a gentle boost of sweetness, coconut oil provides the tender texture, and cardamom adds an exotic accent.

Tips

You can grind your own oat flour in a food processor or blender. Process 1⅓ cups (325 mL) certified GF rolled oats (large-flake or quick-cooking) to the consistency of flour. This will yield a little more than 1 cup (250 mL), enough for the recipe and for dusting.

If using non-dairy milk, try hemp, almond or rice.

Be sure not to chop the pears too finely or they will make the dough overly moist (and lead to tough scones).

Storage Tip

Store the cooled scones in an airtight container in the refrigerator for up to 3 days or in the freezer for up to 3 months. Let thaw at room temperature for 1 to 2 hours before serving.

- Preheat oven to 400°F (200°C)
- Large baking sheet, lined with parchment paper

1 cup	certified GF oat flour	250 mL
1 cup	certified GF large-flake (old-fashioned) or quick-cooking rolled oats	250 mL
2¼ tsp	GF baking powder	11 mL
1 tsp	ground cardamom	5 mL
¼ tsp	fine sea salt	1 mL
⅓ cup	virgin coconut oil, refrigerated until cold and solid, cut into pieces	75 mL
⅓ cup	fine crystal cane sugar	75 mL
1	large egg	1
2 tbsp	milk or plain non-dairy milk	30 mL
1¼ cups	chopped fresh pears (peeled, if desired)	300 mL
	Additional certified GF oat flour	

1. In a large bowl, whisk together oat flour, oats, baking powder, cardamom and salt. Using a pastry blender or two knives, cut in coconut oil until mixture resembles coarse bread crumbs.

2. In a small bowl, whisk together sugar, egg and milk until well blended.

3. Add the egg mixture to the flour mixture and stir until just blended. Gently fold in pears.

4. Turn dough out onto a surface lightly dusted with oat flour. Gently pat into two 6-inch (15 cm) circles, about ½ inch (1 cm) thick. Cut each circle into 6 wedges and place 2 inches (5 cm) apart on prepared baking sheet.

5. Bake in preheated oven for 17 to 22 minutes or until golden brown and firm to the touch. Transfer scones to a wire rack and let cool for 5 minutes. Serve warm or let cool completely.

Scottish Oat and Quinoa Cakes

Oat cakes — part cracker, part scone — are so much more than a teatime treat. Yes, they can be slathered with your favorite marmalade or preserve, but they are also terrific as a savory accompaniment at lunch or dinner, or as a flavorful base for cheese, hummus or other appetizers.

Tips

An equal amount of sorghum or millet flour can be used in place of the quinoa flour.

The butter can be replaced with an equal amount of olive oil or melted virgin coconut oil.

For an extra touch of sweetness, sprinkle the rounds with turbinado sugar before baking.

For a more savory finish, sprinkle the unbaked rounds with sea salt flakes.

Storage Tip

Store the cooled oat cakes in an airtight tin at room temperature for up to 5 days or in the freezer for up to 3 months. Let thaw at room temperature for 1 to 2 hours before serving.

- Preheat oven to 325°F (160°C)
- Food processor
- Large rimmed baking sheet, lined with parchment paper
- 2½-inch (6 cm) round cookie cutter

1½ cups	certified GF large-flake (old-fashioned) rolled oats	375 mL
½ cup	quinoa flour	125 mL
½ tsp	GF baking powder	2 mL
½ tsp	fine sea salt	2 mL
½ cup	hot water	125 mL
¼ cup	unsalted butter, melted	60 mL
2 tbsp	liquid honey	30 mL
	Additional quinoa flour	

1. In food processor, process oats until coarsely ground.

2. In a large bowl, whisk together ground oats, flour, baking powder and salt. Using a wooden spoon, stir in hot water, butter and honey until well blended. Pat dough into a ball.

3. Turn dough out onto a surface dusted with quinoa flour and roll out to a ¼-inch (0.5 cm) thick rectangle. Using the cookie cutter, cut dough into circles, rerolling scraps. Place 1 inch (2.5 cm) apart on prepared baking sheet.

4. Bake in preheated oven for 25 to 30 minutes or until golden and set at the edges. Let cool on pan on a wire rack for 5 minutes, then transfer to the rack. Serve warm or let cool completely.

Golden Buttermilk Biscuits

Makes 9 biscuits

Anytime is a great time for an easy, gluten-free buttermilk biscuit.

Tips

You can grind the chia seeds with a mortar and pestle or seal them in a small, heavy-duty plastic bag with a zipper top and pound them with a mallet or rolling pin until crushed.

Non-dairy buttermilk (see page 29) can be used in place of the buttermilk.

Storage Tip

Store the cooled biscuits in an airtight container at room temperature for up to 2 days or in the freezer for up to 3 months. Let thaw at room temperature for 1 to 2 hours before serving. Serve at room temperature or wrap in foil, enclosing biscuits, and warm in a preheated 350°F (180°C) oven for 15 minutes.

- Preheat oven to 425°F (220°C)
- Large rimmed baking sheet, lined with parchment paper

1 cup	potato starch	250 mL
1/2 cup	tapioca starch	125 mL
1/4 cup	sorghum flour	60 mL
1 tbsp	GF baking powder	15 mL
1 tbsp	chia seeds, ground (see tip, at left)	15 mL
1/2 tsp	fine sea salt	2 mL
3 tbsp	cold unsalted butter, cut into pieces	45 mL
3 tbsp	cold non-hydrogenated vegetable shortening, cut into pieces	45 mL
1 cup	buttermilk	250 mL
	Additional tapioca starch	
1 tbsp	buttermilk	15 mL

1. In a large bowl, whisk together potato starch, tapioca starch, sorghum flour, baking powder, chia seeds and salt. Using a pastry blender or two knives, cut in butter and shortening until mixture resembles coarse bread crumbs. Refrigerate for 10 minutes.

2. Add 1 cup (250 mL) buttermilk and stir until just blended.

3. Turn dough out onto a surface lightly dusted with tapioca starch. Knead briefly until dough comes together. Gently pat into a 6-inch (15 cm) square about 1 inch (2.5 cm) thick. Cut into 9 squares and place 2 inches (5 cm) apart on prepared baking sheet. Brush squares with 1 tbsp (15 mL) buttermilk.

4. Bake in preheated oven for 18 to 23 minutes or until golden brown. Transfer biscuits to a wire rack and let cool slightly. Serve warm or let cool completely.

Gougères

Gougères, airy French cheese puffs, sound like they should be tricky and time-consuming to prepare. Not so! Once you make them, you'll consider them a go-to option for appetizers, snacks and side dishes. Keep in mind that this gluten-free version will have a lighter, less golden hue than their traditional wheat flour counterparts.

Tips

To check that the gougères are done, slit one open with a small, sharp knife; the center should be slightly eggy and moist, but not wet.

The gougères can be made up to 3 hours ahead. Let cool completely on rack. Let stand at room temperature or place in an airtight container. Warm on a baking sheet in a 350°F (180°C) oven for 5 to 10 minutes.

Other grated or shredded cheeses, such as Cheddar, Gouda or Parmesan, may be used in place of the Gruyère.

- Preheat oven to 400°F (200°C)
- 2 large rimmed baking sheets, lined with parchment paper

¾ cup	millet flour	175 mL
¼ cup	tapioca starch	60 mL
½ cup	water	125 mL
½ cup	milk	125 mL
3 tbsp	unsalted butter, cut into pieces	45 mL
¾ tsp	fine sea salt	3 mL
Pinch	ground nutmeg	Pinch
4	large eggs	4
1 cup	shredded Gruyère cheese	250 mL
¼ tsp	freshly cracked black pepper	1 mL

1. In a small bowl, whisk together millet flour and tapioca starch.

2. In a medium saucepan, combine water, milk, butter, salt and nutmeg. Bring to a boil over medium-high heat, stirring until butter is melted. Add flour mixture, stirring vigorously with a wooden spoon until flour absorbs liquid and comes together in a ball. Continue stirring vigorously for 1 minute or until dough no longer appears sticky. Remove from heat, scrape into a large bowl and let cool for 3 minutes.

3. Using an electric mixer on medium speed, beat in eggs, one at a time, making sure each egg is fully incorporated into the dough before adding another. Stir in cheese and pepper.

4. Using a 1-tbsp (15 mL) cookie scoop or a kitchen tablespoon, drop rounded portions of dough about 3 inches (7.5 cm) apart on prepared baking sheets. Gently press down any peaks of dough.

5. Bake in upper and lower thirds of preheated oven for 12 minutes. Reverse positions of pans and bake for 14 to 18 minutes or until golden brown. Transfer gougères to a wire rack. Serve hot or warm.

Goat Cheese Coins with Pecans and Rosemary

Makes 30 coins

Quality crackers — particularly specialty varieties, including gluten-free and organic, and those with unique ingredients or flavorings — can cost a small fortune for a tiny supply. All the more reason to bake your own! They are as easy to make as cookies, and the flavor possibilities are equally vast. These diminutive "coin" crackers are melt-in-your-mouth delicious and unlike anything you can buy in a box.

Storage Tip

Store the cooled coins in an airtight container at room temperature for up to 4 days.

- Food processor
- 2 large rimmed baking sheets, lined with parchment paper

1 cup	toasted pecan halves (see page 26), divided	250 mL
⅓ cup	amaranth flour	75 mL
¼ cup	potato starch	60 mL
1 tsp	minced fresh rosemary	5 mL
½ tsp	GF baking powder	2 mL
½ tsp	fine sea salt	2 mL
2 tbsp	cold unsalted butter, cut into pieces	30 mL
4 oz	semi-firm, creamy-style goat cheese, crumbled	125 g
	Additional potato starch	

1. In food processor, finely grind half the pecans. Add amaranth flour, potato starch, rosemary, baking powder and salt; pulse to combine. Add butter and pulse until mixture resembles coarse meal. Add cheese and pulse 6 to 8 times or until dough comes together.

2. Transfer dough to a work surface lightly floured with potato starch. Divide dough in half. Form each half into a 4-inch (10 cm) long log.

3. Chop the remaining pecans and sprinkle them over a clean work surface. Roll logs in chopped pecans, gently pressing to adhere. Tightly wrap each log in plastic wrap and refrigerate for at least 3 hours, until chilled, or for up to 24 hours.

4. Preheat oven to 350°F (180°C).

5. Slice each log into 15 coins about ¼ inch (0.5 cm) thick. Place 1 inch (2.5 cm) apart on prepared baking sheets.

6. Bake in upper and lower thirds of preheated oven for 6 minutes. Reverse positions of pans and bake for 6 to 9 minutes or until centers are firm to the touch. Let cool in pans on a wire rack for 1 minute, then transfer to the rack to cool completely.

Wheat-Free Thins

Makes about 48 crackers

Crispy, crunchy and satisfying, these crackers showcase the complex flavors of ancient grain flours. Excellent on their own, they are also a perfect accompaniment to soups or salads, or a great platform for a schmear or slice of cheese.

Tip

If the dough is too dry or not quite cohesive in step 1, add 1 to 2 tbsp (15 to 30 mL) additional water to achieve the desired consistency.

Storage Tip

Store the cooled crackers in an airtight tin at room temperature for up to 2 weeks.

- Preheat oven to 450°F (230°C)
- Large rimmed baking sheet, lined with parchment paper, leaving an overhang

1 cup	sorghum flour	250 mL
1/2 cup	teff flour	125 mL
1/4 cup	chia seeds	60 mL
1/4 cup	sesame seeds	60 mL
1 1/4 tsp	GF baking powder	6 mL
1/2 tsp	fine sea salt	2 mL
1/2 cup	water	125 mL
2 tbsp	olive oil	30 mL

1. In a large bowl, whisk together sorghum flour, teff flour, chia seeds, sesame seeds, baking powder and salt. Whisk in water and olive oil until blended and dough is cohesive (see tip, at left). Let stand for 5 minutes.

2. Place dough in center of prepared baking sheet. Using your fingertips, press out dough to cover most of the pan. Place a large sheet of parchment paper or plastic wrap on top of the dough. Using your palm, smooth out dough to even out the surface and completely cover the pan. (The dough should be about $1/16$ inch/2 mm thick.) Remove the top sheet of parchment paper.

3. Bake in preheated oven for 5 minutes. Remove pan from oven, leaving oven on. Using parchment paper overhang, lift cracker from pan onto a cutting board. Cut into $1 1/2$-inch (4 cm) squares or irregular pieces of a similar size. Turn crackers over with a spatula and return parchment and crackers to baking sheet.

4. Bake for 3 to 5 minutes or until crackers are crisp at the edges. Transfer crackers, on parchment paper, to a wire rack and let cool completely.

Multi-Seed Quinoa Crackers

Light, crispy and packed with protein, these delectable crackers are perfect eaten straight up or spread with hummus, nut or seed butter or anything else you fancy.

Tip

Cooked amaranth (see page 8), cooled, can be used in place of the quinoa.

Storage Tip

Store the cooled crackers in an airtight tin at room temperature for up to 2 weeks.

- Preheat oven to 325°F (160°C)
- Large rimmed baking sheet, lined with parchment paper, leaving an overhang

⅓ cup	chia seeds	75 mL
¾ cup	water	175 mL
¾ cup	cooked quinoa (see page 15), cooled	175 mL
⅓ cup	green pumpkin seeds (pepitas)	75 mL
⅓ cup	sesame seeds	75 mL
¼ tsp	fine sea salt	1 mL

1. In a medium bowl, combine chia seeds and water. Let stand for 5 minutes to thicken. Stir in quinoa, pumpkin seeds, sesame seeds and salt. Let stand for 2 minutes.

2. Spread quinoa mixture evenly on prepared baking sheet to form a 10- by 8-inch (25 by 20 cm) rectangle.

3. Bake in preheated oven for 30 minutes or until surface feels dry. Remove pan from oven, leaving oven on. Using parchment paper overhang, lift cracker from pan onto a cutting board. Cut into 2-inch (5 cm) squares. Turn crackers over with a spatula and return parchment and crackers to baking sheet.

4. Bake for 25 to 30 minutes or until crackers are golden at the edges. Transfer crackers, on parchment paper, to a wire rack and let cool completely.

Crispy Cranberry Amaranth Pucks

Makes 12 pucks

Oats and amaranth make these crispy, tart, cranberry-spiked treasures ideal portable snacks.

Storage Tip

Store the cooled pucks in an airtight tin at room temperature for up to 3 days or in the freezer for up to 3 months. Let thaw at room temperature for 1 to 2 hours before serving.

- Preheat oven to 350°F (180°C)
- 12-cup muffin pan, greased

2	large egg whites	2
1/4 cup	pure maple syrup	60 mL
1/4 tsp	ground cinnamon	1 mL
1/4 tsp	fine sea salt	1 mL
1 1/2 cups	certified GF large-flake (old-fashioned) or quick-cooking rolled oats	375 mL
1/2 cup	amaranth	125 mL
1/2 cup	chopped pecans	125 mL
1/2 cup	chopped dried cranberries	125 mL

1. In a large bowl, whisk together egg whites, maple syrup, cinnamon and salt until frothy. Stir in oats, amaranth, pecans and cranberries until combined.

2. Divide mixture equally among prepared muffin cups, pressing down with the back of a spoon to compact.

3. Bake in preheated oven for 17 to 22 minutes or until golden brown. Let cool in pan on a wire rack for 10 minutes, then transfer to the rack. Serve warm or let cool completely.

No-Bake Granola Bars

Makes 10 bars

So easy to prepare, and so delicious to eat, these no-bake bars pack a major punch of protein power.

Tips

If your dates are hard, soak them in warm (not hot) water for 10 to 15 minutes or until soft. Drain and proceed with the recipe.

If using nuts, try pecans or almonds; if using seeds, try green pumpkin seeds (pepitas) or sunflower seeds.

For the nut or seed butter, try peanut butter, almond butter, sunflower butter or tahini.

For even better flavor, toast the oats first. Spread them on a large rimmed baking sheet and bake in a preheated 350°F (180°C) oven for 10 to 15 minutes or until golden and fragrant.

Storage Tip

Store the bars in an airtight container in the refrigerator for up to 2 weeks or in the freezer for up to 3 months. Let thaw at room temperature for 1 to 2 hours before serving.

- Food processor
- 8-inch (20 cm) square metal baking pan, lined with foil (see tip, page 70), foil oiled

1 cup	packed pitted soft dates	250 mL
1½ cups	certified GF large-flake (old-fashioned) rolled oats	375 mL
1 cup	chopped toasted nuts (see page 26) and/or toasted seeds (see page 27)	250 mL
¼ cup	pure maple syrup, liquid honey or brown rice syrup	60 mL
¼ cup	unsweetened creamy nut or seed butter	60 mL

1. In food processor, process dates until finely chopped into a paste.

2. Transfer date paste to a large bowl and stir in oats and nuts.

3. In a small saucepan, over low heat, heat maple syrup and nut butter, stirring until melted and bubbly. Pour over the oat mixture, stirring until well combined.

4. Press mixture into prepared pan and place in the freezer for 30 minutes or until firm. Using foil liner, lift mixture from pan and invert onto a cutting board; peel off foil and cut into 10 bars.

Variations

Chocolate Chip Granola Bars: Add 1 tsp (5 mL) GF vanilla extract and ¼ tsp (1 mL) ground cinnamon to the maple syrup mixture before adding it to the oat mixture. Decrease the nuts to ¾ cup (175 mL) and add ½ cup (125 mL) miniature GF chocolate chips at the end of step 3.

Dried Fruit Granola Bars: Decrease the nuts to ¾ cup (175 mL) and add ½ cup (125 mL) chopped dried fruit (such as apricots, raisins or figs) at the end of step 3.

Desserts

Ancient Grain Chocolate Chip Cookies

Makes 30 cookies

Chocolate chip cookies are iconic treats, and this ancient grain interpretation has just the right balance of flavor, texture and sweetness.

Tips

You can grind the chia seeds with a mortar and pestle or seal them in a small, heavy-duty plastic bag with a zipper top and pound them with a mallet or rolling pin until crushed.

An equal amount of unsalted butter can be used in place of the coconut oil.

Storage Tip

Store the cooled cookies in an airtight container in the refrigerator for up to 5 days or in the freezer for up to 3 months.

- Large baking sheets, lined with parchment paper

1 cup	millet flour	250 mL
1 cup	certified GF large-flake (old-fashioned) rolled oats	250 mL
¼ cup	tapioca starch	60 mL
3 tbsp	chia seeds, ground (see tip, at left)	45 mL
½ tsp	GF baking powder	2 mL
¼ tsp	baking soda	1 mL
¼ tsp	fine sea salt	1 mL
¾ cup	fine crystal cane sugar or packed dark brown sugar	175 mL
⅓ cup	softened (not melted) virgin coconut oil	75 mL
2	large eggs	2
3 tbsp	pure maple syrup	45 mL
1½ tsp	GF vanilla extract	7 mL
¾ cup	GF semisweet chocolate chips	175 mL

1. In a medium bowl, whisk together millet flour, oats, tapioca starch, chia seeds, baking powder, baking soda and salt.

2. In a large bowl, using an electric mixer on medium speed, beat sugar and coconut oil until light and fluffy. Beat in eggs, maple syrup and vanilla until blended. Using a wooden spoon, stir in flour mixture until just blended. Gently stir in chocolate chips. Cover and refrigerate for at least 1 hour, until firm, or overnight.

3. Preheat oven to 350°F (180°F).

4. Drop dough by tablespoonfuls (15 mL) onto prepared baking sheets, spacing cookies 2 inches (5 cm) apart.

5. Bake, one sheet at a time, for 10 to 12 minutes or until golden brown and just set at the edges. Let cool on pan on a wire rack for 2 minutes, then transfer to the rack to cool completely.

No-Bake Chocolate Quinoa Cookies

Makes 24 cookies

Chocolate no-bake cookies are made brand new with the help of an ancient grain. Good luck eating just one!

Storage Tip

Store the cookies in an airtight container, separating layers between sheets of parchment paper, in the refrigerator for up to 1 week or in the freezer for up to 3 months.

- Large rimmed baking sheet, lined with parchment paper

¼ cup	unsweetened natural cocoa powder	60 mL
½ cup	pure maple syrup, liquid honey or brown rice syrup	125 mL
¼ cup	warmed virgin coconut oil	60 mL
½ tsp	fine sea salt	2 mL
½ cup	unsweetened creamy nut or seed butter	125 mL
1 tsp	GF vanilla extract	5 mL
3 cups	cooked quinoa (see page 15), cooled	750 mL

1. In a large saucepan, combine cocoa, maple syrup and coconut oil. Melt over medium heat, whisking until blended and smooth. Bring to a boil and let boil for 1 minute. Remove from heat and stir in salt, nut butter and vanilla until blended and smooth. Stir in quinoa until combined.

2. Drop mixture by small scoopfuls onto prepared baking sheet. Refrigerate for 2 to 3 hours or until firm and set.

Chocolate Snowball Cookies

Makes 36 cookies

Both sophisticated and old-fashioned, these cookies have a deep chocolate flavor and delicate crunch. The snowball eponym comes from the confectioners' sugar coating: the cookies are rolled in sugar while still warm, creating a snowy effect.

Tips

If the coconut oil in your pantry is in a liquid state, measure the amount needed and place it in the refrigerator until semi-solidified, about 15 to 20 minutes.

Pure cane confectioners' (icing) sugar, sometimes labeled "powdered sugar," is made using the same process as regular confectioners' sugar (granulated sugar is crushed to a fine white powder), but is made with less processed cane sugar. Several brands also use tapioca starch or potato starch in place of cornstarch. Regular confectioners' sugar may be used in its place.

Storage Tip

Store the cooled cookies in an airtight container in the refrigerator for up to 5 days or in the freezer for up to 3 months.

- Preheat oven to 350°F (180°C)
- Large baking sheets, lined with parchment paper

1 cup	fine crystal cane sugar	250 mL
¾ cup	millet flour	175 mL
½ cup	unsweetened natural cocoa powder	125 mL
⅓ cup	teff flour	75 mL
¼ cup	tapioca starch	60 mL
½ tsp	baking soda	2 mL
¼ tsp	fine sea salt	1 mL
½ cup	unsalted butter or virgin coconut oil, softened	125 mL
1	large egg, beaten	1
1 tsp	GF vanilla extract	5 mL
2 cups	pure cane confectioners' (icing) sugar (see tip, at left)	500 mL

1. In a medium bowl, whisk together fine crystal cane sugar, millet flour, cocoa powder, teff flour, tapioca starch, baking soda and salt. Using a pastry blender or two knives, cut in butter until mixture resembles coarse crumbs. Using a wooden spoon, stir in egg and vanilla until just blended.

2. Roll dough into thirty-six 1-inch (2.5 cm) balls. Place balls 2 inches (5 cm) apart on prepared baking sheets.

3. Bake, one sheet at a time, in preheated oven for 11 to 13 minutes or until puffed and just set at the edges. Let cool on pan on a wire rack for 1 minute, then transfer to a shallow dish of confectioners' sugar and roll in sugar to coat. Return cookies to the rack to cool completely. Discard any excess confectioners' sugar.

Peanut Butter Cookies

The combination of peanut butter, ancient grain flours and maple syrup produces a delectable, not-too-sweet confection.

Tip

Any creamy nut or seed butter (such as cashew butter, almond butter, tahini or sunflower seed butter) can be used in place of the peanut butter.

Storage Tip

Store the cooled cookies in an airtight container at room temperature for up to 3 days or in the freezer for up to 3 months.

• Preheat oven to 350°F (180°C)
• Large baking sheets, lined with parchment paper

½ cup	millet flour	125 mL
½ cup	sorghum flour	125 mL
⅓ cup	potato starch	75 mL
½ tsp	baking soda	2 mL
½ tsp	fine sea salt	2 mL
1 cup	unsweetened creamy peanut butter	250 mL
½ cup	pure maple syrup or liquid honey	125 mL
½ cup	unsalted butter, melted, or melted virgin coconut oil	125 mL
1 tsp	GF vanilla extract	5 mL

1. In a large bowl, whisk together millet flour, sorghum flour, potato starch, baking soda and salt. Stir in peanut butter, maple syrup, butter and vanilla until blended.

2. Roll dough into 1-inch (2.5 cm) balls. Place balls 2 inches (5 cm) apart on prepared baking sheets. Using the tines of a fork, flatten each cookie slightly, making a cross-hatch pattern.

3. Bake, one sheet at a time, in preheated oven for 13 to 16 minutes or until just set at the edges. Let cool on pan on a wire rack for 10 minutes, then transfer to the rack to cool completely.

Oats and Quinoa Cookies

As soon as the temperature starts to dip and the leaves on the trees turn shades of orange, red and yellow, I'm thinking cookies. These oats and quinoa cookies are a favorite starting point for fall baking because they are equal parts delicious and nutritious. So grab one (or two) for a lunch bag, after-dinner dessert, late-afternoon snack or even breakfast on the run, sans guilt.

Tips

An equal amount of unsalted butter, melted, can be used in place of the coconut oil.

Make these cookies a bit different every time by folding in 1¼ cups (300 mL) chopped dried fruit (such as apricots, cherries or apples), GF chocolate chips, chopped toasted nuts (such as walnuts, pecans or cashews) or toasted seeds (such as green pumpkin seeds or sunflower seeds), or a combination of add-ins totaling 1¼ cups (300 mL), with the oats and quinoa.

Storage Tip

Store the cooled cookies in an airtight container at room temperature for up to 3 days or in the freezer for up to 3 months.

- Preheat oven to 350°F (180°C)
- Large baking sheets, lined with parchment paper

¾ cup	sorghum flour	175 mL
½ cup	quinoa flour or millet flour	125 mL
¼ cup	ground flax seeds (flaxseed meal)	60 mL
1 tsp	GF baking powder	5 mL
¾ tsp	fine sea salt	3 mL
½ tsp	baking soda	2 mL
½ cup	coconut sugar or packed light brown sugar	125 mL
2	large eggs	2
½ cup	melted virgin coconut oil	125 mL
¼ cup	pure maple syrup or liquid honey	60 mL
2 tsp	GF vanilla extract	10 mL
1 cup	cooked quinoa (see page 15), cooled	250 mL
1 cup	certified GF large-flake (old-fashioned) rolled oats	250 mL

1. In a large bowl, whisk together sorghum flour, quinoa flour, flax seeds, baking powder, salt and baking soda.

2. In a medium bowl, whisk together coconut sugar, eggs, coconut oil, maple syrup and vanilla until well blended.

3. Add the egg mixture to the flour mixture, stirring until just blended. Stir in quinoa and oats.

4. Drop dough by heaping tablespoonfuls (15 mL) onto prepared baking sheets, spacing cookies 2 inches (5 cm) apart. Flatten slightly with your fingertips.

5. Bake, one sheet at a time, in preheated oven for 11 to 15 minutes or until just set at the center. Let cool on pan on a wire rack for 5 minutes, then transfer to the rack to cool completely.

Gingerbread Amaranth Cookies

Makes 24 cookies

Tender and spicy, these homey cookies are everything you want a cookie with "gingerbread" in the title to be.

Tip

An equal amount of quinoa flour can be used in place of the amaranth flour, and cooked quinoa (see page 15), cooled, can be used in place of the amaranth.

Storage Tip

Store the cooled cookies in an airtight container at room temperature for up to 3 days or in the freezer for up to 3 months.

- Preheat oven to 350°F (180°C)
- Large baking sheets, lined with parchment paper

1 cup	amaranth flour	250 mL
½ cup	ground flax seeds (flaxseed meal)	125 mL
2½ tsp	ground ginger	12 mL
1 tsp	ground cinnamon	5 mL
½ tsp	baking soda	2 mL
¼ tsp	ground nutmeg	1 mL
¼ tsp	ground cloves	1 mL
¼ tsp	fine sea salt	1 mL
¼ cup	fine crystal cane sugar	60 mL
¼ cup	dark (cooking) molasses	60 mL
¼ cup	unsweetened applesauce	60 mL
3 tbsp	olive oil	45 mL
1 tsp	GF vanilla extract	5 mL
2 cups	cooked amaranth (see page 8), cooled	500 mL

1. In a large bowl, whisk together amaranth flour, flax seeds, ginger, cinnamon, baking soda, nutmeg, cloves and salt. Stir in sugar, molasses, applesauce, oil and vanilla until just blended. Stir in amaranth until blended.

2. Drop dough by tablespoonfuls (15 mL) onto prepared baking sheets, spacing cookies 2 inches (5 cm) apart. Flatten slightly with your fingertips.

3. Bake, one sheet at a time, in preheated oven for 16 to 21 minutes or until just set at the center. Let cool on pan on a wire rack for 10 minutes, then transfer to the rack to cool completely.

Teff Shortbread

Classic shortbread gets an Ethiopian twist with teff flour. The result is a deeply flavored cookie with notes of malt and toffee.

Storage Tips

The wrapped dough can be placed in an airtight container and frozen for up to 3 months. Thaw in the refrigerator for 4 to 6 hours before slicing and baking.

Store the cooled cookies in an airtight container at room temperature for up to 3 days or in the freezer for up to 3 months.

• Large baking sheet, lined with parchment paper

½ cup	tapioca starch	125 mL
¼ cup	teff flour	60 mL
¼ tsp	ground cinnamon	1 mL
¼ tsp	fine sea salt	1 mL
½ cup	unsalted butter, softened	125 mL
¼ cup	fine crystal cane sugar	60 mL
½ tsp	GF vanilla extract	2 mL

1. In a medium bowl, whisk together tapioca starch, teff flour, cinnamon and salt.

2. In a large bowl, using an electric mixer, beat butter and sugar on medium speed for 1 to 2 minutes or until blended and smooth. Scrape sides and bottom of bowl with a spatula. Add vanilla and beat for 1 minute, until blended and smooth.

3. Using a wooden spoon, stir flour mixture into butter mixture until blended.

4. Transfer dough to a large piece of waxed paper. Roll dough into a cylinder about 2 inches (5 cm) in diameter. Tightly wrap in paper, twisting the ends to seal. Refrigerate for at least 1 hour, until very firm, or for up to 24 hours.

5. Preheat oven to 325°F (160°C). Unwrap dough and slice crosswise into ¼-inch (0.5 cm) thick slices. Place cookies 1 inch (2.5 cm) apart on prepared baking sheet. Using a fork, make several shallow pricks in each cookie.

6. Bake for 15 to 18 minutes or until medium brown and just set at the center. Transfer cookies to a wire rack to cool completely.

Gianduja Biscotti

A cup of espresso. An inspiring view. And one of these chocolate and hazelnut biscotti. These crunchy — and surprisingly easy — Italian cookies make a coffee break a quick escape.

Tip
The biscotti will continue to harden after the second bake, as they cool.

Storage Tip
Store the cooled biscotti in an airtight container at room temperature for up to 5 days or in the freezer for up to 3 months.

Variation
Fruit and Nut Biscotti:
Replace the chocolate chips with an equal amount of chopped dried fruit (such as cherries, cranberries or apricots) and use the chopped nuts of your choice (such as almonds, pecans or walnuts) in place of the hazelnuts.

• Large rimmed baking sheet, lined with parchment paper

¾ cup	millet flour	175 mL
⅔ cup	sorghum flour	150 mL
⅔ cup	potato starch	150 mL
1 tsp	GF baking powder	5 mL
¾ tsp	fine sea salt	3 mL
¾ cup	coarsely chopped hazelnuts	175 mL
⅔ cup	miniature GF semisweet chocolate chips	150 mL
1 cup	fine crystal cane sugar or granulated sugar	250 mL
2	large eggs, at room temperature	2
⅔ cup	olive oil	150 mL
2 tsp	GF vanilla extract	10 mL

1. In a medium bowl, whisk together millet flour, sorghum flour, potato starch, baking powder and salt. Stir in hazelnuts and chocolate chips.

2. In a large bowl, whisk together sugar, eggs, oil and vanilla until blended. Gradually add the flour mixture, stirring until just blended. Divide dough in half and shape each half into a rough log. Tightly wrap dough halves in plastic wrap and refrigerate for 1 hour.

3. Preheat oven to 350°F (180°C).

4. Place dough halves on prepared baking sheet and, using moistened hands, shape into two parallel 10- by 3-inch (25 by 7.5 cm) rectangles, spaced about 3 inches (7.5 cm) apart.

5. Bake in preheated oven for 40 to 45 minutes or until set at the center and golden. Remove from oven and decrease oven temperature to 300°F (150°C). Let cool on pan on a wire rack for 15 to 20 minutes or until cool enough to handle.

6. Cut rectangles crosswise into ¾-inch (2 cm) slices. Place slices, cut side down, on baking sheet. Bake for 9 to 11 minutes or until edges are dark golden. Let cool on pan for 1 minute, then transfer to wire racks to cool completely.

Popped Amaranth Energy Treats

These no-bake popped amaranth treats are reminiscent of crispy rice treats, with a major exception: these goodies are good for you, too. Enjoy them any time you need a quick energy boost!

Tips

For the dried fruit, try raisins, cranberries, cherries or chopped apricots.

For the nut or seed butter, try almond butter, peanut butter or sunflower butter.

Storage Tip

Store the amaranth treats in an airtight container at room temperature for up to 3 days or in the freezer for up to 3 months.

- 9-inch (23 cm) square baking pan, sprayed with nonstick cooking spray

3 cups	popped amaranth (see page 9)	750 mL
3/4 cup	certified GF quick-cooking rolled oats	175 mL
1/2 cup	finely chopped dried fruit	125 mL
3 tbsp	ground flax seeds (flaxseed meal)	45 mL
1/2 cup	unsweetened nut or seed butter	125 mL
1/2 cup	pure maple syrup, liquid honey or brown rice syrup	125 mL
2 tsp	GF vanilla extract	10 mL

1. In a large bowl, combine popped amaranth, oats, dried fruit and flax seeds.

2. In a small saucepan, heat nut butter and maple syrup over medium-low heat for 2 to 3 minutes or until warm and blended. Remove from heat and stir in vanilla.

3. Add the nut butter mixture to the amaranth mixture, stirring until combined.

4. Spread and gently press mixture into prepared pan. Cover and refrigerate for 1 hour or until set. Cut into 16 bars.

Honey Tahini Blondies

Makes 16 squares

Butterscotch blondies get a Middle Eastern twist with the additions of floral honey and tahini.

Tip

Other unsweetened nut or seed butters, such as peanut, almond or sunflower, may be used in place of the tahini.

Storage Tip

Store the cooled blondies in an airtight container in the refrigerator for up to 5 days or in the freezer for up to 3 months.

- Preheat oven to 350°F (180°C)
- 8-inch (20 cm) square metal baking pan, sprayed with nonstick cooking spray

¾ cup	millet flour	175 mL
½ cup	potato starch	125 mL
1 tsp	GF baking powder	5 mL
½ tsp	fine sea salt	2 mL
½ cup	tahini	125 mL
¼ cup	unsalted butter, softened	60 mL
1 cup	packed light brown sugar	250 mL
½ cup	liquid honey	125 mL
2	large eggs	2
1 tsp	GF vanilla extract	5 mL

1. In a medium bowl, whisk together millet flour, potato starch, baking powder and salt.

2. In a large bowl, using an electric mixer on medium speed, beat tahini and butter until fluffy. Beat in brown sugar and honey until blended. Add eggs, one at a time, beating well after each addition. Beat in vanilla until smooth. Using a wooden spoon, stir in flour mixture until just blended.

3. Spread batter evenly in prepared pan.

4. Bake in preheated oven for 28 to 32 minutes or until a tester inserted in the center comes out with a few moist crumbs attached. Let cool completely in pan on a wire rack. Cut into 16 squares.

Flourless Fudge Brownies

Makes 16 squares

Good news: the leftover cooked amaranth in your refrigerator can be transformed into fudgy, deep chocolate brownies. You'll likely make extra amaranth all the time, every time, from here on out.

Tips

An equal amount of cooked millet or quinoa, cooled, can be used in place of the amaranth. Information on cooking these grains can be found on pages 11–15.

For the nut or seed butter, try almond butter, peanut butter or sunflower butter.

Storage Tip

Store the cooled brownies in an airtight container in the refrigerator for up to 5 days or in the freezer for up to 3 months.

- Preheat oven to 350°F (180°C)
- Food processor
- 8-inch (20 cm) square metal baking pan, greased

1¼ cups	cooked amaranth (see page 8), cooled	300 mL
½ cup	unsweetened natural cocoa powder	125 mL
½ tsp	baking soda	2 mL
½ tsp	fine sea salt	2 mL
2	large eggs	2
½ cup	unsweetened nut or seed butter	125 mL
½ cup	pure maple syrup, brown rice syrup or liquid honey	125 mL
⅓ cup	unsweetened applesauce	75 mL
¼ cup	melted virgin coconut oil	60 mL
2 tsp	GF vanilla extract	10 mL
½ cup	GF semisweet or bittersweet (dark) chocolate chips	125 mL

1. In food processor, combine amaranth, cocoa powder, baking soda, salt, eggs, nut butter, maple syrup, applesauce, oil and vanilla; process until blended and smooth.

2. Spread batter evenly in prepared pan. Sprinkle with chocolate chips.

3. Bake in preheated oven for 33 to 38 minutes or until just set at the center. Let cool completely in pan on a wire rack. Cut into 16 squares.

Nanaimo Squares

Makes 16 squares

Nanaimo bars (or, in this case, squares) are Canadian classics hailing from the West Coast city of Nanaimo, British Columbia. Traditional recipes for the layered chocolate bars include a cookie crumb crust and buttery custard filling, but I couldn't resist giving them a wholesome, ancient grains spin. My Canadian mother approves!

Tip

It is important to cut the squares very soon after the top chocolate layer has set. If left to chill for too long, the squares will become very difficult to cut.

Storage Tip

Store the squares in an airtight container in the refrigerator for up to 1 week or in the freezer for up to 3 months.

- 8-inch (20 cm) square baking pan, lined with parchment paper, leaving an overhang

Bottom Layer

¼ cup	warmed virgin coconut oil	60 mL
⅓ cup	unsweetened natural cocoa powder	75 mL
¼ cup	pure maple syrup or liquid honey	60 mL
1 tsp	GF vanilla extract	5 mL
1½ cups	popped amaranth (see page 9)	375 mL
1½ cups	unsweetened finely shredded coconut	375 mL

Middle Layer

1 cup	unsweetened almond butter	250 mL
¼ cup	milk or plain non-dairy milk	60 mL
1 tbsp	melted virgin coconut oil	15 mL
1 tsp	GF vanilla extract	5 mL

Top Layer

⅔ cup	GF semisweet chocolate chips	150 mL
2 tsp	virgin coconut oil	10 mL

1. *Bottom Layer:* In a medium saucepan, melt coconut oil over low heat. Whisk in cocoa powder and maple syrup until blended and smooth. Remove from heat and whisk in vanilla. Stir in popped amaranth and coconut until well coated. Press firmly into prepared pan. Cover and refrigerate for 30 minutes or until firm.

2. *Middle Layer:* In a medium bowl, using an electric mixer on low speed, beat almond butter, milk, coconut oil and vanilla for 1 to 2 minutes or until somewhat blended. Beat on medium-high speed until smooth and spreadable. Spread over chilled bottom layer. Cover and refrigerate for 1 hour or until firm.

3. *Top Layer:* In a heatproof bowl set over a saucepan of simmering water, melt chocolate chips and coconut oil, stirring until melted and smooth. Spread over chilled middle layer. Refrigerate for 10 to 15 minutes or until chocolate is set.

4. Using parchment paper overhang, lift layers from pan and cut into 16 squares (see tip, at left). Place squares on a plate and refrigerate for at least 1 hour or until very firm.

Date Squares with Exotic Spices

Enriched with coconut oil, ginger and cardamom, these date bars offer an exotic escape with each bite. The malty flavor of teff flour is a wonderful match with dates, but you can use sorghum flour, millet flour or brown rice flour in its place.

Tips

For the best results, use whole pitted dates and chop them yourself. Pre-chopped dates are typically tossed with oat flour (to prevent sticking) and sugar. In addition, they tend to be fairly hard. If pre-chopped dates are the only option available, give them a quick rinse in hot (not boiling) water to remove any coatings and soften them slightly.

If using non-dairy milk, try hemp, almond or rice.

Storage Tip

Store the cooled squares in an airtight container in the refrigerator for up to 5 days or in the freezer for up to 3 months.

- Preheat oven to 375°F (190°C)
- Blender or food processor
- 8-inch (20 cm) square metal baking pan, sprayed with nonstick cooking spray

1¼ cups	certified GF quick-cooking rolled oats	300 mL
½ cup	teff flour	125 mL
½ tsp	ground cardamom	2 mL
½ tsp	ground ginger	2 mL
½ tsp	GF baking powder	2 mL
¼ tsp	fine sea salt	1 mL
1 cup	chopped pitted soft dates, divided	250 mL
¼ cup	milk or plain non-dairy milk	60 mL
¼ cup	melted virgin coconut oil	60 mL
1 tsp	GF vanilla extract	5 mL
1	large egg, at room temperature	1

1. In a medium bowl, whisk together oats, teff flour, cardamom, ginger, baking powder and salt.

2. In blender, combine half the dates, milk, oil and vanilla; purée until very smooth. Add egg and blend until just combined.

3. Add the date mixture to the flour mixture, stirring until just blended. Gently fold in the remaining dates.

4. Spread batter evenly in prepared pan.

5. Bake in preheated oven for 15 to 20 minutes or until golden brown and set at the center. Let cool completely in pan on a wire rack. Cut into 16 squares.

Maple Espresso Amaranth Cake

Amaranth flour, with its naturally nutty flavor, pairs ever so well with walnuts. Sweeten the deal with maple syrup, then stir in a hefty dose of espresso, and the result is one noteworthy cake.

Tips

Quinoa flour can be used in place of the amaranth flour.

An equal amount of liquid honey, agave nectar or brown rice syrup can be used in place of the maple syrup.

Storage Tip

Store the cooled, unfrosted cake, loosely wrapped in foil or waxed paper, at room temperature for up to 3 days or in the refrigerator for up to 1 week. Alternatively, wrap the unfrosted cake in plastic wrap, then foil, completely enclosing it, and freeze for up to 6 months. Let thaw at room temperature for 4 to 6 hours before serving.

- Preheat oven to 350°F (180°C)
- Food processor
- 9-inch (23 cm) square metal baking pan, lined with parchment paper

1 1/3 cups	chopped toasted walnuts or pecans, divided	325 mL
1 1/2 cups	amaranth flour	375 mL
2 tsp	GF baking powder	10 mL
1/4 tsp	fine sea salt	1 mL
1/3 cup	coconut sugar or packed light brown sugar	75 mL
3	large eggs, beaten	3
1/2 cup	olive oil	125 mL
1/2 cup	pure maple syrup	125 mL
1/2 cup	brewed espresso or extra-strong coffee, cooled	125 mL
2 tsp	GF vanilla extract	10 mL
	Whipped Maple Coconut Cream (variation, page 326)	

1. In food processor, process 1 cup (250 mL) walnuts to a fine meal (be careful not to overprocess into a paste).

2. Transfer walnut meal to a large bowl and whisk in amaranth flour, baking powder and salt. Add coconut sugar, eggs, oil, maple syrup, espresso and vanilla; using an electric mixer on medium-high speed, beat for 1 to 2 minutes or until light and fluffy. Gently fold in the remaining walnuts.

3. Spread batter evenly in prepared pan.

4. Bake in preheated oven for 40 to 45 minutes or until a tester inserted in the center comes out clean. Let cool completely in pan on a wire rack.

5. Spread coconut cream over cooled cake.

Olive Oil Cake with Cherries and Dark Chocolate Chunks

There's no disputing the exquisite flavor of extra virgin olive oil in a host of savory dishes, but it is also worthy of praise as a key ingredient in desserts. This Italian-inspired cake — akin to rustic, sweet polenta cakes — is good-to-the-last-forkful proof.

Tips

You can grind the chia seeds with a mortar and pestle or seal them in a small, heavy-duty plastic bag with a zipper top and pound them with a mallet or rolling pin until crushed.

If using non-dairy milk, try hemp, rice or almond.

Storage Tip

Store the cooled cake, loosely wrapped in foil or waxed paper, at room temperature for up to 2 days or in the refrigerator for up to 1 week. Alternatively, wrap it in plastic wrap, then foil, completely enclosing it, and freeze for up to 6 months. Let thaw at room temperature for 4 to 6 hours before serving.

- Preheat oven to 350°F (180°C)
- 9-inch (23 cm) springform pan, greased

1 cup	millet flour	250 mL
2/3 cup	sorghum flour	150 mL
2/3 cup	potato starch	150 mL
2 tbsp	chia seeds, ground (see tip, at left)	30 mL
2 tsp	GF baking powder	10 mL
3/4 tsp	fine sea salt	3 mL
3	large eggs	3
3/4 cup	fine crystal cane sugar	175 mL
1 cup	olive oil	250 mL
3/4 cup	milk or plain non-dairy milk	175 mL
4 oz	GF bittersweet (dark) chocolate, cut into chunks	125 g
2/3 cup	dried tart cherries, chopped	150 mL

1. In a large bowl, whisk together millet flour, sorghum flour, potato starch, chia seeds, baking powder and salt.

2. In a medium bowl, whisk eggs until very well blended. Whisk in sugar, oil and milk until blended.

3. Add the egg mixture to the flour mixture and stir until just blended. Gently stir in chocolate and cherries.

4. Spread batter evenly in prepared pan.

5. Bake in preheated oven for 40 to 45 minutes or until a tester inserted in the center comes out clean. Let cool completely in pan on a wire rack.

Chocolate, Lime and Coconut Cake

Makes 8 servings

Easy to make, grand to eat and (yes, really!) good for you, too, this is a recipe I suspect you will make again and again.

Storage Tip

Store the cooled, unfrosted cake, loosely wrapped in foil or waxed paper, at room temperature for up to 3 days or in the refrigerator for up to 1 week. Alternatively, wrap the unfrosted cake in plastic wrap, then foil, completely enclosing it, and freeze for up to 6 months. Let thaw at room temperature for 4 to 6 hours before serving.

- Preheat oven to 350°F (180°C)
- 8-inch (20 cm) square metal baking pan, greased

1 cup	amaranth flour	250 mL
1/2 cup	unsweetened natural cocoa powder	125 mL
1/4 cup	potato starch	60 mL
1 tbsp	ground flax seeds (flaxseed meal)	15 mL
3/4 tsp	baking soda	3 mL
1/2 tsp	fine sea salt	2 mL
3/4 cup	fine crystal cane sugar	175 mL
1/2 cup	well-stirred coconut milk (full-fat)	125 mL
1/2 cup	melted virgin coconut oil	125 mL
1/2 cup	water	125 mL
1 tbsp	finely grated lime zest	15 mL
1 tbsp	freshly squeezed lime juice	15 mL

Suggested Topping
Whipped Coconut Cream (page 326)

1. In a large bowl, whisk together amaranth flour, cocoa powder, potato starch, flax seeds, baking soda and salt.

2. In a medium bowl, whisk sugar, coconut milk, coconut oil, water, lime zest and lime juice until blended.

3. Add the coconut milk mixture to the flour mixture and stir until just blended.

4. Spread batter evenly in prepared pan.

5. Bake in preheated oven for 27 to 32 minutes or until a tester inserted in the center comes out with moist crumbs attached. Let cool completely in pan on a wire rack.

6. If desired, spread coconut cream over cooled cake, or serve it alongside.

Loaded Apple Cake

Easier than pie, this moist, fragrant apple cake will always be in style. It's so much easier than pie, but has all of the autumnal apple flavors you're after.

Tips

You can grind the chia seeds with a mortar and pestle or seal them in a small, heavy-duty plastic bag with a zipper top and pound them with a mallet or rolling pin until crushed.

If using non-dairy milk, try hemp, almond or rice.

Storage Tip

Store the cooled cake, loosely wrapped in foil or waxed paper, in the refrigerator for up to 1 week. Alternatively, wrap the cake in plastic wrap, then foil, completely enclosing it, and freeze for up to 6 months. Let thaw at room temperature for 4 to 6 hours before serving.

- Preheat oven to 375°F (190°C)
- 9-inch (23 cm) springform pan, buttered and sprinkled with fine crystal cane sugar

4	tart-sweet apples (such as Gala, Braeburn or Golden Delicious)	4
2 tbsp	fine crystal cane sugar	30 mL
½ tsp	ground cinnamon	2 mL
9 tbsp	unsalted butter, melted, divided	135 mL
½ cup	sorghum flour	125 mL
½ cup	millet flour	125 mL
½ cup	tapioca starch	125 mL
2 tbsp	chia seeds, ground (see tip, at left)	30 mL
2 tsp	GF baking powder	10 mL
½ tsp	fine sea salt	2 mL
2	large eggs	2
¾ cup	packed light brown sugar	175 mL
⅓ cup	milk or non-dairy milk	75 mL

1. Peel and core apples, then cut each apple into 8 wedges and place in a large bowl. Add cane sugar, cinnamon and 2 tbsp (30 mL) butter, tossing to combine.

2. In another large bowl, whisk together sorghum flour, millet flour, tapioca starch, chia seeds, baking powder and salt.

3. In a medium bowl, whisk eggs until well blended. Whisk in brown sugar, milk and the remaining butter until blended.

4. Add the egg mixture to the flour mixture, stirring until just blended.

5. Spread batter evenly in prepared pan. Arrange apple wedges over batter, gently pressing them into batter (only slightly; the tops of the apples should still be visible).

6. Bake in preheated oven for 50 to 55 minutes or until apples are tender and a tester inserted in the center of the cake comes out clean. Let cool completely in pan on a wire rack.

Any Day Carrot Cake

Thanks to its ease and natural goodness, this not-too-sweet cake is not just an "any day" treat but also an "any hour" one, equally perfect for breakfast, dessert, coffee breaks or late-night snacks.

Tips

You can grind the chia seeds with a mortar and pestle or seal them in a small, heavy-duty plastic bag with a zipper top and pound them with a mallet or rolling pin until crushed.

Non-dairy buttermilk (see page 29) can be used in place of the buttermilk.

You'll need about 3 medium carrots to get 1 cup (250 mL) packed finely shredded carrots.

Storage Tip

Store the cooled cake, loosely wrapped in foil or waxed paper, at room temperature for up to 2 days or in the refrigerator for up to 1 week. Alternatively, wrap the cake in plastic wrap, then foil, completely enclosing it, and freeze for up to 6 months. Let thaw at room temperature for 4 to 6 hours before serving.

- Preheat oven to 350°F (180°C)
- 8-inch (20 cm) square metal baking pan, lined with parchment paper

²/₃ cup	quinoa flour or amaranth flour	150 mL
¹/₃ cup	potato starch	75 mL
1¹/₂ tbsp	chia seeds, ground (see tip, at left)	22 mL
1 tsp	baking soda	5 mL
1 tsp	pumpkin pie spice	5 mL
¹/₄ tsp	fine sea salt	1 mL
2	large eggs	2
²/₃ cup	fine crystal cane sugar	150 mL
¹/₃ cup	buttermilk	75 mL
¹/₄ cup	olive oil	60 mL
1 cup	packed finely shredded carrots	250 mL
	Pure cane confectioners' (icing) sugar (optional)	

1. In a medium bowl, whisk together quinoa flour, potato starch, chia seeds, baking soda, pumpkin pie spice and salt.

2. In a small bowl, whisk eggs until well blended. Whisk in cane sugar, buttermilk and oil until blended.

3. Add the egg mixture to the flour mixture, stirring until just blended. Gently fold in carrots.

4. Spread batter evenly in prepared pan.

5. Bake in preheated oven for 40 to 45 minutes or until a tester inserted in the center comes out clean. Let cool completely in pan on a wire rack. Sprinkle with confectioners' sugar, if desired.

Whole-Grain Gluten-Free Pie Crust

Makes one 9-inch (23 cm) pie crust

Tender, flaky and versatile, this easy crust is everything you want and need for your favorite sweet and savory pie fillings.

Tips

If you don't have a food processor, you can whisk the dry ingredients together in a large bowl, then use a pastry cutter or your fingertips to cut in the shortening. Use a fork to mix in the vinegar and water.

If using a metal pie pan, decrease the parbaking time to 8 to 10 minutes, and reduce the complete baking time to 11 to 16 minutes.

- Preheat oven to 375°F (190°C)
- Food processor (see tip, at left)
- 9-inch (23 cm) glass pie plate (see tip, at left)

⅔ cup	sorghum flour	150 mL
⅓ cup	tapioca starch	75 mL
¼ cup	millet flour	60 mL
1½ tbsp	chia seeds, finely ground	22 mL
½ tsp	fine sea salt	2 mL
½ cup	cold non-hydrogenated vegetable shortening, cut into small pieces	125 mL
1½ tsp	cider or white vinegar	7 mL
3 to 5 tbsp	ice water	45 to 75 mL

Additional millet flour or sorghum flour

1. In food processor, combine sorghum flour, tapioca starch, millet flour, chia seeds and salt; pulse to blend. Add shortening and pulse until mixture resembles coarse crumbs. Sprinkle vinegar over flour mixture. Sprinkle water over mixture, 1 tbsp (15 mL) at a time, pulsing just until dough begins to form.

2. Gather dough into a ball, wrap in plastic wrap and flatten into a disc. Refrigerate for 15 minutes.

3. Turn dough out onto a large sheet of parchment or waxed paper lightly sprinkled with millet flour or sorghum flour. Lightly sprinkle dough with the same flour. Using a rolling pin, roll dough out into an 11-inch (28 cm) circle.

4. Invert pie plate on top of dough. Quickly flip both plate and dough over so that the dough rests in the plate. Gently peel away and discard parchment paper. Press dough into pie plate, patching it together, if necessary. Crimp and trim the edges as desired. Using a fork, prick the sides and bottom all over.

Tips

The pie recipes in this chapter call for either a parbaked or a baked crust. Make sure to note which is specified and follow the appropriate version of step 5, including letting the crust cool as instructed, before proceeding with the recipe.

This recipe is easily doubled: simply double the ingredients and divide the dough into two equal portions.

To Parbake

5. Bake in preheated oven for 10 to 12 minutes or until golden. Let cool slightly on a wire rack, then fill and bake as directed in the pie recipe.

To Bake Completely

5. Bake in preheated oven for 15 to 20 minutes or until golden brown and set at the edges. Let cool completely on a wire rack. Fill as desired.

Chocolate Cream Pie

Makes 10 servings

This intensely chocolate pie is every bit as luxurious as it sounds. Because it is very rich, cut the pie into smaller-than-usual wedges.

Storage Tip

Prepare the pie through step 3 and store, loosely wrapped in foil or waxed paper, in the refrigerator for up to 2 days.

12 oz	GF semisweet chocolate chips	375 g
2 cups	well-stirred coconut milk (full-fat)	500 mL
2 tsp	GF vanilla extract	10 mL
1/4 tsp	fine sea salt	1 mL
1	baked Whole-Grain Gluten-Free Pie Crust (page 308)	1
1 1/2 cups	Whipped Coconut Cream (page 326)	375 mL
	GF chocolate shavings (optional)	

1. Place chocolate chips in a large bowl.

2. In a medium saucepan, heat coconut milk over medium heat until hot but not boiling. Pour over chocolate chips. Let stand for 2 minutes, then whisk until blended and smooth. Let cool at room temperature for 30 minutes.

3. Whisk the chocolate mixture and pour into baked pie crust. Cover surface of filling with plastic wrap and refrigerate for at least 3 hours, until firm, before serving.

4. Spread coconut cream over chilled pie filling. Sprinkle with chocolate shavings, if desired.

Chocolate Truffle Pie

This rich chocolate pie is at once decadent and simple. Coconut milk adds depth of flavor and richness without overwhelming the chocolate — no one will notice (or care!) that the dish is both egg- and dairy-free.

Tip

You can grind the chia seeds with a mortar and pestle or seal them in a small, heavy-duty plastic bag with a zipper top and pound them with a mallet or rolling pin until crushed.

Storage Tip

Store the pie, loosely wrapped in foil or waxed paper, in the refrigerator for up to 3 days.

¼ cup	unsweetened natural cocoa powder	60 mL
3 tbsp	tapioca starch	45 mL
1½ tbsp	chia seeds, ground (see tip, at left)	22 mL
3 cups	well-stirred coconut milk (full-fat)	750 mL
⅓ cup	pure maple syrup	75 mL
½ cup	GF semisweet chocolate chips	125 mL
1 tsp	GF vanilla extract	5 mL
1	baked Whole-Grain Gluten-Free Pie Crust (page 308)	1

Suggested Toppings

Whipped Coconut Cream (page 326)
Raspberries

1. In a medium saucepan, whisk together cocoa powder, tapioca starch, chia seeds, coconut milk and maple syrup until blended. Heat over medium heat, whisking, until starting to bubble. Remove from heat and add chocolate chips and vanilla. Let stand for 1 minute, then whisk until blended and smooth. Let cool in pan for 20 minutes.

2. Spread filling in baked pie crust. Cover surface of filling with plastic wrap and refrigerate for at least 4 hours, until firm, before serving. Serve with the suggested toppings, if desired.

Key Lime Pie

Makes 8 servings

Limes have the power to transport you to a tropical island, even in the depths of winter. Here, they shine in a gloriously (and naturally) green pie.

Tips

Some brands of coconut milk now add emulsifiers to their products to prevent separation of the coconut fats and liquid. Separating the coconut cream from the remaining liquid is not possible with these brands because the cream will not solidify properly when chilled. Be sure to check the ingredients on the coconut milk label; if emulsifiers are included on the list, opt for a different brand.

Flipping the can upside down places the solidified cream at the bottom and the milky coconut water on top; this makes it easier to pour off the liquid and scoop out the cream.

Storage Tip

Store the pie, loosely wrapped in foil or waxed paper, in the refrigerator for up to 3 days.

- Food processor

2	cans (each 14 oz/400 mL) coconut milk (full-fat), refrigerated for 24 hours	2
2	large ripe Hass avocados, cut into quarters	2
2 tsp	finely grated lime zest (Key lime or regular)	10 mL
¾ cup	freshly squeezed lime juice (Key lime or regular)	175 mL
⅓ cup	liquid honey or brown rice syrup	75 mL
2 tbsp	chia seeds, ground (see tip, page 311)	30 mL
⅛ tsp	fine sea salt	0.5 mL
1	baked Whole-Grain Gluten-Free Pie Crust (page 308)	1

1. Remove coconut milk from refrigerator and flip cans upside down. Open cans and pour off liquid into a container or measuring cup. Scoop thick coconut cream into 2-cup (500 mL) measuring cup. Add enough of the coconut liquid to total $1\frac{1}{4}$ cups (300 mL). (Store excess liquid in an airtight container in the refrigerator for another use.)

2. In food processor, combine avocados, lime zest, lime juice and honey; purée until smooth. Add chia seeds, salt and coconut cream; purée until smooth.

3. Spread filling in baked pie crust. Cover surface of filling with plastic wrap and refrigerate for at least 4 hours, until firm, before serving.

Gingery Pumpkin Pie

Here, pumpkin gets a tropical spin thanks to coconut milk, ginger and cardamom. The verdict? Sensational.

Tip
If you use homemade pumpkin purée instead of canned, or if only larger cans are available, you'll need 1¾ cups (425 mL).

Storage Tip
Store the cooled pie, loosely wrapped in foil or waxed paper, in the refrigerator for up to 3 days.

- Preheat oven to 350°F (180°C)

2½ tsp	ground ginger	12 mL
¾ tsp	ground cardamom or allspice	3 mL
½ tsp	fine sea salt	2 mL
2	large eggs	2
1	can (15 oz/425 mL) pumpkin purée (not pie filling)	1
1 cup	well-stirred coconut milk (full-fat)	250 mL
⅔ cup	pure maple syrup or liquid honey	150 mL
1	parbaked Whole-Grain Gluten-Free Pie Crust (page 308)	1

1. In a large bowl, whisk together ginger, cardamom, salt, eggs, pumpkin, coconut milk and maple syrup until well blended.

2. Spread filling in parbaked pie crust.

3. Bake in preheated oven for 60 to 70 minutes or until center is set. Let cool completely on a wire rack. Serve at room temperature or refrigerate until ready to serve (see tip, at left).

Tipsy Sweet Potato Pie

Makes 8 servings

No one has to know how easy this impressive and decadent pie is to make. A combination of whiskey, coconut milk and a hint of spice in the filling makes the sweet potatoes sing.

Tips

To make 1¾ cups (425 mL) sweet potato purée, you'll need 1⅓ lbs (675 g) sweet potatoes (about 2 large). Using a fork, prick sweet potatoes all over. Place on a large plate and microwave on High, turning every 5 minutes, for 15 to 20 minutes or until very soft. Immediately cut in half to release steam. When cool enough to handle, scoop flesh into a bowl and mash until smooth. Measure 1¾ cups (425 mL), reserving any extra for another use.

Store the cooled pie, loosely wrapped in foil or waxed paper, in the refrigerator for up to 1 day.

• Preheat oven to 350°F (180°C)

¾ cup	packed dark brown sugar	175 mL
3 tbsp	tapioca starch	45 mL
1 tsp	ground cinnamon	5 mL
¼ tsp	fine sea salt	1 mL
⅛ tsp	ground nutmeg	0.5 mL
1¾ cups	cooked sweet potato purée (see tip, at left)	425 mL
1¼ cups	well-stirred coconut milk (full-fat)	300 mL
3 tbsp	whiskey or bourbon	45 mL
1	parbaked Whole-Grain Gluten-Free Pie Crust (page 308)	1

1. In a large bowl, whisk together brown sugar, tapioca starch, cinnamon, salt, nutmeg, sweet potato, coconut milk and whiskey until well blended.

2. Spread filling in parbaked pie crust.

3. Bake in preheated oven for 50 to 55 minutes or until center is set. Let cool completely on a wire rack. Serve at room temperature or refrigerate until ready to serve (see tip, at left).

Peanut Butter and Raspberry Jam Pie

Classic flavor combinations are always in style, but you can still make them brand new. Here, PB&J is given just such a renovation, with oh-so-delicious results.

Storage Tip

Store the cooled pie (without raspberries), loosely wrapped in foil or waxed paper, in the refrigerator for up to 2 days.

- Preheat oven to 375°F (190°C)

3 tbsp	seedless raspberry jam	45 mL
1	baked Whole-Grain Gluten-Free Pie Crust (page 308)	1
4	large eggs	4
1 tsp	GF vanilla extract	5 mL
1¼ cups	evaporated milk	300 mL
⅔ cup	unsweetened creamy peanut butter	150 mL
¼ cup	packed light brown sugar	60 mL
2 cups	raspberries	500 mL

1. Spread jam on bottom of baked pie crust.

2. In a large bowl, whisk together eggs and vanilla.

3. In a medium saucepan, over medium-low heat, combine milk, peanut butter and brown sugar. Cook, stirring, for 4 to 5 minutes or until sugar is dissolved. Slowly pour into the egg mixture, whisking constantly, until well blended.

4. Carefully spread filling over jam in pie crust.

5. Bake in preheated oven for 23 to 27 minutes or until edges are just set but center still jiggles slightly when shaken. Let cool completely on a wire rack. Serve at room temperature or refrigerate until ready to serve (see tip, at left). Top with raspberries before serving.

Berry Crisp with Brown Sugar Ginger Topping

With its crisp gingery topping and lush berry filling, this summery dessert is both simple and sophisticated.

Tip

You can grind the chia seeds with a mortar and pestle or seal them in a small, heavy-duty plastic bag with a zipper top and pound them with a mallet or rolling pin until crushed.

Storage Tip

Store the cooled crisp, loosely wrapped in foil or waxed paper, in the refrigerator for up to 2 days. Serve cold, or warm in the microwave on Medium (70%) for about 1 minute.

- Preheat oven to 375°F (190°C)
- 9-inch (23 cm) square glass baking dish, oiled

6 cups	assorted fresh or thawed frozen berries	1.5 L
3 tbsp	fine crystal cane sugar	45 mL
2 tbsp	chia seeds, ground (see tip, at left)	30 mL
⅔ cup	millet flour	150 mL
⅔ cup	certified GF large-flake (old-fashioned) rolled oats	150 mL
½ cup	packed light brown sugar	125 mL
1½ tsp	ground ginger	7 mL
¼ tsp	fine sea salt	1 mL
⅓ cup	cold unsalted butter or virgin coconut oil, cut into small pieces	75 mL

1. In a large bowl, combine berries, sugar and chia seeds. Transfer to prepared baking dish.

2. In a medium bowl, whisk together millet flour, oats, brown sugar, ginger and salt. Using a pastry blender or two knives, cut in butter until mixture resembles coarse crumbs. Sprinkle over berry mixture.

3. Bake in preheated oven for 28 to 33 minutes or until berry mixture is bubbling and topping is golden brown. Let cool on a wire rack for 10 minutes before serving.

Vanilla Rhubarb Crumble

Rhubarb is an old-fashioned addition to pies and crisps, evoking nostalgia and comfort with ease. But here it feels modern in a cozy amaranth and oat crumble that is understated and not too sweet.

Tips
You can grind the chia seeds with a mortar and pestle or seal them in a small, heavy-duty plastic bag with a zipper top and pound them with a mallet or rolling pin until crushed.

You can use frozen sliced rhubarb in place of fresh. Measure the 10 cups (2.5 L) while the rhubarb is frozen, then let it thaw before adding it to the filling.

Removing the foil halfway through baking allows the topping to become crisp and browned.

Storage Tip
Store the cooled crumble, loosely wrapped in foil or waxed paper, in the refrigerator for up to 2 days. Serve cold, or warm in the microwave on Medium (70%) for about 1 minute.

- Preheat oven to 375°F (190°C)
- 13- by 9-inch (33 by 23 cm) glass baking dish, sprayed with nonstick cooking spray

Crumble

1¼ cups	certified GF large-flake (old-fashioned) oats	300 mL
¾ cup	amaranth flour	175 mL
½ cup	fine crystal cane sugar or packed light brown sugar	125 mL
1 tsp	ground cinnamon	5 mL
½ tsp	fine sea salt	2 mL
½ cup	unsalted butter, melted and cooled slightly	125 mL
1 tsp	GF vanilla extract	5 mL

Filling

⅔ cup	fine crystal cane sugar	150 mL
2 tbsp	chia seeds, ground (see tip, at left)	30 mL
½ cup	unsweetened apple juice	125 mL
1 tsp	GF vanilla extract	5 mL
10 cups	sliced rhubarb (½-inch/1 cm slices)	2.5 L

1. *Crumble:* In a medium bowl, whisk together oats, amaranth flour, sugar, cinnamon and salt. Stir in butter and vanilla until moist and crumbly.

2. *Filling:* In a large bowl, whisk together sugar, chia seeds, apple juice and vanilla. Add rhubarb and toss to coat.

3. Spoon filling into prepared baking dish and sprinkle with crumble. Cover with foil.

4. Bake in preheated oven for 30 minutes. Remove foil and bake for 25 to 30 minutes or until browned and bubbling and rhubarb is tender. Let cool on a wire rack for 30 minutes. Serve warm or at room temperature.

Variations
Mixed Berry Crumble: Replace the rhubarb with an equal amount of assorted berries (such as blackberries, blueberries, raspberries and diced strawberries). Reduce the sugar in the filling to ¼ cup (60 mL).

Apple Cranberry Crumble: Replace the rhubarb with 8 cups (2 L) sliced peeled tart-sweet apples (such as Braeburn or Gala) and 1½ cups (375 mL) fresh or thawed frozen cranberries.

Clafouti

Clafouti is a traditional dessert — part cake, part pie, part custard — from the Limousin region of France. The French opt for cherries in their clafouti, but almost any fruit can take its place. Because this one is not too sweet, it is equally excellent for breakfast or brunch as for dessert.

Storage Tip

Store the cooled clafouti, loosely wrapped in foil or waxed paper, in the refrigerator for up to 2 days.

Tip

If using non-dairy milk, try hemp, rice or almond.

Variations

Spiced Pear Clafouti: Replace the cherries with an equal amount of diced firm-ripe pears, and add 1 tsp (5 mL) pumpkin pie spice with the salt.

Lemon Berry Clafouti: Replace the cherries with an equal amount of fresh or thawed frozen blueberries or raspberries, and replace the vanilla with 1 1/2 tsp (7 mL) finely grated lemon zest.

- Preheat oven to 325°F (160°C)
- 9-inch (23 cm) glass pie pan or cast iron skillet, oiled

2 cups	pitted sweet cherries	500 mL
1/3 cup	millet flour	75 mL
1/2 cup	fine crystal cane sugar	125 mL
2 1/2 tbsp	potato starch	37 mL
1/8 tsp	fine sea salt	0.5 mL
3	large eggs	3
1 cup	milk or plain non-dairy milk	250 mL
1 tsp	GF vanilla extract	5 mL
2 tbsp	unsalted butter or virgin coconut oil, melted	30 mL

1. Arrange cherries in prepared pan.

2. In a large bowl, whisk together millet flour, sugar, potato starch and salt. Whisk in eggs, milk and vanilla until blended. Whisk in butter. Pour batter over cherries.

3. Bake in preheated oven for 35 to 40 minutes or until puffed and golden. Let cool on a wire rack for 15 minutes. Serve warm or at room temperature.

Honey and Cardamom Baked Apples

Spring and summer aren't the only seasons for fresh fruit desserts. Case in point: these honey-sweetened, cardamom-scented, ancient-grain-stuffed apples.

Tips

Cooked amaranth, quinoa or sorghum, cooled, can be used in place of the millet. Information on cooking these grains can be found on pages 8–17.

Ground cinnamon, ginger or allspice can be used in place of the cardamom.

Other dried fruits, such as blueberries, cranberries or chopped apricots, may be used in place of the raisins.

An equal amount of pure maple syrup or brown rice syrup can be used in place of the honey.

Storage Tip

Store the cooled apples, loosely covered in foil or plastic wrap, in the refrigerator for up to 1 day. Serve cold, or warm in the microwave on Medium (70%) for about 1 minute.

- Preheat oven to 350°F (180°C)
- 8- or 9-inch (20 or 23 cm) square glass baking dish or glass pie plate

4	tart-sweet apples (such as Braeburn, Gala or Fuji), cored	4
½ cup	cooked millet (see page 11), cooled	125 mL
⅓ cup	raisins	75 mL
⅓ cup	chopped toasted walnuts (see page 26)	75 mL
½ tsp	ground cardamom	2 mL
6 tbsp	liquid honey, divided	90 mL

Suggested Topping

Plain Greek yogurt or Whipped Coconut Cream (page 326)

1. Using a vegetable peeler, peel top 1 inch (2.5 cm) of apples. Place apples, top side up, in baking dish.

2. In a small bowl, combine millet, raisins, walnuts, cardamom and 2 tbsp (30 mL) honey. Stuff millet mixture into apple cavities. Drizzle 1 tbsp (15 mL) honey over each apple.

3. Bake in preheated oven for 45 to 55 minutes, brushing occasionally with accumulated juices, until apples are tender.

4. Transfer apples to a plate and pour pan juices over top. Serve with yogurt, if desired.

Jeweled Amaranth Pudding

Easy enough to make as a weeknight dessert, nutritious enough to eat for an energizing snack or breakfast, this fruit-studded amaranth pudding is cool, creamy comfort food.

Tips

For the dried fruit, try raisins, cherries, blueberries, currants or chopped apricots.

If using non-dairy milk, try coconut, almond, rice or hemp.

Ground cardamom, cinnamon or ginger can be used in place of the allspice.

Storage Tip

Store leftover pudding in an airtight container in the refrigerator for up to 2 days.

Variation

Almond Amaranth Pudding: Omit the dried fruit and allspice, and replace the vanilla with ½ tsp (2 mL) GF almond extract. If desired, sprinkle the pudding with toasted sliced almonds before serving.

1 cup	amaranth	250 mL
½ cup	dried fruit	125 mL
¼ cup	fine crystal cane sugar or granulated sugar	60 mL
¼ tsp	ground allspice	1 mL
⅛ tsp	fine sea salt	0.5 mL
3 cups	milk or plain non-dairy milk	750 mL
⅔ cup	water	150 mL
2 tsp	GF vanilla extract	10 mL

1. In a medium saucepan, combine amaranth, dried fruit, sugar, allspice, salt, milk and water. Bring to a gentle boil over medium heat. Reduce heat to medium-low, cover, leaving lid ajar, and simmer, stirring occasionally, for 30 to 35 minutes or until amaranth is very soft and mixture is thickened. Remove from heat and stir in vanilla.

2. Transfer amaranth mixture to a medium heatproof bowl and let cool to room temperature. Serve at room temperature or cover and refrigerate until cold.

Butterscotch Rice Pudding

Makes 4 servings

Home-style comfort food at its best, this easy rice pudding gets subtle sweetness from brown sugar, plus loads of flavor from a bit of browned butter and a splash of whiskey.

Tips

If using non-dairy milk, try hemp, soy, almond or rice.

The rice pudding is also delicious made with an equal amount of maple syrup or liquid honey in place of the brown sugar.

Storage Tip

Store leftover pudding in an airtight container in the refrigerator for up to 2 days.

1 tbsp	unsalted butter or virgin coconut oil	15 mL
2 cups	cooked medium- or short-grain brown rice (see page 16), cooled	500 mL
1/3 cup	packed dark brown sugar	75 mL
1/8 tsp	fine sea salt	0.5 mL
1 1/2 cups	milk or plain non-dairy milk	375 mL
1 tbsp	whiskey or bourbon	15 mL
1 tsp	GF vanilla extract	5 mL

1. In a medium saucepan, melt butter over medium heat. Heat for 1 to 2 minutes or until butter begins to brown.

2. Stir in rice, brown sugar, salt and milk; increase heat to medium-high and bring to a simmer. Reduce heat and simmer, stirring constantly, for 20 to 25 minutes or until thickened.

3. Remove from heat and stir in whiskey and vanilla. Let cool to room temperature. Serve at room temperature or cover and refrigerate until cold.

Coconut Chia Pudding

This simple pudding is as good for you as it is good to eat. It couldn't be easier to make, but you do need to plan ahead, since it requires chilling for at least 4 hours. The chia seeds plump up overnight, resulting in a texture akin to tapioca pudding.

6 tbsp	chia seeds	90 mL
1/8 tsp	fine sea salt	0.5 mL
1	can (14 oz/400 mL) coconut milk (full-fat)	1
1/3 cup	water	75 mL
3 tbsp	liquid honey or pure maple syrup	45 mL
1/2 tsp	GF vanilla extract	2 mL

Suggested Toppings

Fresh berries or chopped fruit (blueberries, raspberries, mango, apple)

Plain or toasted flaked or shredded coconut

Toasted nuts or seeds (hemp, sunflower, green pumpkin, sesame)

Dried fruit (raisins, cherries, cranberries)

Tips

If you do not like the tapioca consistency of chia seeds, in step 1 blend the ingredients in a blender until smooth. Refrigerate and serve as directed.

You can vary the flavor of this pudding in countless ways: for example, add a small amount of a ground spice (such as cinnamon, cardamom or ginger), or replace the vanilla with finely grated citrus zest (such as lemon, lime or orange) or GF almond extract.

1. In a small bowl, whisk together chia seeds, salt, coconut milk, water, honey and vanilla until blended. Cover and refrigerate for at least 4 hours, until thickened, or for up to 5 days.

2. Divide chia mixture among four bowls and top with any of the suggested toppings, as desired.

Chocolate Chip Millet Pudding

Makes 6 servings

Creamy, comforting and studded with melting bits of dark chocolate, this easy dessert is reminiscent of old-fashioned bread pudding. It can be varied in countless ways, with different chips, dried fruits, flavorings and other add-ins.

Tip

If using non-dairy milk, try coconut, almond, rice or hemp.

Storage Tip

Store leftover pudding in an airtight container in the refrigerator for up to 2 days.

- Preheat oven to 325°F (160°C)
- 8-cup (2 L) baking dish, sprayed with nonstick cooking spray
- Large baking dish or roasting pan (to fit baking dish)
- Large rimmed baking sheet

½ tsp	ground cinnamon	2 mL
½ tsp	fine sea salt	2 mL
3	large eggs	3
½ cup	pure maple syrup	125 mL
2 tsp	GF vanilla extract	10 mL
2 cups	milk or plain non-dairy milk	500 mL
3 cups	cooked millet (see page 11)	750 mL
¾ cup	GF semisweet chocolate chips	175 mL
	Boiling water	

1. In a large bowl, whisk together cinnamon, salt, eggs, maple syrup and vanilla until blended. Whisk in milk. Stir in millet. Gently fold in chocolate chips.

2. Pour mixture into prepared 8-cup (2 L) dish. Place large baking dish on baking sheet. Set filled dish inside larger dish. Transfer baking sheet to the oven and carefully add enough boiling water to the larger dish to reach halfway up the sides of the smaller dish.

3. Bake for 23 to 28 minutes or until golden and set at the center. Transfer baking dish with pudding to a wire rack and let cool for 20 minutes. Serve warm or let cool completely.

Chocolate Teff Pudding

Not only does this chocolate pudding trump any and all store-bought varieties, but it is also rich in antioxidants and other nutrients. Go ahead, have seconds.

Storage Tip

Store leftover pudding in an airtight container in the refrigerator for up to 2 days.

• Blender

½ cup	teff	125 mL
¼ cup	unsweetened natural cocoa powder	60 mL
¼ cup	fine crystal cane sugar	60 mL
⅛ tsp	fine sea salt	0.5 mL
1⅓ cups	water	325 mL
1 cup	well-stirred coconut milk (full-fat)	250 mL
1 tsp	GF vanilla extract	15 mL

1. In a medium saucepan, whisk together teff, cocoa powder, sugar, salt, water and coconut milk. Bring to a gentle boil over medium heat. Reduce heat to medium-low, cover, leaving lid ajar, and simmer, stirring occasionally, for 15 to 20 minutes or until teff is very soft and mixture is thickened. Remove from heat and stir in vanilla.

2. Transfer teff mixture to a medium heatproof bowl and let cool to room temperature.

3. Transfer cooled mixture to blender and blend until smooth.

4. Divide mixture among four ramekins or dessert cups. Cover loosely and refrigerate until cold.

Coco-Cocoa Chia Gelato

This is a sublime chocolate ice cream–like frozen dessert. The processed chia seeds help thicken the ice cream, resulting in a particularly rich, velvety texture.

- Blender
- Ice cream maker

½ cup	unsweetened natural cocoa powder	125 mL
⅓ cup	packed pitted soft dates	75 mL
¼ cup	chia seeds	60 mL
1	can (14 oz/400 mL) coconut milk (full-fat)	1
¼ cup	pure maple syrup or liquid honey	60 mL
1 tsp	GF vanilla extract	5 mL

1. In blender, combine cocoa powder, dates, chia seeds, coconut milk, maple syrup and vanilla; process until smooth. Cover and refrigerate for at least 4 hours or until cold.

2. Pour into ice cream maker and freeze according to manufacturer's instructions.

3. Spoon into an airtight container, cover and freeze for 4 hours, until firm, or for up to 3 days.

Polka-Dot Mango Ice Pops

These ice pops are a serious ode to summer fruit.

Tips
Taste the mango before blending; depending on its sweetness, you may not need to add any sugar.

You can use 4-oz (125 mL) paper cups as ice-pop molds. Place them on a baking sheet, then fill until almost full. Cover with foil, then make a small slit to insert ice-pop sticks or small bamboo skewers and freeze as directed.

- Blender
- 8-serving ice-pop mold

3½ cups	fresh or frozen mango chunks	875 mL
2 tbsp	fine crystal cane sugar (see tip, at left)	30 mL
2 tbsp	chia seeds	30 mL

1. In blender, purée mango and sugar until smooth.

2. Transfer mango purée to a bowl and let stand for 5 minutes to allow sugar to dissolve. Stir in chia seeds.

3. Pour purée into ice-pop molds, insert sticks and freeze for 4 to 6 hours, until solid, or for up to 3 days. If necessary, briefly dip bases of mold in hot water to loosen and unmold.

Whipped Coconut Cream

**Makes about
¾ cup (175 mL)**

This lush, snow-white whip is likely to become your new favorite dessert topping. It also makes a great instant frosting for cakes and cupcakes.

Tips

Some brands of coconut milk now add emulsifiers to their products to prevent separation of the coconut fats and liquid. Making whipped coconut cream is not possible with these brands because the cream will not solidify properly when chilled. Be sure to check the ingredients on the coconut milk label; if emulsifiers are included on the list, opt for a different brand.

Flipping the can upside down places the solidified cream at the bottom and the milky coconut water on top; this makes it easier to pour off the liquid and scoop out the cream.

Storage Tip

Store any unused whipped coconut cream in an airtight container in the refrigerator for up to 2 weeks. Rewhip with an electric mixer before using.

- Electric mixer

| 1 | can (14 oz/400 mL) coconut milk (full-fat) | 1 |

1. Place the can of coconut milk in the refrigerator. Refrigerate for at least 24 hours.

2. Just before whipping the coconut cream, place a medium bowl (preferably metal) and the beaters from the electric mixer in the freezer for 5 minutes.

3. Remove can from refrigerator and flip upside down. Open can and pour off liquid (store liquid in an airtight container in the refrigerator for another use). Scoop thick coconut cream into chilled bowl.

4. Whip the coconut cream with the electric mixer on high until soft peaks form. Use immediately.

Variations

Whipped Lemon Coconut Cream: Add 2 tsp (10 mL) coconut sugar, 1½ tsp (7 mL) finely grated lemon zest and 1 tbsp (15 mL) freshly squeezed lemon juice near the end of whipping in step 4.

Whipped Vanilla Coconut Cream: Add 2 tsp (10 mL) coconut sugar and 1 tsp (5 mL) vanilla extract near the end of whipping in step 4.

Whipped Maple Coconut Cream: Add 1 tbsp (15 mL) pure maple syrup near the end of whipping in step 4.

Index

Library and Archives Canada Cataloguing in Publication

Saulsbury, Camilla V., author
    Bob's Red Mill everyday gluten-free cookbook : 281 delicious whole-grain recipes / Camilla V. Saulsbury.

Includes index.
ISBN 978-0-7788-0500-7 (pbk.)

    1. Gluten-free diet—Recipes. 2. Cooking (Cereals). 3. Grain. 4. Cookbooks. I. Title. II. Title: Everyday gluten-free cookbook.

RM237.86.S38 2015   641.5'638   C2014-907744-0